Unsettling Settlements – Cities, Migrants, Climate Change

Studien zur internationalen Umweltpolitik

Studies on International Environmental Policy

begründet von / founded by
Prof. Dr. Dr. h. c. Gerhard W. Wittkämper,
Prof. Dr. Horst Zilleßen

herausgegeben von / edited by

Prof. Dr. Miranda Schreurs
Hochschule für Politik München

Prof. Dr. Dr. h. c. Udo E. Simonis
Wissenschaftszentrum Berlin

Prof. Dr. Helga Weisz
Potsdam-Institut für Klimafolgenforschung

Band / Volume 18

LIT

Kira Vinke

Unsettling Settlements – Cities, Migrants, Climate Change

Rural-Urban Climate Migration as Effective Adaptation?

LIT

This book is printed on acid-free paper.

Bei diesem Buch handelt es sich um eine Dissertation an der Humboldt-Universität zu Berlin, Kultur-, Sozial- und Bildungswissenschaftliche Fakultät.

Bibliographic information published by the Deutsche Nationalbibliothek
The Deutsche Nationalbibliothek lists this publication in the Deutsche Nationalbibliografie; detailed bibliographic data are available on the Internet at http://dnb.d-nb.de.

ISBN 978-3-643-91130-8 (pb)
ISBN 978-3-643-96130-3 (PDF)
Zugl.: Humboldt-Universität Berlin, Univ., Diss., 2019

A catalogue record for this book is available from the British Library.

Klosbachstr. 107
CH-8032 Zürich
Tel. +41 (0) 44-251 75 05
E-Mail: zuerich@lit-verlag.ch http://www.lit-verlag.ch
Distribution:
In the UK: Global Book Marketing, e-mail: mo@centralbooks.com
In North America: Independent Publishers Group, e-mail: orders@ipgbook.com
In Germany: LIT Verlag Fresnostr. 2, D-48159 Münster
Tel. +49 (0) 2 51-620 32 22, Fax +49 (0) 2 51-922 60 99, e-mail: vertrieb@lit-verlag.de
e-books are available at www.litwebshop.de

Contents

Foreword by Prof. Dr. H. Weisz 13
Foreword by Prof. Dr. Dr. h.c. H. J. Schellnhuber 15
Part I: Departure 19
Prologue 21
Abstract 23
1. Introduction 25
1.1. Thesis Structure 28
2. Terminology and Literature Review: Climate Change, Adaptation, Migration 29
2.1. Definitions of Climate Change, Environmental Change and Global Change 29
2.2. Climate Migrants, Refugees and Disaster Displacement 30
2.3. Migration and the Adaptation Discourse 33
3. Theoretical Framework 41
3.1. Climate Migration in the Context of Global Change 41
3.2. Theories Explaining Migration 44
3.3. Knowledge Gaps in Climate Impact Research 46
3.4. Operationalization of Effectiveness 49
4. Research Design: Grounded Theory Driven Multi-Level System Analysis Based on Two Cases 55
4.1. Grounded Theory 56
4.2. Conceptual Systems Model & Case Study 59
4.3. Case Selection 60
4.4. Structure of Analysis 65
5. Methods 67
5.1. Techniques of Data Collection 67
5.2. Analysis of Interview Data 71

Part II: Unsettling Settlements 75
6. Case Study 1: Southwestern Bangladesh - Migration as Adaptation to Rapid Onset Disasters 77
6.1. Methods of Field Research 79
6.2. Current Climate Hazards in Southwestern Bangladesh 88
6.3. Future Climate Change Impacts and their Implications for Migration 93
6.4. Interactions of Physical Climate Impacts with Human Systems 96
6.5. Migration Patterns Bangladesh 102
6.6. Migrant Household Profiles 112
6.7. Effective or Not? Migration as Adaptation in Southwestern Bangladesh 121
6.8. Synergetic System Analysis 150
6.9. Discussion of the Bangladesh Case Study Results 154
7. Case Study 2: Migration in the Marshall Islands as a Response to Sea Level Rise and related Crop Failure 159
7.1. Methods of Field Research 162
7.2. Current Climate Hazards on the Marshall Islands 170
7.3. Future Climate Impacts and their Implications for Migration 175
7.4. Interactions of Physical Climate Impacts with Human Systems on RMI 176
7.5. Foreign Imposed Migration Patterns in the Marshall Islands: Nuclear Legacy and Climate Change 186
7.6. Household Profiles 197
7.7. Effective or Not? Migration as Adaptation on the RMI 201
7.8. Synergetic System Analysis 229
7.9. Discussion of Results 233

Part III: Settling Unsettlements 239
8. Conclusions: Risk Exchange through Migration 241
8.1. Effectiveness of Migration in Reducing Risks 244
8.2. Generation of Hypotheses 246
8.3. Implications for the Adaptation Discourse 251
8.4. Climate Migration in the Context of Divisive Urbanization 253
9. Recommendations for Addressing Climate Migration 257
9.1. International Level 257
9.2. National Level 260
9.3. Regional Level 261
9.4. City / Village Level 262

Part IV: Arrival 265
10. Outlook: Migration as Adaptation in this Century 267
11. Epilogue: Tales of Hope 271
12. "It takes a village to raise a child" (Acknowledgements) 273
13. Bibliography 275
14. Annex 305
14.1. Summary / Zusammenfassung 305
14.2. Interview Guide 308
14.3. Annex Bangladesh 309
14.4. Annex Marshall Islands 322

List of Figures

Figure 1 The Two-Fold Gap in our Understanding of the Links between Climate Change and Migration 47
Figure 2 Research Process Overview. 65
Figure 3 Map of Bangladesh Interview Locations. 81
Figure 4 Location of Bangladesh (source: TUBS, 2011a) 82
Figure 5 Themes of Effectiveness of Migration as Adaptation for Migrants Bangladesh. 88
Figure 6 Possible Climate Migration Pathways in Bangladesh............. 104
Figure 7 Simplified Migration Pathways of Respondents to Khulna.... 104
Figure 8 Perceived Reason for Environmental Change of Respondents in Bangladesh. 120
Figure 9 System Analysis of Migrants' System of Origin and Destination Bangladesh 141
Figure 10 Synergetic System Analysis of Climate Change and Migration in Southwest Bangladesh 152
Figure 11 Location of the Republic of the RMI 165
Figure 12 Themes of Effectiveness of Migration as Adaptation for Migrants RMI 169
Figure 13 Observed Monthly Maximum Sea Level Change at Uliga Dock, Majuro 171
Figure 14 Observed Monthly Minimum Sea Level Change at Uliga Dock, Majuro 171
Figure 15 Observed Monthly Mean Sea Level Change at Uliga Dock, Majuro 172
Figure 16 Map of the Marshall Islands, including Research Location Sites Majuro, Ailuk, Maloelap. 188
Figure 17 Possible Climate Migration Pathways in the RMI 188
Figure 18 Perceived Reason for Environmental Change from Respondents on the Outer Islands and Migrants Interviewed in Majuro................... 201
Figure 19 System Analysis of Migrants' System of Origin and Destination, Marshall Islands 219

Figure 20 Synergetic System Analysis of Climate Change and Migration in the Republic of the Marshall Islands 231
Figure 21 Conceptualization of Impact Response 252
Figure 22 Typology of Climate Migration. 253

List of Tables

Table 1 Most Different Inductive Case Study Design............................. 60
Table 2 Most Different Inductive Case Study Design 64
Table 3 Overview of Interview Partners in Bangladesh.......................... 80
Table 4 Climate Migration and its potential Effects on Health............ 101
Table 5 Overview of Interview Partners RMI 163
Table 6 Overview of Expert Interviews. 164

List of Pictures

Picture 1: Typical House in Bangladesh's Coastal Communities 113
Picture 2 Typical Urban Informal Settlement in S.W. Bangladesh 128
Picture 3 Informal Settlement in Barisal 135
Picture 4 Pandanus Fruit 177
Picture 5 Water Desalinization Units 183
Picture 6 Okeanos Marshall Islands Anchored in Majuro.................... 189
Picture 7 Sand Exploitation for Cement Construction 189
Picture 8 Ailuk Atoll 190
Picture 9 Maloelap Atoll 190
Picture 10 Typical Housing on Maleolap Atoll 199

List of Abbreviations

ADB	Asian Development Bank
CC	Climate Change
CIA	Central Intelligence Agency
FAO	Food and Agriculture Organization of the United Nations
GIZ	German Corporation for International Cooperation
ILO	International Labor Organization
IOM	International Organization for Migration
IPCC	Intergovernmental Panel on Climate Change
RMI	Republic of the Marshall Islands
SLR	Sea Level Rise
TC	Tropical Cyclone
UN	United Nations
UNEP	United Nations Environmental Programme
UNFCCC	United Nations Framework Convention on Climate Change
UNHCR	United Nations High Commissioner for Refugees
WBGU	German Advisory Council on Global Change
WFP	World Food Programme
WHO	World Health Organization

Foreword

by Prof. Dr. Helga Weisz

Climate migration is high on the political and scholarly agenda, but it remains a controversial issue. Will there be millions of migrants in the future putting further pressure on already polarized political landscapes? Or is migration in the face of increasing environmental damage simply a way to adapt to the impacts of anthropogenic global warming? Does such a thing, as climate migration, at all exist? After all, people have always migrated and did so for a variety of reasons.

The scientific literature on climate migration meanders between outright denial of the phenomenon to projections of hundreds of millions of climate migrants in the coming decades, from downplaying the phenomenon as an adaptation rather than a problem, to diluting any meaningful analysis through endless semantic quibbles and squishy generalities.

This book takes a different approach and thus tells a much more coherent and compelling story. Kira Vinke conducted dozens of interviews with migrants in the urban slums of Bangladesh and in the Marshall Islands. Most of her interview partners used to be subsistence farmers, who migrated in the aftermath of tropical cyclones, sea level rise, or droughts often to the nearest city where they ended up in urban slums.

These persons typically do not migrate strategically but involuntarily, as a reaction to a hazard as a last option to survive. As migration is often from rural to urban areas, their situation worsens, because in urban settings they are excluded from the labor market, from education and health systems, but there is no more a subsistence farming alternative or an established social network. In fact, the exclusion of persons from core social provision systems, such as health, education and labor market, prior to migration, is an important predictor of maladaptive migration.

This study demonstrates that characterizing this form of climate migration as adaptation is an euphemism that serves to justify political inaction and shifts the responsibility to adapt from the society and the polluters to the affected individuals. It would be much more appropriate to talk about forced displacement or survival migration in the face of climate change impacts. These results commend themselves to be picked up in future research and international policy.

With many original quotations from the interviews, this book gives a voice also to those who typically are not heard. The quotations provide an authentic, albeit depressing, account of the burdensome reality of the extreme poor under climate change and how slim their options are. The almost complete absence of policy attention that is apparent in the interviews should be a wake-up call.

More than anything this study reveals the severe institutional and policy failures at municipal, national and international levels and a lack of acknowledging the scale of the problem. Today 1 to 2 billion people still live as subsistence farmers - smallholders and pastoralists - in rural areas in developing countries. Their livelihoods have always been poor and risk prone, even without impacts from global warming. The scientific community has devoted a substantial body of work to study such smallholder and pastoralist communities. Too often, however, they have focused on their complexity and diversity, stressing for example the variety of scoping strategies they have developed.

This diverted the attention from what they all have in common: a direct dependence on local biological productivity, the exclusion from education, health and other provisioning systems and the unfavorable terms of their increasing inclusion in global food markets. The damaging impacts of global warming come on top of this. They hit those most severely and immediately who are the least prepared and who have least contributed to the problem. It is the joint duty of academic communities and international policy to face the urgency and scale of threatened livelihoods among the world's poor in the face of climate change.

Foreword

by Prof. Dr. Dr. h.c. Hans Joachim Schellnhuber

The first „Conference of the Parties to the Framework Convention on Climate Change“, abbreviated as COP1, took place in Berlin in 1995. The conference president was a young environment minister from Germany named Angela Merkel. I attended that "climate summit" as an advisor to the host government in my capacity as a member of the "German Advisory Council on Global Change" (WBGU). In the run-up to COP1, the WBGU had developed a global *mitigation* concept called the "tolerable windows approach" that argued in favour of a planetary-warming boundary of 2°C. There were several encounters with Merkel in that year where we discussed our concept.

20 years later, at the COP21 in Paris, the 2°C guardrail became international law, and the world community was even called upon to limit anthropogenic global warming to 1.5°C, if at all possible. So eventually an extremely simple, yet extremely challenging mitigation target emerged as a reference point for each and every action to reduce greenhouse-gas emissions. In order to "avoid the unmanageable", as I put it a long time ago. Climate science is currently piling up overwhelming evidence that beyond the 2°C-warming line all types of disruptive events lurk – such as the collapse of major ice sheets, circulation patterns and ecosystems ("tipping elements").

Yet even if we are able to keep global warming significantly below 2 degrees, there will be severe impacts which must be dealt with by decision makers and individuals in all walks of life. This is about "managing the unavoidable", the notion that completes my quote which has become sort of a classic. And this, in turn, is about the sister strategy of mitigation, namely *adaptation* to man-made climate change.

While mitigation efforts can be deduced from and orchestrated by the Paris Agreement within a global framework, there is nothing comparable with respect to the adaptation side of the dilemma coin. This has many diverse reasons, not least the persistent confusion regarding the very meaning of the word "adaptation", which has led to dozens of scholastic, if not futile, debates among climate-change experts. In my view, a specific measure implemented by any decision maker – whether it is a nation state or a single farmer – only qualifies as global-warming adaptation if it is an *anticipatory strategic action based on projective information provided by science*. Everything else is merely a reaction to the pressures a rapidly changing is generating, in other words, a climate impact.

So the distinction between re-action and pro-action is key, particularly when it comes to the biggest of all challenges associated with anthropogenic global warming: the potential relocation of people (and their supporting infrastructures) due to the shifting living conditions – such as sea-level rise, glaciers melting, desertification and alteration of extreme-events regimes. Some studies estimate that hundreds of millions of human beings will need to move in geographic space even if the 2°C-line can be held against most odds. And the all-important question is whether that relocation will happen as forced displacement (impact) or planned migration (adaptation). A worldwide strategy for the latter would actually constitute the adaptation equivalent of the Paris Agreement. However, the international community still appears to be lightyears away from such a grand scheme.

This is one of the reasons why climate-related motion only happens in a predominantly reactive manner at the individual-to-household level so far. And even this motion is a completely under-researched topic. The study presented by Kira Vinke here is a pioneering attempt to shine bright rays of light into that dark room where millions of people may strive for survival, often under abominable circumstances. Her book provides evidence in the starkest possible form about an existential challenge largely ignored by the academic elite. In other words, this book is a must-read. Also because her work goes beyond documenting and organizing the empirical data by conceptualizing and contextualizing the overall displacement phenomenon and the social dynamics it brings about. But see for yourself…

Let me conclude by highlighting a fundamental problem when it comes to discuss migration as a genuine (and possibly effective) adaptation measure. The ultimate decision to be made (by humankind, two hundred or so nation states, the UN Security Council or some other institution) is whether the relocation of the many millions severely exposed to anthropogenic global warming will happen in a centrally-planned, top-down manner or in a self-determined way by individuals and families empowered and enabled to find a better life elsewhere than in their traditional place of residence. Looking back in relocation history, one quickly realizes that the first approach tends to generate chaos, misery and death. The second approach is not only the preferred ethical choice but could actually work on the ground – if the right means and institutions for "migration in dignity" are established and offered.

Kira Vinke's study does not fail to touch upon this highly controversial issue and thus constructs a tenuous bridge towards the intellectual territory where just and effective climate adaptation can be truly addressed.

Part I: Departure

Prologue

“This is where I buried my first child“, he says as we step through a small patch of salty marshland behind a shack on the embankments of Shyamnagar, Bangladesh. “We had never seen such a high wave, it had never happened before, we were not prepared.” The students translate and we hear another account about the reality of our research on people who migrated, those who stayed and those who perished in the storms and floods of a changing climate. It was after these personal encounters which formed the basis of data for my research that I decided not to question whether or not “climate migrants” exist, nor to project how high exactly their numbers may be, but to find out whether and under which circumstances humans are able to effectively adapt to climate impacts through migration. This research could not have been carried out without the people who were interviewed and I owe them my deepest gratitude for sharing their life stories with me.

Abstract

The nexus between climate change and migration is complex and its investigation leads to crucial implications for mitigation, adaptation and development policies. In developing countries the general trend of rural-urban migration may be amplified by the negative effects of climate change on agricultural production as sources of livelihoods in the countryside, and on human health and safety. In Asia and the Pacific many people are highly vulnerable to climate change. Deltaic regions such as the Bay of Bengal and island nations like the Marshall Islands are at the forefront of expected climate impacts. Already, in many cities informal and poor settlements are growing, leaving little capacity to absorb migrants with no skills for the urban labor market. This leads to the question of this dissertation: **Is migration an effective adaptation to the impacts of climate change?** Following a Grounded Theory approach, a theory building multilevel qualitative systems analysis, which takes into account empirical data from two case studies, is carried out. As different actors employ different criteria for effectiveness, three levels of analysis are included: the individual migrant, the sending community and the receiving community. Methods include semi-structured qualitative interviews with migrants, sending communities and relevant experts, focus group discussions, participatory observation, a literature review and a critical discussion of the existing scientific debate. A key insight of this study is that individual agency in migration decision-making and in shaping migration outcomes is strongly limited by the vulnerabilities of the social group to which the individual belongs. Therefore, migration effectiveness is determined by wider structural inequalities. The study also arrives at the conclusion that migration should only be categorized as adaptation if it is of a preventative nature. If it is a reaction to the already occurred effects of climate change, it should be seen as an impact response. This study intends to inform policies of climate mitigation, adaptation and migration management.

1. Introduction

The assessment of the link between climate change and migration is becoming increasingly important as climate impacts intensify and damages surface, which may induce migratory movements. However, much of the related research has caused controversies in the scientific community as well as in the political discourse (Piguet, 2018). Meanwhile, compensation demands for losses as well as legal cases of migrants pleading for residence permits in foreign countries due to climate change impacts have started to emerge (Farber, 2007; United Nations Environment Programme and Sabin Center for Climate Change Law, 2017). Subsequently, the definitions of climate migration and therefore also the determinants of who could be considered a "climate migrant" are subject to extensive debate (Behrman, 2018; Berchin et al., 2017; Felli, 2013; Gill, 2010; Hartmann, 2010; Hingley, 2017; Piguet, 2013).

Regardless of the debates around definitions and in the absence of an international legal framework granting protection or refugee status to climate migrants – with a locked-in future warming level of about 1.5°C increase in global mean temperature compared to pre-industrial levels (Stocker et al., 2013; The World Bank, 2014) and continuously rising emissions – the problem will not lose its scope. Recent projections for three regions, Latin America, South Asia and Sub-Saharan Africa, estimate that the numbers of internal climate migrants by 2050 could be 31 to 72 million in a climate-friendly scenario and more than 143 million in a pessimistic scenario (Kumari Rigaud et al., 2018).

In the 2015 Paris Agreement the international community decided to limit global warming to 1.5 to 2°C above pre-industrial levels. However, so far not enough action has been taken to reduce emissions and stay within those temperature boundaries (Figueres et al., 2017; Rockström et al., 2017). Even such moderate warming levels of 1.5 to 2°C which would be the result of the most optimistic emissions reduction scenarios will have severe impacts on livelihoods in some regions of the world (IPCC, 2018; The World Bank, 2012). Climate change will render parts of the now fertile land barren or flooded and will cause some coastal areas to erode into non-existence. One of the already observable effects is internal migration (Adger et al., 2014). In the two case studies analyzed in this dissertation, covering rural to urban climate migration in the Southwest of Bangladesh and the Republic of the Marshall Islands, people are presently experiencing climate impacts which may affect other countries in the coming decades, too. Such damages, often connected to additional anthropogenic influences, are already requiring adaptive measures to maintain livelihoods.

In the literature there are opposing views on whether migration is an adaptation strategy. One group sees migration as the result of failed adaptation, a measure of last resort in face of grave threats of climate change and often as a sudden response to disasters (Brown, 2007; Felli, 2013). It generally emphasizes negative consequences of migration, namely pressure on migrant-receiving communities and loss of heritage and community for the migrants, especially if the diaspora is dispersed to various locations. The other group underlines the argument that migration has been used as a strategy to adapt to new socio-economic realities and can improve the situation not only for the migrant, but also for remittance-receiving home communities (Barnett and Adger, 2003; Foresight, 2011; Martin and Warner, 2012). This could be the case for example if their land is not rendered entirely uninhabitable and not all members relocate, but only a few people migrate to substitute losses in agricultural income of their families and thereby enhance resilience. It may therefore be an adequate coping mechanism reducing the vulnerability of climate impact-affected communities. Moreover, communities with low birthrates that receive migrants may benefit from an expansion of their workforce. Migration could therefore arguably be viewed as a form of adaptation (Gemenne and Blocher, 2017; McLeman and Smit, 2006).

The discussion of whether migration can be considered a form of adaptation, eventually leads to the question: If it is considered to be adaptation – how effective is it? It is clear that through migration people move not only geographically but also along social strata, their departure marking a point from which they are confronted with new socio-economic conditions. This may lead to an upward movement, e.g. because of better job opportunities in urban areas that provide higher income security in comparison to rural regions. But migration or displacement may also be detrimental to the movers' living standard or overall household income. In fact, it can lead into a poverty trap. The movements in the social strata are harder to evaluate than geographic routes and may not be limited to one generation. Migration can thus lead to intergenerational movements in the social strata by improving or impairing the offspring's capacities to succeed in life. Determining factors could be, for instance, access to education or healthcare. A professional training or traditional education which may have placed a person in the middle-income group among their peers in their place of origin, may place them near the lowest-income group in their new location. Therefore, migrants may not be sufficiently prepared for integration into urban labor markets. These considerations form the basis of the research question: **Is migration an effective adaptation to the impacts of climate change?**

In the attempt to decipher whether migration is an effective means of adaptation, this analysis also intends to shed light on the circumstances under which climate migration is socially successful in enhancing the migrants' resilience as well as highlighting factors that may push migrants into impoverishment. This will expand the existing literature beyond the scope of outlining of causal links between climate change and migration flows. Despite well-known uncertainties, the debate needs to shift from a discourse about the existence of climate migration and its definitions to a discussion on how such migration can be managed. Should communities be relocated if they are situated in high risk areas? What rights do they have and where do the responsibilities lie? What are the economic costs of involuntary climate migration? What are the non-economic costs of involuntary migration such as loss of cultural diversity and the uprooting of communities? Who benefits from climate migration if not the migrants themselves? While this thesis will not give a uniform answer to these fundamental questions, it will provide validated patterns through the analysis of two case studies, on the Southwest of Bangladesh and on the Republic of the Marshall Islands, adding value to the contemporary scientific discourse.

1.1. Thesis Structure

This dissertation is structured in four sections. The first part "Departure" reflects the current scientific debates around the concept of migration as an adaptation to climate change, and the uncertainties which persist around the nexus of climate change and migration. Through this a specification of significant variables for the selection of case studies and a first set of criteria for the evaluation of effectiveness will be identified. The second part "Unsettling Settlements" is the body of the analysis, including the two case studies in which the effectiveness of migration as a means of adaptation is analyzed. The first case study, based on fieldwork in Southwest Bangladesh, focuses on the migrants' perspective on their migration outcome. The second case study investigates internal and transboundary migration in the Marshall Islands and analyzes in depth how migration choices affect sending communities and migrants. The two case studies explore the different social, cultural, economic and natural systems from which the migrants come from and to where they migrate into. The third part of the dissertation "Settling Unsettlements" builds upon the findings of the case studies and develops hypotheses regarding the effectiveness of migration. It provides an overview of defining elements in migration management that can affect migration effectiveness. The fourth part "Arrival" provides an outlook on the future dynamics of climate change and migration and develops policy recommendations for migration management grounded in the fieldwork.

2. Terminology and Literature Review: Climate Change, Adaptation, Migration

Definitions of terms used in this research have evolved through scientific and political discourses and are used incoherently in the pertinent literature. I therefore introduce, discuss and define the core terms as used in my study below. Following the Straussian approach of Grounded Theory, I conducted a literature review, covering the scientific publications and reports of international organizations before the field research (Corbin and Strauss, 2015; Halaweh et al., 2008). Particularly relevant to the research question are the differentiations between climate change and changes in the natural environment connected to other anthropogenic drivers, the discourse on adaptation and how to evaluate it, and the contested definition of the term 'climate migrant'.

2.1. Definitions of Climate Change, Environmental Change and Global Change

Although a clear separation of migration drivers is often not possible, it is necessary to outline briefly the differences between climate, environmental and global change, as possible influences on migration patterns. The three terms are frequently used by different disciplines and authors without clear differentiation and sometimes even interchangeably. In this dissertation I rely on the following definitions. Climate change is defined by the United Nations Framework Convention on Climate Change (UNFCCC) as "*a change of climate which is attributed directly or indirectly to human activity that alters the composition of the global atmosphere and which is in addition to natural climate variability observed over comparable time periods*" (United Nations, 1992). Climate-change impacts, or short climate impacts, are "*the consequences of climate change – both expected and realised – for natural and human systems*" (Nature, 2018). In the field of climate change there are two other major terms which dominate both scientific and political debates. These are mitigation, the "*human intervention to reduce the sources or enhance the sinks of greenhouse gases*", and adaptation the "*process of adjustment to actual or expected climate and its effects*" (IPCC, 2012).

Environmental change can result from climate change, but also other natural or anthropogenic drivers, such as pollution, or excessive use of natural resources, such as raw materials, water or land. In this dissertation environmental change is used synonymously with environmental degradation that is linked to both climate change and other anthropogenic factors. Environmental change solely because of non-climate related anthropogenic drivers, such as industrial pollution is not the subject in this research.

Global change is yet broader, denoting the planetary dimensions of human activities, including environmental change. The German Advisory Council on Global Change (WBGU) gives the following definition, global change "*refers to the linkages between global environmental changes, economic globalization, cultural transformation and a widening North-South divide*" (WBGU, 2004). This definition makes clear that global change needs to be addressed through both, environmental and development policies. To conclude, climate migration is in its complexity and multicausality a phenomenon of global change.

2.2. Climate Migrants, Refugees and Disaster Displacement

In both the academic and in the grey literature, a variety of terms and concepts for the interlinkage between climate change and migration exists. The term "*climate refugee*" or "*environmental refugee*" has been widely used by nongovernmental organizations and the media. It also appeared in some (earlier) academic publications on the topic (Brown, 2007; Myers, 1993). The term "refugee", however, is defined in international law through the Geneva Convention Relating to the Status of Refugees of 1951 (UNHCR, 2010). This convention specifies "refugee" as a person who "*owing to well-founded fear of being persecuted for reasons of race, religion, nationality, membership of a particular social group or political opinion, is outside the country of his nationality and is unable or, owing to such fear, is unwilling to avail himself of the protection of that country; or who, not having a nationality and being outside the country of his former habitual residence as a result of such events, is unable or, owing to such fear, is unwilling to return to it*" (UNHCR, 2010). The circumstance of being persecuted is decisive for the applicability of the term refugee. Contemporary interpretation of the law does not view climate impacts as persecution (McAdam, 2011). Therefore, people who flee from natural disasters or environmental degradation are not included in this definition and therefore do not hold the right to press for asylum under the application of this protection regime. Moreover, a persecutor to flee from would have to be identified, this in turn would be the industrialized countries responsible for climate change that would likely be also the destinations to seek shelter for those affected by climate change (McAdam, 2011). Actually, the Geneva Convention applies only to persons who are outside of their home country and thus have migrated across borders. However, most of the people who are migrating because of environmental change, or who will do so in the future, will migrate within their own country (McAdam, 2011). This owes to the fact that international migration is generally more difficult, as it requires greater financial resources and more preparation. Also, many people prefer to stay within their country of origin, where their language and culture are practiced, in proximity of friends and family.

Climate displacement or *disaster displacement* are also regularly used descriptions, highlighting the often involuntary nature of movement. The term *disaster displacement* would be considered forced migration as per definition of the term through the International Association for the Study of Forced Migration: "*a general term that refers to the movements of refugees and internally displaced people (those displaced by conflicts) as well as people displaced by natural or environmental disasters, chemical or nuclear disasters, famine, or development projects*" (FMO, 2012). The link between climate change and forced migration has been challenged by Zetter (2012), who argues that because the changes in the environment may be slow and thus the migration multicausal, it cannot be categorized as forced migration. But likewise, a political conflict may arise slowly, forcing people out of a certain region gradually and not at some specific point in time. Moreover, climate change-induced environmental change may not always be slow, but can occur as extremes, such as floods or storms. Overall, it would be difficult to consider the determining factor of forced migration to be time. If only sudden or instant migration could be considered forced migration, the boundary timeline of such migratory movements would have to be strictly defined also for forced migration that happens due to conflicts. Then it would be in question whether the definition of conflict-induced migration includes people fleeing out of an affected region within a few hours of a bombardment, or over days, weeks, or even years. Therefore, making multicausality or time exclusion into factors for the definition of forced migration seems implausible and does also not relate to common definitions of the phenomenon. As environmental degradation due to climate change is a factor which the affected people probably cannot control (this is particularly true for the poor who have little or no capacities for adaptive measures), the migration due to climate change impacts can be seen as forced, even though it may be multicausal. While most human behaviors are multi-causal, the degradation of the environment can still be a trigger for migration. This discussion also shows that climate migration can take many forms (Warner, 2011).

In conclusion, the above considerations led me to apply the definition of environmental migrants as defined by the International Organization for Migration: *"Environmental migrants are persons or groups of persons who, for compelling reasons of sudden or progressive change in the environment that adversely affects their lives or living conditions, are obliged to leave their habitual homes, or choose to do so, either temporarily or permanently, and who move either within their country or abroad"* (Laczko and Aghazarm, 2009). Accordingly, I define the term climate migrants as environmental migrants who are affected by environmental change that has likely been caused or significantly influenced by anthropogenic climate change. The use of the rather neutral terms *climate migration* or *climate migrant* also avoids unduly limitations regarding legal status and spatial extent, as connected to the term refugees. It also allows me to include displacement as well as planned outmigration in face of climate change-induced degradation. This does not mean that climate change impacts and related environmental change were the only drivers of migration, other push and pull factors (Lee, 1966) may have contributed to the migration decision of the individual. These connections and the location-specific circumstances are elaborated in the respective case studies. Not covered in this dissertation are displacements which are caused by infrastructural projects, such as the building of dams, or displacement that happens due to geological events, such as earthquakes and tsunamis which have no correlation with climate change.

2.3. Migration and the Adaptation Discourse

Before exploring the potential effectiveness of migration as adaptation, it has to be established whether or not migration can be viewed as adaptation. This question arises from the literature because authors from various disciplines have taken different approaches in framing climate migration, as either adaptation to climate change or as an impact of climate change. However, so far it has not been sufficiently determined why or under which circumstance the first or the second interpretation applies to climate migration. It is clear that migration can result in better opportunities or also in hardship (Opitz Stapleton et al., 2017).

Whereas mitigation aims to avoid causes, not effects, adaption seeks to avoid effects, not to avoid causes. Therefore, the goal of adaptation is not to experience effects of climate change. The academic literature on adaptation is quite fragmented. Several authors provide definitions and classifications of adaptation (Brooks and Fisher, 2011; Kates et al., 2012; Nelson et al., 2007). The IPCC, building a consensus on the definition described that "*in human systems, adaptation seeks to moderate or avoid harm or exploit beneficial opportunities. In some natural systems, human intervention may facilitate adjustment to expected climate and its effects*" (IPCC, 2012). It is important to note that when humans are at the center of analysis, the definition of the effects of climate change cannot be limited to the physical event itself. They include secondary or tertiary effects, such as the consequences for livelihoods in agriculture, productivity and potentially even more fundamental effects such as the reduced ability to lead a self-determined life. For example, if the impact of climate change is ultimately poverty caused by a loss of livelihood, adaptation should at the very least seek to prevent poverty if it is not possible to protect or reestablish the same livelihood. The physical environmental changes and their effects on socio-economic conditions constitute the impacts of climate change, perhaps along with other factors, which cause a person to migrate. The migration itself can thereby be seen as either an adaptation, especially if it is a planned movement in anticipation of effects of climate change and thus a strategic decision, or as a mere reaction to an impact or a set of impacts. This understanding of adaptation would require a revision of the IPCC definition which includes both strategic behavior and the plain exploitation of opportunities in face of climate change impacts.

What emerges from the literature is that adaptation can take place in various forms, in different spatial settings and on different timescales (Nelson et al., 2007). For this reason, another prominent discussion in the literature is concerned with categorizing different types of adaptation. Some authors distinguish between different types of adaptation varying in the degree of depth of the intervention from incremental to transformational, with several overlapping concepts and grey areas of adaptation measures which are both continuous and transformative (Brooks and Fisher, 2011; Kates et al., 2012; Termeer et al., 2017). In the fifth assessment report the IPCC introduces a more systematic approach and determines three categories of adaptation based on the type of intervention: structural/physical, social and institutional (Noble et al., 2014). "*Assisted migration*" is mentioned under structural ecosystem-based adaptation, and social behavioral adaptation (Noble et al., 2014). Furthermore, the IPCC resumes that "*migration may be adaptive or maladaptive or both depending on context and the individuals involved*" (Noble et al., 2014). Mal-adaptation can be defined as follows: "*actions undertaken to adapt to climate impacts that do not succeed in reducing vulnerability but increase it instead*" (OECD, 2009). The investigation in this dissertation falls under the IPCC category of social behavioral adaptation because the movements researched occurred unassisted.

Another important debate in academics and policy is concerned with the definition of a successful adaptation (Noble et al., 2014). This debate has very practical implications for the international development community of NGOs, policy makers and financing institutions as they have to evaluate projects (Spearman and McGray, 2011). Yohe & Tol (2002) use feasibility, acceptability and efficacy as measurements and define adaptation efficacy rather generally as "*reducing either sensitivity or exposure.*" Equally general Brooks & Fisher (2011) define "*successful adaptation* [as keeping] *inclusive development on track.*" This would in turn mean that adaptation leading to greater inequalities could not be considered successful.

As evaluation criteria for successful adaptation, Brooks & Fisher (2011) building upon Yohe & Tol (2002) and Neil Adger, Arnell, & Tompkins (2005) suggest: "feasibility, efficacy/effectiveness, efficiency, acceptability/legitimacy, equity, sustainability". Regarding the evaluation of effectiveness of adaptation they suggest to distinguish between the impact of an adaptation measure (1) at the institutional level, (2) the individual or group levels, or (3) on outcomes (for example regarding mortality, health or poverty) (Brooks and Fisher, 2011). As the migration as adaptation in this research falls into the category of social behavioral adaptation of the IPCC, the effectiveness of this means of adaptation is assessed specifically with regard to points (2) and (3). Overall, it is important to note that "defining adaptation success requires consideration of the context in which adaptation activities occur"(Spearman and McGray, 2011). Consequently, there is no uniform indicator or metric to measure successful adaptation (Adger and Barnett, 2009; Brooks and Fisher, 2011). To address migration as adaptation in this research I choose the criteria of effectiveness. I develop an operationalization of effectiveness based on several pre-defined categories which are linked to the categories of the Human Development Index (HDI) and further adapted to the findings of the field research which originate from the application of Grounded Theory (see chapter 4.1.).

Migration as an Impact versus Migration as Adaptation

Besides the academic debate on defining and systemizing the concept of adaptation, there are also different approaches with regard to whether migration is labeled as an impact of or an adaptation to climate change. Whereas linkages of climatic events and migration have existed throughout history, the nexus between anthropogenic climate change and migration has only emerged since the beginning of this century as a topic of academic investigation. The research around this connection between climate change and migration is growing (Piguet, 2018), but still the phenomenon is insufficiently understood and causes controversies in the scientific community and likewise in political or public debates. Key insights related to the question of migration as adaptation to climate change versus migration as an impact and the evolving scientific discourse are summarized below.

The scientific debate gained momentum after Myers's article "Environmental Refugees in a Globally Warmed World" was published in the early 1990s (Myers, 1993). This study estimates the numbers of "environmental refugees" at that time as well as numbers of people who would be displaced in the future. The analysis was based on rough assessments of environmental impacts amplified by climate change in several locations, compared to a baseline scenario without climate change. The resulting estimate was 150 to 200 million "*environmental refugees*" until 2050. Although Myers did acknowledge the weaknesses in his methodology and emphasized that it should be seen only as an approximation to the scale of the problem, it still caused vehement opposition (see for example: Piguet, 2008). The widely-cited analysis triggered discussion largely around two topics: the estimates and the terminology "*environmental refugee*". Nevertheless, the estimates which Myers again pronounced in 2005 were included in the IPCC and the 2006 Stern Review on the Economics of Climate Change (Myers, 2005; Stern, 2007).

The variation of possible climate change impacts on the extent and nature of migratory movements in a 2°C- or 4°C-world are addressed by Gemenne (2011). While also criticizing the simplicity of deterministic approaches towards the scale of future climate change-induced migration, Gemenne emphasizes that these predictions are all based on a 2°C-increase in global temperature. Migration as a consequence of a 4°C warmer world may not only change in terms of numbers of people shifting locations, but will also be altered in its characteristics as people may react differently if climate change impacts are so severe that they pose a threat to their lives. Furthermore, he argues that while (temporary) migration is a traditional adaptation strategy to changes in the environment, climate change and especially warming levels beyond the 2°C-threshold may make migration difficult because they would diminish the available resources needed to relocate (Gemenne, 2011).

Frequently, the estimates about the future scale of climate migration have been labeled alarmist. While political stakeholders frequently demand projections of the numbers of future climate migrants, it is futile to make such an attempt in the absence of a definition of the term (see chapter 2.1.). It may however be possible to make estimates of temporary or permanent internal displacement due to specific climate impacts such as sea level rise or zones whose climate conditions would exceed the upper limit for human's thermoregulatory capacity for more than half of the year because of "*deadly heat*" (Mora et al., 2017). One advance to estimate future migration flows within countries was made by a transdisciplinary team of the World Bank which projects that in a high emissions scenario with rising developmental inequalities more than 143 million people could move by 2050 within their respective countries in Latin America, South Asia and Sub-Saharan Africa due to slow onset events, including rising sea levels, crop failure and water insecurity (Kumari Rigaud et al., 2018).

The notion of migration as an adaptation strategy to climate change has just recently been developed, in response to the rather negative contemplations over climate change-induced migration. It has been criticized that "doomsday" scenarios of millions of migrants relocating across borders are used to pressure governments to act on mitigation. The argument is embedded in the criticism of an evolving perception of migrants as threats to security which has gained foothold in the media and public opinion since the 9/11 terror attacks of 2001 in the United States (Castles, 2003; Karyotis, 2007). The intention of framing migration as one of many adaptation measures may therefore be to avert negative images of millions of poor migrants crossing international borders that could paralyze (political) action, or even instigate greater anti-immigration policies on the national level (Black et al., 2011). Therefore, the interpretation of migration as an accepted and effective form of adaptation could serve to establish and fund mechanisms for a managed outmigration from high-risk areas.

Tacoli argues that migration provides the opportunity of income diversification for vulnerable households and thereby should also be viewed as adaptation (Tacoli, 2009). The author calls for a more in-depth analysis of the causal relations between climate change and migration. For instance, the very poor may not have the adaptive capacity and resources to leave their home and could thus not be counted into the estimates of people likely to migrate. Tacoli sees the possibility that climate change may reduce the capacity to migrate because of diminishing (financial) resources. In this case, the immobility of groups should then be seen as an impact of climate change.

Jacobson et al. (2018) found through a case study in Cambodia that migration may be a maladaptive response to the effects of climate change because it does not address the climate impacts on food security which contributed to the migration decision. At the same time, the migration investigated in this case study has led to negative consequences for sending communities. The authors established that problems in the sending communities included a diminishing labor force and social challenges, for example in connection with the safety of women left behind in the villages (Jacobson et al., 2018).

Some recent articles use the concept of translocality which was conceptualized by Greiner et al. (2015) in the context of climate change migration (Greiner et al., 2015; Sakdapolrak et al., 2016). Translocality refers to the interconnections between people and places, for example households securing their livelihood and diversifying their risk of income loss by working in multiple places (Greiner et al., 2015). Greiner et al. do not address the linkages between climate change and migration but evaluate the effects of migration on home communities, for instance through remittances or knowledge transfers. Parts of the former scientific discourse are portrayed as a dialogue between alarmists and skeptics (Greiner et al., 2015).

Gemenne & Blocher (2017) lay out a research agenda on "*how can migration serve adaptation to climate change?*". They highlight methodological and conceptual pitfalls and reject the notion of migrants as victims of climate change. In this, they arrive at the conclusion that there is no consensus on "*whether the adaptive benefits of migration outweigh the 'costs' to the home community*" and that more research is needed. Furthermore, the authors stress that such research should take into account migrants, sending and receiving communities.

Raleigh, Jordan and Salehyan (2008) argue that also the IPCC's view of the nexus between migration and climate change has shifted over the last decades, from the notion of migration as a consequence of a changing climate towards a more complex analysis of broader vulnerabilities and adaptive capacities of communities or regions where migration may be a factor. In its 1990 report it was emphasized that "*the gravest effects of climate change may be those on human migration as millions are displaced by shoreline erosion, coastal flooding and severe drought*" (IPCC, 1990) whereas the "*reference to* human *migration as a* consequence *of climate change was eliminated from the 2001 Policy Maker's Summary*" (Raleigh et al., 2008). Ober (2014) emphasizes that in the 2014 IPCC report the views on climate migration remain diverse between different chapters and working groups.

From the outlined literature, migration could be seen as a strategy to "*moderate or avoid harm or exploit beneficial opportunities,*" as adaptation is defined (IPCC, 2012). However, the case in which migration is seen as harm in itself, for instance when it is an involuntary movement, or the case in which migration is ineffective in averting harm, may constitute reasons not to label migration as a form of adaptation. Because of the unclear definition of what migration as adaptation would constitute, the debate on climate change and migration is characterized by conceptual pitfalls. If migration is categorized as adaptation, it must imply that through migration the exposure and / or vulnerability to climate change impacts are reduced. Even more important than the classification of migration and theoretical advancements of the concept of adaptation is the presumption that such an analysis may give insights into the circumstances which make migration an effective or successful adaptation strategy to climate change and thus outlines possibilities to replicate such conditions. However, to decipher such conditions, one has to understand the reasons for migratory movements and how these interact with climate change. Therefore, to form the basis of the qualitative systems analysis it needs to be discussed how uncertainties in the nexus of climate change and migration can be addressed.

3. Theoretical Framework

To explain the relevance of the research question, this chapter begins exploring the topic of climate migration in the context of global change. Through a review of the existing literature and the theories around migration I identify both a research and a theory gap in the topic of migration as adaptation. For this reason I chose the approach of Grounded Theory combined with the methods of a multilevel system analysis based on two case studies.

3.1. Climate Migration in the Context of Global Change

Climate migration is closely intertwined with other phenomena of global change, notably urbanization and population growth (Price & Benton-Short, 2007). In this century the population in most regions will likely reach its maximum accompanied by an unprecedented increase in the urban population (Basten et al., 2013; UN Department of Economic and Social Affairs, 2014, 2017, 2018; WBGU, 2016). Rapid urbanization and human development in cities, which began with the advancements of the industrial revolution and accelerated through various stages, rest on an excessive resource exploitation that is unequally distributed among world regions and income groups (Lenton et al., 2016). Climate change is one of the negative consequences of the intensive energy input from fossil fuels and is becoming more and more a push factor for migration. In general, the majority of migrants seeks to live in cities (International Organization for Migration, 2015), often in hope of a higher or more stable income. Displaced people who are affected by natural disasters also seek refuge in nearby cities where food security is higher. Climate migration is not an isolated occurrence, but is taking place along with other forms of migration that are directed towards cities and culminating in high demands for urban housing and services. Much of the recent urbanization in developing nations has happened without a concomitant growth in urban labor markets. Current trends, however, imply that regardless of this, migration into cities is likely to continue with migrants often settling in city slums (International Organization for Migration, 2017). Displacement of people from their homeland due to climate change impacts would add pressure to already instable urban systems. As even a moderate 2°C warming would lead to significant impacts in many regions and as infrastructural adaptation is often not deployed or not feasible, it is reasonable to assume that climate migration may come to constitute a significant challenge in the 21st century.

More in-depth research on the different links between climate impacts and the effectiveness of adaptation measures is thus urgently needed. Whereas several governments of small island nations such as Tuvalu, Kiribati or the Maldives have raised concerns over having to relocate populations and have engaged in exploring the possibility of purchasing land elsewhere, larger nations are also becoming increasingly aware of areas that will no longer be suitable for habitation (McAdam, 2012). The general trend of rural-urban migration may be amplified by the negative effects of climate change impacts on agricultural production. A variety of rural push and urban pull factors are leading people to migrate to cities (Jedwab et al., 2014; Lee, 1966). Rural push factors include the underdevelopment of rural areas and persistent poverty, limited access to healthcare and education infrastructure, lack of opportunities and the absence of insurances against risks of crop failure and other forms of social protection (Poelhekke, 2011; Yuki, 2007). Some farmers also use circular or seasonal migration to diversify their income (FAO, 2016). Especially in regions where agriculture is largely rain-fed, subsistence farming and livelihood creation of smallholder farmers may become more difficult. Technological advancements could lessen detrimental effects, but may also decrease the demand for rural labor, which consequentially could increase outmigration. Migration of a family member to urban areas can have positive effects for the sending community through the provision of remittances and knowledge transfers (Skeldon, 1997). Castles (2008) sees the destruction of agricultural livelihoods as part of a wider social transformation and argues to view migration in the context of these changes (Castles, 2010). In many rural areas, extreme weather events, such as tropical storms, droughts or flooding, pose increasing risks for human health and safety. Urban pull factors include employment opportunities, better education and healthcare, higher wages, better provision of services and fewer risks to livelihoods (International

Organization for Migration, 2015). However, if push factors are strong enough rural-urban migration can occur even in the absence of opportunities in cities (Fay and Opal, 2000; Jedwab et al., 2014; Poelhekke, 2011). Moreover, governmental policies regarding migration, city development and investments can also shape migration patterns (Ades and Glaeser, 1995; Seto, 2011). Although migrants seek a safer environment in cities, many urban settlements are also affected by risks of climate change impacts and the poor are especially affected (Revi et al., 2014; Roy et al., 2016).

Unmanaged or badly managed migration can be a determining factor for the quality of the migrants' life and integration into their receiving communities. The lack of livelihood options and basic services for migrants may cause societal friction or even contribute to emerging conflicts. Kelley et al. (2015) observed this in Syria where they show that an unusually severe and badly managed drought displaced farmers to the peripheries of cities, together with Iraqi and Palestinian refugees (Kelley et al., 2017, 2015). Against the backdrop of the Arab spring, many factors, including long-term political oppression of the Assad regime, dire living conditions in the cities, rising food prices and declining GDP during the drought led people to protest (Polk, 2013). The drought and the government's failure to address it added to the political instability and the people's disillusionment with the Assad regime (Kelley et al., 2015).

Further, the reoccurring deaths of refugees drowning in the Mediterranean during their passage to Europe and overcrowded camps in wealthy receiving communities arguably mark the failure of policy to adequately address problems in places of origin as well as the incapacity to manage migration. In light of current and future climate impacts, possibly leading to further migration flows, it should be established under which circumstances migration can be an effective and thus a desirable adaptation strategy in response to climate change. In order to avoid policy failure, the limitations or conditions of migration as an adaptation option need to be defined.

Even more important than the political or security implications of climate migration are the closely connected questions of risks, responsibility, and justice. Whether migration is an effective adaptation strategy cannot be evaluated solely on the basis of economic considerations. Factors such as the loss of hereditary land or of traditions in the diaspora cannot be adequately expressed in monetary terms.

It further has to be considered that those who may have to move are not responsible for anthropogenic climate change. For instance, many of the rural poor in developing countries will be severely affected by climate change and thereby may need to leave their land. They often live in areas exposed to hazards because property prices are low and they have the least resources to adapt to a changing environment in situ (Mitlin and Satterthwaite, 2014; Revi et al., 2014). The poor have not contributed to climate change, as in general their lifestyles produce very little or net-zero anthropogenic greenhouse gas emissions (Oxfam, 2015; Rao et al., 2014). Thus following a causative principle for assigning responsibility, it would be unfair for these people to have to relocate. This leads to the question: Can an adaptation strategy be considered effective if it is inherently unjust? These aspects make the topic highly relevant to contemporary societal discourses on climate justice, transboundary obligations and the connected allocation of responsibilities. The loss of homeland may have severe implications on whether migrants themselves see their movement as an effective adaptation strategy for the changing environment.

3.2. Theories Explaining Migration

Theoretical approaches to migration are divergent, varying among disciplines but also depending on the units of analysis (Brettell and Hollifield, 2015). Economic theory on migration is largely based on rational choice models for the explanation of movements and economic models' predominantly look at labor migration. The migrant in the economic models thus acts as a maximizer of individual utility and therefore bases his decision on a cost-benefit analysis. In economic theorems, labor markets are examined to predict or explain migratory movements. In the Harris-Todaro Model, rural to urban migration is explained by the differences in incomes

(Harris and Todaro, 1970). Hence, despite high unemployment rates in cities, people may still be inclined to migrate from rural areas to cities if urban incomes are disproportionately higher than rural incomes (for an expansion of the Harris-Todaro Model, see also Fields, 1975). This model does not take into account environmental factors explicitly; it only implicitly includes them through the effects of environmental degradation on rural incomes and agricultural productivity. Since the development of the Harris-Todaro Model, concepts emerged which go beyond assessments of labor markets when explaining migration but fall short of explaining the interaction of climate extremes with migration. In "*The new economics of labor migration*" Stark & Bloom (1985) arrive at the conclusion that migration is not only an individual's choice driven by "*desperation*" or "*boundless optimism*," but a strategy to manage risks for the entire family or household. It takes into consideration the remittance system existent between diaspora and home communities and states that it also serves to help people stay in their home communities. In sociological theory the topic of migration is often approached with regard to assimilation of migrants into receiving communities, the influence of the social capital like networks on the decision to migrate as well as the situation of migrants in the diaspora.

Because numbers of migrants and also refugees have risen dramatically and the nature of migratory movements has changed in times of globalization, migration scholars have called for the development of an altered theory of migration and also specifically for a better framework to understand forced migration, a field insufficiently reflected in existing migration research (Castles, 2003). As Castles (2003) explains, "*Migration is an existential shift which affects every part of human life. No single discipline can adequately describe and analyse this experience on its own.*" Climate migration can be involuntary and thus be forced migration. In the literature, it is generally categorized as "*Disaster Induced Displacement*" together with migration after earthquakes and industrial accidents (FMO, 2012). Ahsan, Karuppannan, & Kellett, (2011) suggest "*that we are witnessing a new kind of migration that has not been seen in the past.*" For climate migration it is thus even more essential to take an interdisciplinary approach.

Nevertheless, the literature is divided and consists of perspectives from the humanities to perspectives from the natural sciences. Cross-cutting, interdisciplinary research is scarce, but has started to emerge in recent years (see for instance: Kelley, Mohtadi, Cane, Seager, & Kushnir, 2015 on the 2007-2010 drought in Syria and the resulting rural-urban migration). For advancement in the field of climate migration research it is crucial to collect more data and to base the generation of hypotheses on this information. Due to the lack of applicable theory which could explain the phenomenon of climate migration as adaptation adequately, I am using a Grounded Theory approach for my analysis.

3.3. Knowledge Gaps in Climate Impact Research

The knowledge about climate change impacts has increased tremendously over the last decades, and as the 5th report of the Intergovernmental Panel on Climate Change (IPCC) has shown in detail, climate change has led to observable impacts across all continents and oceans and therefore already affects livelihoods (Field et al., 2014). However, there are regional and sectoral disparities in the state of knowledge of observed and future impacts, some of which derive from a lack of capacity for local scientific research. Nevertheless, "*The scarcity of robust scientific evidence supporting the attribution of observed impacts to climate change in some vulnerable regions does not indicate that no such impacts have occurred*" (Hansen and Cramer, 2015). There is high regional variability in the existence of scientific assessment of observed impacts: "*In some cases, despite the expectation that impacts might have occurred, individual elements of the causal chain leading from changes in climate to changes in the respective impact system were not addressed in scientific studies, making attribution impossible*" (Hansen and Cramer, 2015). Despite progress in climate impact research, some gaps in our knowledge of causal chains are likely to persist in the near future. For research on climate migration there is a particular need to address these knowledge gaps. From the literature review, I draw the conclusion that a large part of the debate around the causal links between climate change and migration has circled around a two-fold gap in our understanding (figure 1).

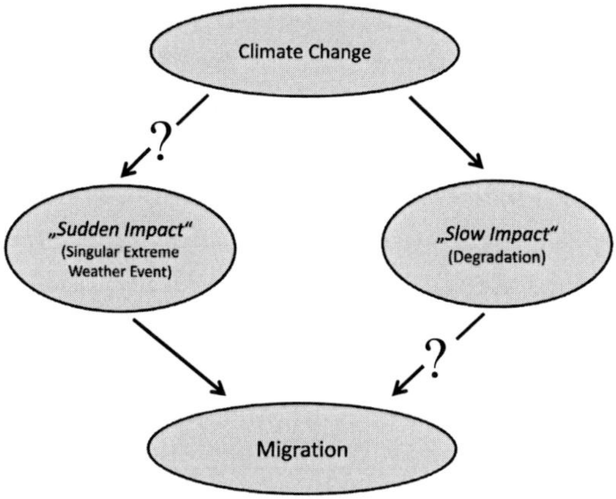

Figure 1 The Two-Fold Gap in our Understanding of the Links between Climate Change and Migration. In a conceptual division of sudden and slow impacts, there are two gaps in our knowledge on the links between climate change and human migration (source: own).

To demonstrate this, a distinction between "sudden impacts," such as tropical storms, and "slow impacts" such as degradation or sea level rise, is useful (McLeman and Hunter, 2010; Siegele, 2012). While this division is methodologically contestable because sudden events can also be the result of long-term changes in the environment and the impacts of degradation may as well appear to be sudden, it nonetheless serves to illustrate the debate around the existence of climate migrants. Whereas during the occurrence of sudden extreme events the migratory movements can easily be linked to the event, as everyone moves during roughly the same time period, the specific extreme event cannot individually be linked to climate change (Burkett et al., 2014; Cramer et al., 2014). With tropical storms, for instance, one can make projections about the increases of intensity and frequency of storms, but one cannot attribute a singular event clearly to the effects of climate change (Cramer et al., 2014) because it could also be explained with natural variability. Conversely, with regard to slow impacts, such as degradation, rising temperatures and sea levels, the knowledge base for attribution to climate change is solid. However, it is extremely difficult to link migratory movements to slow onset impacts because people generally leave the affected area at different points in time. For example, some parts of the population may leave right at the beginning of a degradation process; some may leave after crops have failed consecutively, etc. The individual's decision for migration would depend on varying factors, making a clear attribution to the changes in the environment difficult. Still, the absence of the decisive evidence does not indicate that climate migration does not exist. Given the already existing evidence about climate impacts and migration, it is more important to accept the knowledge gaps and evaluate policy implications than solely aim at further evidence on causal linkages between climate change and migration.

Knowledge gaps should not prevent scientific analysis from going beyond the debate on causal chains. Nonetheless, the presently available assessments of the evidence on observed climate impacts must be considered. I therefore take a pragmatic approach. Instead of avoiding the topic of climate change-induced migration or questioning its existence on the basis of the lack of causal evidence (Black, 2001), the gaps in our knowledge need to be bridged with relevant information about the place-specific push factors of migration and how they relate to observed climate regional or local climate impacts. This entails a rigorous analysis of the occurring changes in the environment which have led to or been a factor in the migratory movements, whether or not it is plausible that climate change has been a significant factor in these changes. Where uncertainties exist, these are clearly identified and accounted for. Although in some cases a lack of data may remain a problem, there is a chance to make reasonable assumptions about present cases of migration. Furthermore, the comparison of migrations may lead to conclusions about "*a number of factors that determine the outcome of the migration experience*" (Foner, 1998). The isolation of such factors over others may form ground for further research and assist the development of policies for the management of climate migration. This thesis does therefore not claim causality in the singular case of an individual migrating because of climate change. In contrast it establishes that migration is happening at a time of observable climate impacts that can influence migration decisions along with other environmental, economic, demographic or political push and pull factors (Black et al., 2011). Whereas "*the migration literature has focused theoretically and empirically on questions related to why individuals move or to their process of leaving altogether*" (Mallick, 2015) this study goes one step further. It investigates the cases when people move because of environmental changes which are likely to have a connection to observed changes in the climate system and asks if their movement is an effective adaptation.

3.4. Operationalization of Effectiveness

Following the Straussian approach of Grounded Theory, this research begins with a specification of effectiveness by introducing an operationalization. At the center of this research are the people who were affected by climate change and who migrated as a response or adaptation to the new environmental conditions and the communities who stayed behind. While some research has focused on adaptive capacity of countries or regions, the effectiveness of the individual's adaptation to climate change – which links to the adaptive capacity of the individual – is crucial for a thorough understanding of the phenomenon and future policy making. As Saroar & Routray (2012) note "*ultimately, it is the people, not the country, who suffer because of their poor adaptive capacity. Therefore, for enhancing individuals' adaptive capacity against particular impacts that make their livelihood insecure, it is more logical to assess the adaptive capacity of people, not the country.*"

Through the interviews, as well as complementary research methods, such as observations and literature review, the effectiveness of migration as a form of adaptation to climate change will be evaluated on three levels of analysis: First, the individual level, including the distinct experiences of migrants; second, the level of the sending community, recognizing the effect of migration on those who stay behind; and third, the level of the receiving communities, referring to challenges at the level of the city administration. These evaluations will be made separately but on the same case studies or migration routes. This will not only enrich the overall analytical depth of the study, but also allow for a triangulation of sources, reducing possible bias in the data set. In the conclusion, the results of this multilevel analysis will be reflected upon conjointly. This approach of addressing migration as adaptation on these three different levels has also been emphasized as an important future research direction of climate migration (Gemenne and Blocher, 2017) and is common practice in migration studies (Castles et al., 2013; Lall et al., 2006).

Because climate change poses a threat to the homeland of humans, the effectiveness of migration as a form of adaptation cannot be evaluated solely in terms of economic gains and losses, like it could potentially be the case for exclusively economic migration. If the reason to migrate is economic, effectiveness could possibly be measured in the overall financial situation after relocation. However, measuring effectiveness of migration as adaptation to climate change by just assuming a homo economicus perception of migrants does not suffice. If a person is displaced from their traditional land, other factors, such as the inability to perform one's type of employment, may contribute to the overall outcome of migration for the individual. Thus it is not enough to compare income and living conditions before and after a migratory movement, although it will form part of the evaluation.

It is important to emphasize that this study does not compare migrants with a group of non-migrants. The effectiveness of adaptation is not addressed by asking: 'Who is better off, the migrant or the person who stayed?' This question could only be addressed in a larger quantitative analysis of migrants and sending communities. Then, for example, the method of Propensity Score Matching could be used to estimate how people with similar biographic and socio-economic backgrounds from sending communities fare in terms of income or other quantitative indicators after a climate impact has occurred in comparison with those who migrated. Ideally, this comparison of people who have the same propensity for outmigration would be based on a dataset over a longer period of time that captures the situation before and after the climate impact or which includes several time points in the years after the climate event. There could even be a third control group in the receiving communities, to see whether migrants are worse off over a period of several years than their statistically identical counterparts in the receiving locations. However, this would require a larger research consortium, as the necessary data in areas which are marked by a high degree of informality is hard to obtain. Such a study would certainly produce valuable insights into the economic success of migrants and would be complimentary to my research objectives. For the question of effectiveness a comparison between the economic indicators of these three indicators does not suffice. This is due to the fact that many of the analyzed movements are within the spectrum of forced migration which means, the person who has stayed could be always worse off than the one who left. That would make an analysis based on a possibly trapped control group biased. Therefore, effectiveness is instead based on the following operationalization.

For the individual, relocation is entirely ineffective if the migrant ends up worse off than he would have been had he stayed put. Following this, a relocation is the more effective the greater the improvement is, compared to the situation the migrant would have been in, had he or she stayed in their home community. A relocation can be deemed a truly effective adaptation strategy if the migrant ends up at least as well off as she would have been without the push factors, e.g. had there been no climate change. This goes beyond the question of the fulfillment of the individual's intentions of migration which are risk minimizing strategies to reduce their vulnerability and or individual exposure to a hazard. For example, the migrant's intentions for migration may be to save his life, or to secure livelihood for his family. In this, he or she may have been successful; however, they may be still worse off than they would have been if they could have stayed in their home community and had not experienced the climate change impacts that forced their migration decision. For the individual it has to be established to which degree the demolition of the migrant's property through the effects of climate change constitutes the preconditions for a forced movement and how this violates the migrant's rights. This may prompt the question whether a migration that occurs due to a violation of the inalienable rights of a person can be considered effective, even if it is economically profitable. Rather than adhering to a strictly causative principle, in which it would have to be proven by the migrant that his or her migration has been induced by climate change, this study will take into account the responsibilities that result from a precautionary principle. This is examined by identifying the key rights which migrants and non-migrants alike are entitled to on the basis of the Universal Declaration of Human Rights and more specifically through the International Covenant on Economic, Social and Cultural Rights (UN General Assembly, 1966)[1]. Basic rights identified in the covenant are workers' rights, the right to social security and social protection, the right to an adequate standard of living, the right to health, the right to education and cultural rights. The degree of achievement of these entitlements, such as fair wages, may be altered through the migration or displacement which is why they are a relevant factor in the determination of the nation states' responsibility for achieving effectiveness of migration for the individual.

To choose adequate indicators for effectiveness which can be covered in interviews with the migrants themselves I used the Human Development Index (HDI) as a guiding tool. This index covers three general areas of human development: life expectancy at birth, education (expected and mean years of schooling) and gross national income per capita (UNDP, 2018). Migration as adaptation needs to aim at maintaining or improving these areas of life if it is considered to be effective. Although a qualitative analysis cannot deliver a complete assessment of these indicators, I used the general topics of economic situation, health and education based on the core areas of the HDI and identified proxies for these to be included in the set of questions. Because the interviews are semi-structured, it allowed for

---

[1] Article 2.1 of the Covenant on Economic, Social and Cultural Rights states: "*Each State Party to the present Covenant undertakes to take steps, individually and through international assistance and cooperation, especially economic and technical, to the maximum of its available resources, with a view to achieving progressively the full realization of the rights recognized in the present Covenant by all appropriate means, including particularly the adoption of legislative measures*" (United Nations, 1966).

other areas that arose during the process of field research to evolve and be addressed. This approach therefore goes beyond a quantitative analysis and captures the experience of the migrants in these areas of human development. Hence it is possible to identify shortages or crises which may not be visible in a quantitative analysis because only annual averages are considered or because the experience simply cannot be captured in numbers. Thus the first sets of indicators and their preliminary proxies are included as follows: economic situation (access to income, does the migrant send or receive remittances), health (access to hospitals and healthcare, access to sanitary facilities such as toilets, access to food, access to drinking water, health risks associated with the migration itself), and education (access to schooling and vocational training). From the field research the category of self-determination (access to former or preferred type of employment, freedom of movement, freedom of choosing a place to live, owning land rights or secure lease) and preservation of culture (the ability to engage in and preserve one's own culture) and knowledge about the destination (information about labor market opportunities and living situation, information about the rule of law when migrating internationally) emerged. To conclude the semi-structured interview, migrants were asked how their current living situation related to the conditions they experienced in their places of origin. The indicators and proxies for effectiveness developed also through the interviews and focus group discussions with migrants because their evaluation which criteria have to be fulfilled to consider a migration an effective option for adaptation is key to the understanding of the problem. Furthermore, the analysis of overall effectiveness will not only include the outcome of the movement for the migrating person but also extend to the effects such migration flows have on receiving and sending communities. This analysis can potentially contradict the outcome of the evaluation of effectiveness of adaptation on the level of the individual migrant. For example, the individual's migration could be effective, in that he is doing as well in his place of arrival as he was in his home place without the effects of climate change. Nevertheless, his outmigration could have negative (or positive) effects on his place of origin and in the receiving community alike.

In the home communities of the migrants, this would be analyzed through information on remittances and a comparison of how people who had adapted in-situ had fared in terms of income and food security, as well as their own evaluation whether or not they assume resettlement to be the better option. One supposition could be that migrant envoys – people who have been sent by the home community to work in a different location – support the non-migration and resilience of the community or their own family by sending remittances. In this case it would also have to be analyzed what the social effects are if, for example, the male breadwinners work in a city away from their families.

In the receiving communities it will be discussed what the midterm absorptive capacities of the labor and housing market are and to what degree the interim capacities of the infrastructure of health and schooling systems can be extended to absorb an influx of migrants. Effectiveness for receiving communities may strongly depend on the overall state of the urban economy and on the numbers of migrants, just as whether or not policies are in place to manage the migration so that migrants can successfully integrate. Moreover, the effects of international climate migration – if applicable – on relations between countries and regional stability can be a factor.

While all three groups; migrants, home and receiving communities, are addressed in this research, the aim is not to weigh one experience of the phenomenon of migration against the other, but to make visible the different effects on groups or communities it can have. Through this a more holistic analysis of climate migration and its effectiveness can be developed that may also help to formulate coherent policy advice.

4. Research Design: Grounded Theory Driven Multi-Level System Analysis Based on Two Cases

Like most phenomena of global change, climate migration can only be understood by interlinking the research of various disciplines (Castles, 2003; WBGU, 1997). The multiplicity of determining factors for migration and its outcome requests an analysis, which at the same time includes and reduces complexity. Building upon the existing research of migration (Harris and Todaro 1970; Castles 2003; Brettell and Hollifield 2015), I developed a conceptual systems model that considers multiple levels of analysis. It takes into account two case studies which are evaluated within the larger international structural setting in which the migrations occur. This method is suitable because in order to understand the nature of migration and its effects, a system composed of migrants, sending and receiving communities and the relevant governance bodies must be analyzed under the impacts of climate change. Therefore, to gain a full overview, it is not sufficient to isolate one group or component from another. Because research question could not be fully answered without capturing and understanding the experience of climate migration, qualitative research methods are used in this thesis. As Pope & Mays (1995) explain: "*The goal of qualitative research is the development of concepts which help us to understand social phenomena in natural (rather than experimental) settings, giving due emphasis to the meanings, experiences, and views of all the participants.*"

Using quantitative methods would not be a feasible option to find answers to the research question. While there are quantitative studies with regard to the nexus of climate change and migration (Beine and Jeusette, 2018; Carvajal and Pereira, 2010; Findley, 1994; Thiede et al., 2016), the overall data availability and quality is insufficient for a detailed analysis of migration effectiveness. Especially the data quality and quantity on internal migration is highly dependent on what countries provide. The most exposed countries with large vulnerable populations often do not have good datasets. This often leads to the fact that the effect of environmental change on migration patterns cannot be fully accounted for and behavioral responses to it remain unidentified (Piguet, 2010). Moreover, a large-n survey study could in this case only deliver very general results, which would not allow for conclusions that inform national or regional migration policy or would support capacity building for climate adaptation. Qualitative methods, on the contrary, make it possible to capture viewpoints of different groups on the phenomenon and take into account the concrete local conditions under which people decide to migrate and where they arrive at.

4.1. Grounded Theory

Grounded Theory is "*the discovery of theory from data*" (Glaser & Strauss, 1967). It has been introduced by Glaser and Strauss in 1967 to advance sociological research and theory building. The aim of this approach is to capture "*emerging patterns in data*" (Walsh et al., 2015). Glaser and Strauss developed Grounded Theory in distinction to the verification of existing theories. In their work the authors differentiate the purposes of research between the testing of grand theories by applying specific hypothesis on the one hand and the generation of hypothesis through analysis of empirical data on the other. Whereas some theories are derived from logical deduction, Grounded Theory aims at building theory through the analysis of data. In this study qualitative data is primarily used, however Grounded Theory can also be derived from quantitative data. The authors emphasize that "*generating hypotheses requires evidence enough only to establish a suggestion – not an excessive piling up of evidence to establish proof*"(Glaser & Strauss, 1967:39). This makes qualitative research methods applicable to grounded research, for often the number of cases investigated is small compared to quantitative methods. Working with small samples is necessary for research in areas where big datasets are not available, which is often the case when focusing on a new phenomenon, as is the case with climate migration. Building theory from data suggests that field research develops over time. The first steps of investigations are completed without preconceived conceptions about possible hypotheses (Glaser and Strauss, 1967). Then an iterative process begins that closely intertwines data collection and analysis. It is important to note that Glaser and Strauss later developed different methodologies for Grounded Theory with regard to conceptualization, coding and the role of the researcher (Halaweh et al.,

2008). The interpretative approach of Strauss allows for a literature review and first specification of concepts before the field research. As there is already significant literature available, I follow the Straussian version of Grounded Theory (Corbin and Strauss, 2015).

To generate solid hypotheses, the collection and analysis of data is systematic. A common method for Grounded Theory work is interviewing. For this, the first step is theoretical sampling (see chapter 5). The design for the chosen sample aims not at representing the entire population, but at a specific set of interview partners whose information could lead to the development of a new theory or hypothesis. After such interviews, transcriptions are made and then coded (see chapter 5.2.). This means to group information of interviews into specific sections. After each field research session, I check my preliminary results and first assumptions with the incoming data. Subsequently, the gathered information can again be contextualized with significant background information. Therefore, the statements from the interviews are weighed against one another and also against the relevant background information. In the case of this study, such contextual information includes climatic data, demographic developments or the political situation of a country or region. The insights gained may lead to new categories to be explored during the course of research. Overall, the newly developed hypotheses which stand at the end of the analysis are not seen as static, but as a point of beginning for further alterations and development. This dynamic methodology helps to work on current issues where new evidence is mounting every day, like in the case of migration due to emerging climate impacts. Hence, for new phenomena Grounded Theory is a suitable way to formulate a new theory.

For the interaction of the environment with human systems such an approach is particularly adequate because they represent highly complex causal networks and are not easily disentangled into their different logical compartments. While each element or process may be simple, their interactions and possible feedback loops, such as negative or positive reinforcements, can make the whole system intricate and multifaceted (Swilling and

Annecke, 2012). One of the advantages of Grounded Theory is that it incorporates new insights of such interactions over the course of the research.

There are several reasons why building theory through analysis of new empirical data is a suitable approach for this thesis' research question. For once, at the outset of this study it is not completely clear what constitutes the system in which a migration occurs. While some variables, such as the financial situation of the migrant, are known to be significant factors for the effectiveness of migration as adaptation, others, however, are at the outset not yet defined and are expected to be identified over the course of the research (see chapter operationalization of effectiveness 3.4.). Furthermore, Grounded Theory can be developed from small sample sizes. When investigating climate migration, a challenge is that a large share of migrant movements is undocumented. For example, internal migration is often not fully captured by local administrations, especially when the destination is an informal settlement. Using qualitative methods helps to gain deeper understanding of climate migration, specifically in the context of adaptation. The lack of existing data and the incompleteness of current knowledge mean that logical deduction, a hypotheses-testing design may not expand or advance the field. It may even lead to misconceptions of the phenomenon. When assessing the effectiveness of adaptation of migration, it is crucial to include the migrant's experience and form hypotheses which encompass this viewpoint. There is also no sufficient data on how climate migrants fare after their migration.

It is important to stress that Glaser & Strauss (1967) argue that theory must be comprehensible not only for scholars of the field, but also to non-scientists who work in a relevant area. While the authors specifically refer to sociology when they propose their concept of Grounded Theory, it can be argued that the same standards hold for the field of political science. Advancements in theory building and hypotheses generation that fulfill these criteria are enhancing the relevance of scientific research for the public discourse, the political and the field practice. Since the question whether or not migration is an effective adaptation to climate change is relevant to future policy planning, theoretical insights into this matter should also hold value for field experts.

4.2. Conceptual Systems Model & Case Study

Following the Straussian Grounded Theory approach, I conduct a theory building multilevel qualitative systems analysis, taking into account empirical data from two case studies. Theory building case study research has been conducted in different social sciences (Eisenhardt, 1989). A case study is "*an empirical inquiry that investigates a contemporary phenomenon within its real-life context, especially when the boundaries between the phenomenon and the context are not clear*" (Yin, 2003). The phenomenon of climate migration occurs in very different geographic, political, cultural and socio-economic contexts and the ways in which these influence the phenomenon are not sufficiently understood. In case study research the several viewpoints can be assessed in the evaluation, including both actors, which in this case are the migrants, and the groups with whom they interact, in this case sending and receiving communities (Feagin et al., 1991). Case study research is a common methodology of qualitative investigation (Thomas, 2011), and the body of case study research on climate change and migration has grown substantially since the turn of the millennium (Piguet, 2018). I will compare two cases. The advantage of a comparative approach over a single case study is that the strength of the hypotheses developed from this comparative research is higher than it would be from a single case study because of a larger empirical base of evidence (Herriott and Firestone, 1983). As migration is multi-causal and therefore context-specific, I want to develop hypotheses from two cases in which the climate-related migration takes place under different circumstances. The research therefore takes a comparative perspective (Levy, 2008) based on a most different case study design (first introduced by Mill, 1843) and will juxtapose two cases in which people had to migrate because of changes in the environmental conditions linked to climate change under different geographical, political and socioeconomic conditions. By making comparisons of two very different cases, I aim to find out whether there are similarities in the effectiveness or ineffectiveness of migrations which can then be generalized. These are the variable(s) ("Q") which are to be identified through the Grounded Theory guided research. Table 1 provides an overview of this hypotheses generating comparative case study design. The two cases selected should differ in terms of their exposure, the hazards which affect them, the vulnerability of the population at risk and the types of migration flows (Tacoli, 2009).

Variable	**Case Study I**	**Case Study II**
Geography & Exposure	**W**	**A**
Hazard	**X**	**B**
Vulnerability and Population at Risk	**Y**	**C**
Climate Migration Flow	**Z**	**D**
Unknown „Q" = ?	**Q = ?**	**Q = ?**

Table 1 Most Different Inductive Case Study Design

In table 1 Q is the variable which is not yet known and may lead to the generation of hypotheses. Two sub-questions are of guidance to the research design: Are there similarities between the two cases leading to an effective or ineffective migration? What could Q be if the outcome is similar? If the outcome is dissimilar, for example, when there are groups in both countries achieving different migration outcomes, the analysis intends to deliver whether there are similarities within those groups valid for both cases. This could in turn lead to a split in Q, into $Q_{1effective}$ and $Q_{2ineffective}$, signifying that the variable Q1 leads to effective adaptation whereas Q2 leads to ineffective adaptation.

4.3. Case Selection

The selection of cases is based on the need to find two different regions in which migration has occurred clearly connected to a climate hazard. To identify such climate migration hotspots, the case selection will be done in accordance with the following simplified scheme (1) which follows the factors of risk as outlined in the Fifth Assessment Report of the IPCC (Cardona et al., 2012):

$$\text{Risk}_x = f_x(\text{Hazard, Exposure, Vulnerability}) \qquad (1)$$

The risk for an occurrence x is henceforth a function of three dominant factors: hazard, exposure and vulnerability. Herein, x can refer to the potentiality of climate change-related displacement (climate migration as an impact of climate change) or it refers to climate risks to which migration is used as an adaptation strategy. These risks are largely determined by the occurrence of climate hazards, the exposure and vulnerability of population or assets to these hazards. Hazards are slow onset or sudden events that "*may have adverse effects on vulnerable and exposed elements*" (Cardona et al., 2012). In this study, I only consider hazards which are likely to be linked to climate change, according to the state of the scientific literature. Geophysical events such as earthquakes are not considered here. Hazards are a necessary but not a sufficient condition for risk because it is not the only determinant of risk; rather exposure and vulnerability are other key factors (Cardona et al., 2012). Exposure refers to people and assets located in the area potentially affected by hazard. Exposure is a necessary condition for risk because "*if population and economic resources were not located in (exposed to) potentially dangerous settings, no problem of disaster risk would exist*"(Cardona et al., 2012). Vulnerability, which has been used as a concept by various disciplines (Weisz et al., 2013), can be defined for climate change research as the "*propensity of exposed elements such as human beings, their livelihoods, and assets to suffer adverse effects when impacted by hazard events*" (Cardona et al., 2012). The predisposition of people or human systems to be affected by climate change impacts can also be altered by non-climate-change-related anthropogenic environmental stressors, such as the over-usage of groundwater. It is important to note that "moderate" levels of vulnerability could already lead to outmigration, while an extremely high vulnerability is not a sufficient condition for displacement as it may result in no movement. For example, in extreme cases where the exposure is very high, but people have too few resources to move, they may be forced to remain on their (degraded) land. However, from the same communities, more affluent groups or individuals may have migrated. This is why at the outset of finding adequate case studies for high displacement risks, I looked for cases which were characterized by an occurrence of strong climate hazards and a high exposure of very vulnerable populations.

This thesis will focus on Asia and the Pacific as it is one of the most affected regions of climate change and also a region of high mobility, population growth and rapid urbanization (see also: Graeme, 2010). The two case studies used for the analysis will focus on different groups of migrants in Bangladesh and the Marshall Islands. These countries were chosen because they are highly vulnerable to climate change, and the current warming level of almost 1°C has already led to observable impacts that, along with other factors such as rural poverty, have caused people to migrate (ADB, 2012; Gautam, 2012). They are on the forefront of what is to be expected in other regions as well as under various warming scenarios. A variety of climate impacts affect livelihoods in Bangladesh and the Marshall Islands such as extreme weather events, sea level rise or erosion. Furthermore, these two nations are characterized by limited availability of land. In both places, the inhabitants of the affected regions are directly dependent on ecosystem services since their livelihoods are often closely intertwined with the environment. Furthermore, many communities often have limited resilience and limited capacities to respond or adapt to climate impacts. Changes in the environment have induced or contributed to a variety of movements, such as temporary, seasonal or permanent migration. Nevertheless, some parts of the communities remained in the affected areas, whereas others migrated.

Although both countries are impacted by climate change and people are moving away from high risk areas, the two cases are substantially different. Bangladesh is a nation of 163 million people, situated in a vast river delta. The Marshall Islands on the contrary are a small island state of 29 remotely located Atolls which host just over 74 500 people (CIA World Factbook, 2017b). Whereas in the Southwest of Bangladesh most people were migrating because of the impacts of tropical cyclones, in the Marshall Islands droughts in connection with rising sea levels were the biggest push factors. The nature of movements and their destinations are also different. To move from one island to another in the Marshall Islands requires some degree of preparation and planning, due to the lack and cost of transport. In Bangladesh, people are able to move relatively spontaneously to urban centers which in general have a large population. Whereas both cases are undergoing a fast urbanization, the scale of it is dissimilar. In the case of Bangladesh, the capital city of Dhaka has developed into a megacity of almost 17.6 million people over the past decades (CIA World Factbook, 2017a). Other secondary cities in Bangladesh have also experienced high levels of urbanization, their populations multiplied, migrants often settled informally in the peripheries and slums of the cities. These growth rates are due to the general trend of rural to urban migration and high birthrates. Presently and in the near future, climate change will induce movements which will add to existing flows, posing further challenges to city governments and receiving communities. In Bangladesh, migratory routes largely lead from the rural areas to nearby medium-sized cities which may also be vulnerable to the effects of climate change (Vinke et al., 2017). The measures of effectiveness, such as an analysis whether or not the rights of migrants have been violated, can be evaluated on the basis of these studies. The key differences relevant to the study are summarized in the overview table (table 2).

Variable \ Case	**Bangladesh (South-West)**	**Marshall Islands**
Geography & Exposure	**W** Deltaic Country	**A** Small Island State
Hazard	**X** Tropical Cyclones (storm surges in combination with SLR), Riverine Flooding	**B** Droughts, Salinization (in combination with SLR), Coastal Erosion, Crop Failure
Vulnerability & Population at Risk	**Y** Large & dense Population at Risk (63 Mio in LECZ)	**C** Small & dispersed Population at Risk (74 500 total pop.)
Climate Migration Flow	**Z** Large internal Migration, undocumented Immigration to India	**D** Small Movements, ultimately going Abroad, Legal Immigration to the US
Q = ?	**Q = ?**	**Q = ?**

Table 2 Most Different Inductive Case Study Design Bangladesh and Marshall Islands

This design bears the risk of all outcomes being dissimilar, meaning that in the two cases the migration outcomes are different for completely different reasons. From this, only context-specific hypothesis could be generated. However, if the design works as expected it will deliver replicable results with regard to other vulnerable populations facing climate hazards such as extreme tropical cyclones and sea level rise. Evidently, not all possible variables which could have an influence on effectiveness can be researched. But by using techniques such as theoretical sampling, triangulation of sources and semi-structured interviews, the risk of an omitted variable bias is minimized. Whereas each individual's decision to migrate is generally an intricate and multifold process, the phenomenon of climate migration can nevertheless be researched by addressing complexity and discovering the most significant patterns which lead to an effective or ineffective adaptation outcome.

4.4. Structure of Analysis

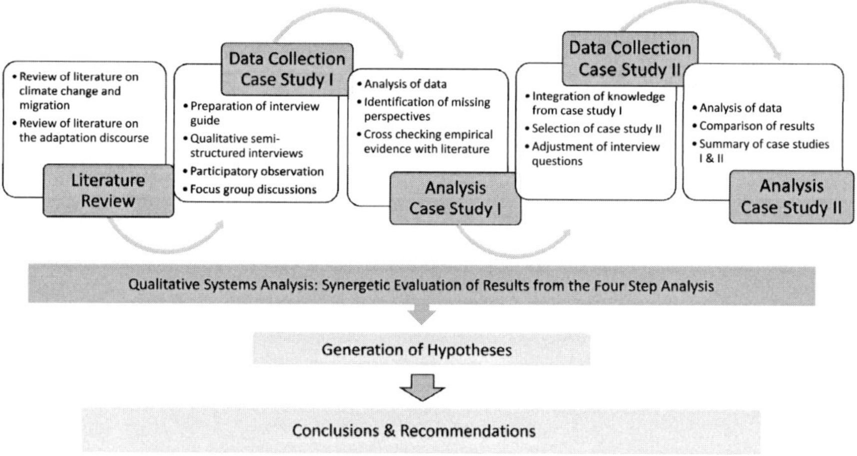

Figure 2 Research Process Overview (source: own).

After the literature review the first case, South-Western Bangladesh, is identified. The tools (interview guide, set of questions, etc.) for the field research are prepared. After completion of the first field research, missing elements and perspectives are identified through the analysis of the empirical data and an extensive literature review of case-relevant scientific publications. The second case is chosen and the field research builds upon the preliminary results.

The analysis of the two cases will be structured as follows: At the outset of each case study it will be established through an evaluation of existing literature what changes in the environment have been observed. This is succeeded by a summary of the case-relevant future changes in a 1.5 – 2°C world and under a business-as-usual scenario of a 4°C world by the end of the century. Afterwards, the interactions of climate impacts with human systems and the elements shaping migration patterns are discussed as portrayed in the literature and complemented by new empirical evidence from the field research. The characteristics of the migrant households are introduced. Here then follows the evaluation of the effectiveness of migration as adaptation on three levels; migrant, sending and receiving communities. This evidence is used for the system analysis of the migrant's system of origin and destination as well as the synergetic system analysis of the system of climate migration of the respective case. Based on the analysis, hypotheses regarding the effectiveness of migration as adaptation are developed. The implications of the research findings for the adaptation discourse are presented. The dissertation concludes with recommendations for the governance of migration as adaptation and an outlook for future research directions and development of the topic.

5. Methods

This work aims at finding patterns of effective and ineffective migration as adaptation from qualitative empirical research. Interviews are herein used to inform the qualitative systems analysis and to aid the evaluation of effectiveness by following the principle that migrants and sending communities are experts of their own lives. In addition to the qualitative analysis described below, where there is pertinent quantitative data and literature available, existing data will be used to complement and reflect on the case studies and to identify relevant processes and feedback loops. Such data includes migration flows as registered by the International Organization for Migration (IOM), UNHCR as well as survey studies which have been conducted in the respective region and census data. The complementary use of the existing quantitative data intends to reduce the possibility of an omitted variable bias and aims at adequately addressing the complexity of the phenomenon.

5.1. Techniques of Data Collection

Three different techniques were used to collect empirical data, allowing for a triangulation of the evidence. The main technique was qualitative semi-structured interviews. I gathered additional information through participatory observation. Moreover, for each case, one focus group discussion was held to discuss and cross-check preliminary findings. Qualitative semi-structured interviews (n=87) were held with three different groups: migrants, sending communities, city planners and migration experts from international organizations form the basis of this analysis of the effectiveness of migration as adaptation. Qualitative interviews make it possible to gain information that is not accessible through the analysis of quantitative data, such as surveys, or the in- and out-migration rates. While it may be feasible – depending on the location – to analyze economic data on incomes of migrants, this is not sufficient to evaluate effectiveness (see section Operationalization of Effectiveness). Moreover, particularly in poor areas, data availability on migratory movements is strongly limited.

In comparison with other subjects of investigation, such as climate impacts on coral reefs or glacier ecosystems, the analysis of human-environment interactions can and should make use of the unique circumstance that humans can communicate. As Bertaux (1981) puts it bluntly, "*If given a chance to talk freely, people appear to know a lot about what is going on.*" Interviewing migrants themselves will add information that is not reflected in the current literature. In his book on "Interviewing as Qualitative Research" Seidman (2006) describes the reason for this method as follows: "*At the root of in-depth interviewing is an interest in understanding the lived experience of other people and the meaning they make of that experience.*" Qualitative interviews provide the opportunity to capture migration experiences and perceptions. An approach that includes views of migrants will add to the current debate in which this perspective on the issue is often underrepresented. While a small or medium number of qualitative interviews may not be adequate to test hypothesis deducted from existing theory (Seidman, 2013), they can be an important tool to generate hypothesis out of the newly acquired information.

Using semi-structured interviews leaves the possibility of asking additional questions or probing for more information if a new relevant issue is addressed which has not been included in the set of questions. Each interview partner is representative for the social system in which he or she lives. For example, migrants who share their experience have followed their own rational logic of action within their realm of the system they operate in. The information they provide can, if contextualized, represent a part of the system to be analyzed. Expert or key informant interviews can contribute to the systemic analysis of the phenomenon, by adding viewpoints of practitioners who work on solutions for migrant integration, planned relocation or in-situ adaptation. Following the iterative process of interviewing and henceforth adjusting probing questions or design, additional interviews may be conducted to complement or verify the knowledge derived from the previous interviews. The sample size for each case study was not predetermined. Interviews were held until a point of theoretical saturation was reached, in which sufficient evidence was accumulated to generate hypothesis and no new patterns or themes emerged from interviews.

Interview Guide for Semi-Structured Interviews

The topics for the interviews are chosen in line with the research question "Is migration an effective adaptation to climate change?" The sets of questions asked are specific to the group which is to be interviewed (migrant and household / city or village representative / international expert) and to the case study. While the topics of questions will be the same in all case studies, some questions needed to be adjusted to the regional context. For example, in Bangladesh the occurrence of storms is particularly relevant to the migration history, whereas drought was a significant factor in the case study on the Marshall Islands. The format is semi-structured interviews, where a set of questions is pre-defined, but can be expanded through additional questions which may arise from the course of the interview. When necessary, probing questions were used for clarifications or more detailed analysis. In these cases, the additional questions were included in the transliterations. When several people migrated together, focus group interviews and discussions were held. Introductions were not recorded. The interviewees were selected through theoretical sampling. First an initial set of interviews was held in Bangladesh with migrants. This group was predetermined to be able to provide information that held value to the research question. From the overview of the first set of interviews, the next set of interviewees, which were sending communities and local leaders, was selected. Overall, the Bangladesh case study and the categories which emerged from the coding process then provided insights into which sample may add significant data in the second case study, until a point of theoretical saturation is reached. Because of the nature of this process, the number of interviewees is not predetermined at the outset of the study.

For interviews with migrants an interview guide was developed which follows three sets of questions covering the biographical data; the reasons for migration and migration pathways; and the living situation and challenges before and after the migration. During observations, attention was given to environmental factors affecting the decision to migrate as well as the current living situation. For the interviews in the climate change-affected areas i.e. the places of origin, the interview guide was modified and included a shorter set of questions, addressing why some people moved and some remained in these regions. In the Bangladesh case study, all interviews with migrants were held in Bangla, with intermittent translations by student translators. On the Marshall Islands, interviews were held in Marshallese or English. The interview guide, including the translations into Bangla and Marshallese, can be found in the Annex.

Informed Consent

Before all interviews, the participants were informed about the intent of the study, time frame and that they would not receive any direct benefits from participation in the study. The consent form was read out loud and also handed to the participants. All interviewees volunteered to participate and signed the form, sometimes with fingerprints if they could not read or write. In the case of a minor under the age of 18 the legal guardians were also asked for their consent. It was also stated that if they did not wish to answer a particular question or did not wish to continue the interview, the process would be stopped at any time. If the situation allowed for it, the researchers provided some snacks and drinks during the interview, in order to create a more relaxed atmosphere of dialogue. The consent forms used in the case studies and their translations are included in the Annex. Signed consent forms by individual participants can be provided by the author on request.

Sampling Procedures

As this dissertation follows a Grounded Theory approach, I used theoretical sampling to gather data which would inform the emerging concepts and hypotheses of migration effectiveness (Corbin and Strauss, 2015). Theoretical sampling requires data analysis and concept development throughout the research process. The evolving concepts drive the selection of the interviewees. The data collection ends when theoretical saturation is reached and the concepts around migration effectiveness have been specified. A detailed description of the sampling process is included at the beginning of the case studies (chapter 6.1. and 7.1.). In both cases sample selections were discussed with local researchers and experts of the institutions described below.

In Southern Bangladesh I conducted a set of 39 interviews with migrants, sending communities and one expert. My field research was supported by the German Development Cooperation (GIZ), and I summarized findings regarding economic survival strategies of the climate migrants in the urban areas for an internal GIZ working document (Vinke, 2014). This unpublished data has been newly analyzed for the first case study of this dissertation.

On the Marshall Islands, I collaborated with the Okeanos Foundation for the Sea and the GIZ office Marshall Islands to plan and conduct 48 interviews with Migrants, sending communities and experts. The GIZ and the Okeanos Foundation assisted with translators and local guides, and the collaboration with these two institutions was key to the success of this research as it minimized risks for personal security and facilitated the research in informal settlements or remote areas.

Selection of Sites

The initial selection of sites will be discussed with local development experts who work on migration and climate change-related topics in the regions which have been determined as case studies. In general, I aim to identify urban destinations of climate migrants and their places of origin, the sending communities. Moreover, the theoretical sampling procedure may also influence the selection of specific sites insofar as additional information may have to be gathered in another location. The specifics of each site selection are described in the case studies.

5.2. Analysis of Interview Data

The interviews in Bangla and Marshallese are transcribed by native speakers following the order of the interview guide, so that the loss of meaning in the process of translation is minimized. The wording in the transcriptions may be moderately smoothed (without altering the meaning) if there are distracting grammatical errors in the sentence (Fuß & Karbach, 2014). More substantial text additions for understanding are marked with [text]. In the excerpts text omissions from the quotes are marked with […]. Speech sound, pauses and fill words ("mmh") are not transcribed, unless necessary for the understanding of the content. Background sounds (cell phone ringing etc.) are also not transcribed as the interviews took place in noisy surroundings and the mentioning of all sounds would disrupt the text flow substantially. Words which are not understood by the transcriber are marked in the transcription. After complete translation and transcription, the interviews are transferred to QDA Miner, a computer-assisted qualitative data analysis software. With this software, I use basic coding techniques to analyze the text. I conducted all interviews personally with the help of translators. In between sessions I wrote memos on important insights and observations. For this reason I already have a general overview of the material when I begin the analysis of the transcriptions. Once all interviews are transcribed, I re-read all the material in one or two sittings before I begin with the analysis. Then I take each interview individually and start the coding process. For this I prepare an initial coding scheme for categories which are relevant to evaluating the effectiveness of migration. This initial set of categories emerged from the overview of the samples and the operationalization of effectiveness. Furthermore, I try to find statements which provide insights into the former social system of the interviewed person and the system he or she had migrated into. Moreover, I want to capture some information about the migration experience, why people migrated, whether they had gone there directly and how they observe the environmental problems in their home communities. During the course of the field research or between the two cases, I added categories that emerged as relevant to the case (Glaser and Strauss, 1967). From the coding exercise, I seek to identify patterns which may give information whether migration is an effective adaptation to climate change. For example, in the Bangladesh case study the themes of typical livelihoods and debt in urban areas emerged as very important for answering the research question. From the patterns or themes I identify, I conduct a text reduction process and quote interview excerpts which reflect the pattern as a whole, or introduce a new aspect (Froschauer and Lueger, 2003). The text-reduction process follows the questions "*what are in summary the most important characteristics of a theme and in which contexts do they occur?* [...] *To what extent are there differences in themes occurring in the interviews?* [...] *How can the thematic characteristics be integrated into the context of the research question?*" (translated from Froschauer & Lueger, 2003). The order in which themes are brought up in the conversations is not considered because this is largely provided by the sequence of the interview guide. To conduct the concluding system's analysis of the social system of origin and destination of the migrants, I use theoretical sampling to select from the interview set several interviews which I analyze in depth. This analysis of codes in the end should lead to the system analysis of the migrants' system of origin and destination and form the basis for the generation of hypotheses and the process of theory building.

Part II: Unsettling Settlements

6. Case Study 1: Southwestern Bangladesh - Migration as Adaptation to Rapid Onset Disasters

The case of climate migration in the Southwest of Bangladesh is representative for other highly populated deltaic regions because the situation there has many characteristics which apply to other deltas and bays or could apply in the future as climate impacts intensify. These significant characteristics include rural poverty and exposure to climate impacts as well as rapid urbanization in connection with the formation of slums. Since Bangladesh is already severely affected by climate change today, one can derive and analyze patterns which may also occur elsewhere in the coming decades. As Susmita Dasgupta, chief environmental economist of the World Bank put it "*Bangladeshi households are in the forefront of climate change. Their behavior and their path to adaptation can help us understand how millions of households around the world will behave in the future*" (The World Bank, 2016). Since the country's independence in 1971 migration has occurred within Bangladesh for various reasons, but climate change poses new threats especially to coastal populations which may cause substantial population shifts from one area to another. For this reason, current migratory patterns due to storms and floods and their effects on people have to be assessed more in depth and with different focal points than what has been addressed by migration studies so far. For this case study I focus on the southwestern region of the country which is both, highly exposed to climatic risks such as cyclones, flooding and sea level rise and extremely vulnerable because of few livelihood opportunities, low incomes and high food insecurity.

Bangladesh lies in the Ganges-, Brahmaputra- and Meghna- Delta, along the Bay of Bengal. Considering the whole territory, 80% of Bangladesh's landmass are floodplains (Brouwer et al., 2007). Because of this geographic location large parts of Bangladesh are naturally exposed to hydrological extremes such as floods. Less than half of the country lies more than five meters above sea level which means that a big area of Bangladesh's landmass is already affected by sea level rise and storm surges.

Moreover, the country is densely populated. In 2016, Bangladesh's population density was 1,252 people per square kilometer and continues to rise (The World Bank, 2017a). By comparison, Germany's population density was 237 people per square kilometer the same year. While the fertility rate has already decreased from 6.7 children per women in 1960 to 2.2 in 2014 (The World Bank, 2017a), the population is expected to continue to grow from currently 163 Million (2016) to approximately 202 Million by 2050 (The World Bank, 2017a). At the same time, the country is rapidly urbanizing. Since 1990, the urban population has almost tripled from about 21 million to more than 57 million in 2016 (The World Bank, 2017a). Today 35% of the country's population lives in cities. By 2030, through rural-urban migration dynamics and population growth, it is expected that more than 83 million Bangladeshis will live in urban centers. This number will rise to 112 million in 2050 when more than half (55.7%) of the country's population could live in cities (The World Bank, 2017a). These rapid urbanization dynamics pose significant challenges to city planners and local administrations. 61.6% of Bangladesh's urban population lives in slums (UN Habitat, 2013). While this percentage has decreased from 87.3% in 1990, the absolute numbers of slum dwellers rose from almost 20 000 000 in 1990 to 27 542 000 in 2009. However, it should be noted that the definition of slums varies between institutions. The Bangladesh national census, for example, cites overall lower numbers of slum residents.

The problem of different data sources holds also for internal migration. There are several sources of migration data describing different migration flows, such as the (temporary) displacement of people due to natural disasters, rural-urban migration, migration to particular cities and from district to district. These often have different conditionalities for the definition of who is a migrant (for example the minimum number of months away from the former habitation can differ). In this case study, several migration datasets are quoted to give an impression of the dimension and patterns of migration in Bangladesh. However, the numbers should largely be taken into account with the understanding of the existing uncertainties, which are data collection and coverage, methods and definitions. Because of the multicausality of migration, there are methodological limitations of quantitative approaches to analyze climate related migration. It can be said however that rural-urban migration will increase because of diminishing sources of livelihood in the countryside due to climate impacts. This urbanization dynamic can be seen as representative for the region. In South Asia, the urban population increased by 130 million within just one decade (2001-2011). It is expected that it will further grow by 250 million until 2030 (Ellis and Roberts, 2016).

Although national and international efforts have led to a reduction of poverty in Bangladesh, development for the poor remains a substantial challenge. Between 1990 and 2010 the number of people living below 1.90 USD per day has decreased from 49 million to 28.1 million. Also the rate of poverty, the poverty headcount ratio, has decreased from 44.2 to 18.5% in the same time span. This reduction of extreme poverty is remarkable. However, when taking a slightly higher poverty line of 3.10 USD per day as an indicator, the extent of poverty and the limited scope of poverty reduction surface. According to this indicator, in 1991 more than 91.4 million people lived below this poverty line, which corresponds with 82.4% in the poverty headcount ratio. This number only saw a minimal decrease by 2010 when still 86.1 million people lived below the 3.10 USD poverty line. Nevertheless, the corresponding poverty headcount ratio decreased to 56.8% in 2010. In absolute terms this could be interpreted as population growth outpacing the speed of advancements in development, in the absence of a redistribution of wealth in favor of the lower socio-economic classes. This in turn leads to continuously high levels of people living in poverty but to a falling rate of poverty.

6.1. Methods of Field Research

This case study builds upon the previous quantitative and qualitative research that has analyzed the connection between climate change and migration in Bangladesh and assessed the observed migration patterns within the country. It is grounded in qualitative field-research that I undertook in September and October 2014. The cyclones Aila and Sidr, which displaced many of the interviewees, occurred 5 and 7 years before the field research was done, respectively. Therefore, the interviews with people who were displaced by these sudden events are not accounts of temporary relocation but narratives of long-term displacement. The field research's core is a set of interviews with migrants in Southern Bangladesh who had settled in urban or peri-urban areas after emigrating from rural regions due to mostly sudden-onset climatic events. To cross check the interviews with the migrants, additional interviews were held in rural locations where some of the migrants had emigrated from.

Category:	Migrants	Sending Community	Local Experts	Total
Number of households:	31	7	1	39 (24 Women 15 Men)

Table 3 Overview of Interview Partners in Bangladesh

The purpose of these interviews in sending communities was to assess how climate change-related environmental conditions were affecting livelihoods in the villages and how people who had stayed in the villages had fared after cyclones or floods. One expert interview with the town planner of Khulna was conducted, in order to gain insights from the perspective of urban development and administration.

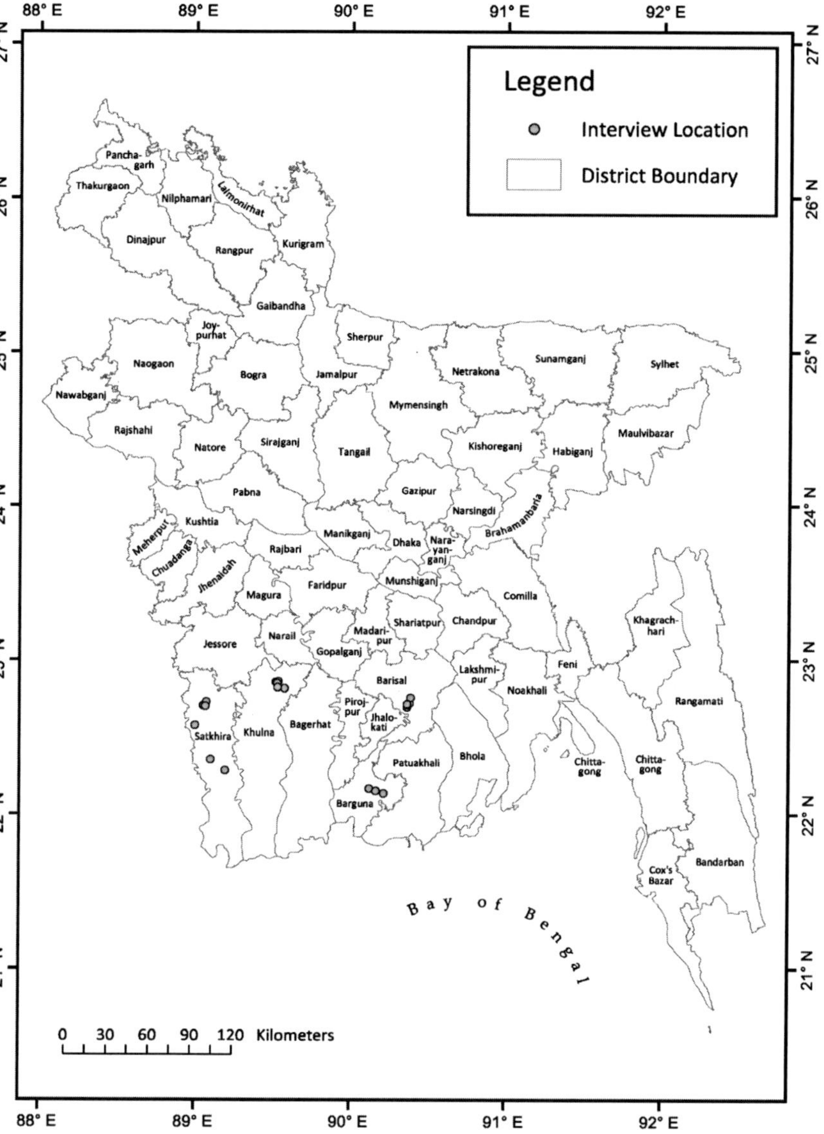

Figure 3 Map of Bangladesh Interview Locations (source: own, Vinke, 2014).

The qualitative semi-structured interviews followed the interview guide as outlined in chapter 5.1. The research team in Bangladesh consisted of two student translators and me. A test-run of the interview guide was held in Bangladesh's capital city, Dhaka, in the Korail Slum area. In this slum migrants from distant locations were present, some of whom had migrated because of various environmental factors. After this initial set of interviews, the questions were slightly adjusted to avoid misunderstandings because of translational problems which became apparent during the process of interviewing.

Site Selection in Bangladesh

Figure 4 Location of Bangladesh (source: TUBS, 2011a)

This case study focuses on the South of Bangladesh because it "*sits at the confluence of climate risks*" (Yu et al., 2010) and is home to large populations with low incomes that have presently little capacity to adapt in-situ through seeking alternative income sources to subsistence agriculture. The impoverished population in coastal Bangladesh is as large as 12 million people (The World Bank, 2016). For the field research three urban areas were predetermined due to their function as destination points for rural migrants of the respective region: Khulna, Satkhira Pourashava and Barisal, including informal settlements in the periphery of these cities. Ullah (2004) found in a study on migration to Dhaka that "*a significantly higher percentage of migrants lives in slums as compared to other places*" which is why informal settlements are of particular interest. The three locations were chosen because in the respective regions a variety of climate impacts is currently affecting communities. By conducting research in at least three different locations, the overall validity of the results for the region is strong. For example, whereas in one location a very specific set of circumstances may have led to effective or ineffective migration, an increase in the variance would avoid or balance such bias. It was thus assumed that by conducting interviews in these areas it would be possible to encounter people who had left for various reasons, including slow-onset climate impacts as well as sudden disasters. Within the urban areas poor and informal settlements were identified and then visited. The researchers asked local habitants, such as tea stall owners or rickshaw pullers, who often have a wealth of information about current city developments, where new settlements were to be found in the city.

In addition to the three pre-identified urban locations, the researchers visited other areas after consultation with experts from GIZ offices in the field research sites. Some sites were selected because migrants were known to have settled there, such as the location in Barguna. Moreover, some affected areas were inspected, for example villages close to the Sundarban forest where cyclones impact communities frequently, and the settlement in Charbaria, Barisal where a short time before the visit a large area of land had vanished due to river erosion. In the cyclone-affected region the intention of the research was to talk to families about whether or not family members had migrated and how the remaining families had adapted to the situation of frequent disasters. In the village where river erosion had taken place several people had died or were missing as the river had carried away the land at night time. Here, the researchers wanted to find out why people were still living in the disaster-prone areas.

Selection of Interviewees

Because there is no comprehensive theory regarding the effectiveness of climate migration, the selection of interviewees starts based on the existing knowledge on climate migration (Strübing, 2001). I use theoretical sampling in which the selection of interview partners evolves during the course of the field research (Corbin and Strauss, 2015; Glaser and Strauss, 1967). The initial selection of interviewees was conducted through sampling in locations that were identified as arrival points of migrants from exposed rural areas. It was intended to interview several migrants who differed not only in age and gender but also in profession or source of income. This research did not aim at representing the entire migrant community and analyzing why people had migrated, but focused on those who had migrated due to various climate impacts and then documented and assessed in depth their experiences connected to the relocation. For the selection of migrant interviewees it was first evaluated whether climate impacts played a role in the decision to migrate. Secondly, if the answer was positive meaning that they had migrated because of climate change-related environmental factors, it was inquired how living conditions were at the time of arrival, what living conditions are currently prevailing and what amenities and services are lacking (see interview guide in the chapter 14.3. and description of interview conduct in chapter 5.1.). Interviews were held with people who had migrated to the urban areas up to ten years ago. In this time period the impacts of climate change on the natural environment were stronger and could have had influence on migration, compared to migrations which had occurred decades ago. Within one family or household generally only one person was interviewed, unless family members had migrated for different reasons or households had formed after the migration. The respondent generally told the story of their family and thereby can be seen as a representative of the migratory history of several people in the household. If the interviewee was female and the women did not provide the major source of income in the family, they were asked what their husbands' occupation was.

Following a snowball system, the participants were asked after the interview was finished whether they knew any other families who had recently moved to the urban areas, or people who had been affected by cyclones. This in some cases led to other areas within the city where other new settlements of climate migrants were located. As the research evolved, the researchers looked more specifically for locations where typical employment options were available to migrants. Also, local GIZ offices helped with the orientation in the town and gave location-specific information on the effects of climate change and human mobility. Towards the end of the field study, researchers frequently addressed rickshaw pullers who were often themselves migrants and had settled in areas where many migrants lived. While I first focused on migrants in different locations in the city and with different occupations, the replies to the set of questions guided me to also visit sending communities and talk to an expert on city administration in the south of Bangladesh.

Methodological Problems and Possible Bias

Unless people had migrated directly after a cyclone, identifying climate migration in an interview setting is often challenging. Many of the participants in the study who were asked about why they had left the villages first gave the prospect of work opportunities as an explanation for their migration. Only after enquiring about why they needed to find employment, they revealed that changes in the environment had induced their jobs search and thereby their movement. Another problem that arose was that – although participants had been informed about the intent and limited scope of the study (see informed consent in chapter 14 annex) – people frequently hoped that through participation benefits would come to them at a later point in time. It was clearly stated by the researchers that this was not the case, but due to the generally very difficult socio-economic situation and the prevalence of aid programs from various international organizations the researchers were under the impression that some participants were at least hoping for support. If areas are frequently visited by scientists, research fatigue can occur, meaning that local residents may not be eager to participate in research. Part of the problem is that often the results of the research are not communicated to participants and are perceived to have no effect. As the research in Bangladesh was carried out under the support of the GIZ, which has a longstanding presence in many parts of the country, research fatigue was not a major problem.

Another difficulty the research team faced was that it was generally not possible to conduct interviews one on one. After entering the slum areas people took interest in the researchers and wanted to hear what questions were asked and what exactly the research team was doing. Therefore, the group of researchers with the interviewee was usually surrounded by about 20-50 people, sometimes more. This can lead to bias in the answers of the participants as they are not anonymous to their immediate surroundings. Information may be excluded or altered due to individual reasons. In one case, the participant told the researchers when accompanying them out of the village that he was not feeling comfortable talking about the extent of his economic misery because he did not want to worry his wife and family. He then told researchers he was skipping meals to feed his children. Sometimes this information was added as additional observations to the interview guide form. Because the researchers usually interviewed several families within one area the information provided was cross-checked as much as possible, and through this the risk of an omitted variable bias was minimized.

Structure & Application of Interview Data

Whereas the next chapter 6.2. provides an overview of the most significant observed climate impacts on livelihoods in Southwestern Bangladesh based on the state of the art literature, the other chapters draw upon the newly collected qualitative interview data. The data is used in this chapter as follows: Some interview quotes are used to complement and contextualize the information given in chapter 6.4. on the interactions of climate change with human systems and in chapter 6.5. explaining the migration patterns in Bangladesh. Both chapters, however, are grounded in the existing literature on climate change impacts, livelihoods and migration in Bangladesh. In chapter 6.6. it is analyzed what the significant commonalities amongst the interviewed migrant households were. These are themes which emerged from coding the interviews and structuring them through a thematic analysis based on a text reduction process (Froschauer and

Lueger, 2003). Then, the central systematic evaluation of the interviews with regard to the research question, whether migration is an effective adaptation strategy or not, is written in chapter 6.7. For all chapters, the interview excerpts are derived from the coding process (see chapter 5.2). The coding sheet which emerged from this chapter includes a variety of categories relevant to the research question and can be found in the Annex Bangladesh.

From the operationalization of effectiveness and the codes which have emerged through the interview analysis, themes and subthemes can be identified which are used for the written analysis. These themes are A "Economic Situation", including the subthemes: Typical Livelihoods, Begging, Debt, Lack of Access to Education and Social Services. B "Migrant Health," including the subthemes: Cost of Healthcare, Sanitation and Living Conditions, Climate Impacts on Urban Population Health, Mental Health and Wellbeing. C "Self-determination" including the subthemes: mplications of Forced Migration, Trapped Populations at Migration Destinations, Constraints of Debt (see figure 5). These themes are reflected in the structure of chapter 6.7. Effectiveness of Migration as Adaptation.

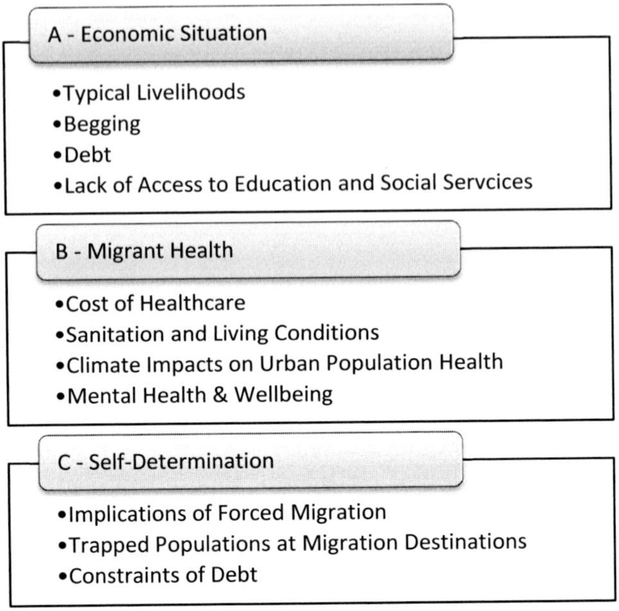

Figure 5 Themes of Effectiveness of Migration as Adaptation for Migrants Bangladesh (source: own).

6.2. Current Climate Hazards in Southwestern Bangladesh

More and more, the progress in human development in Bangladesh is up against the intensification of climate impacts on human livelihoods. Significant independent variables determining the risk of displacement, or simply put, the climate change-related environmental drivers of migration in Southwestern Bangladesh, are hazards such as floods, salinization, riverbed erosion and tropical cyclones.

Floods

Already today, the effects of floods are prevalent in various sectors of the country. Economic losses from floods can be devastating. For example, "*in 2007, Bangladesh was hit by successive riverine and storm surge floods. Estimated loss from the riverine flood was $1.4 billion*" (Mirza, 2010).

Natural hazards and food insecurity pose existential threats to rural communities in the south of Bangladesh. Areas of high food insecurity in the south are also areas frequently affected by flooding and high risk regions for cyclones (WFP, 2005). In 2007, floods caused food losses of 1,2 million tons (Mirza, 2010). These risks have become more substantial in the past decades: "*The frequency of extreme floods is also apparently on the rise. Bangladesh experienced five large floods from 1987 to 2007. (...) In addition to this, there is a tendency of expansion of flood-prone areas*" (Mirza, 2010). While the high frequency of extreme floods over the past decades could still be attributed to natural climate variability, many studies see it as the beginning of an emerging pattern of rising frequency and magnitude of floods and storms, which could determine the development prospects of the nation (Agrawala et al., 2003; The World Bank, 2011; Vinke et al., 2017). These unusual flooding events are furthermore connected to an increase in regional intraseasonal and interannual rainfall variability, which is giving rise to extreme precipitation and periods of dry spells (The World Bank, 2013). The changing precipitation pattern causes substantial difficulties for rainfed agriculture, which is the basic income source in the rural areas of Bangladesh besides fisheries. Only in some northwestern parts of the country irrigation systems are used, whereas the southern coastal agricultural areas are completely dependent on rainfall (Warner et al., 2012).

Salinization

The combined effect of overusage of existing freshwater resources and groundwater intrusion of saline ocean water due to sea level rise leads to salinization of drinking water and soils. Another significant anthropogenic stressor is the expansion of shrimp farming in coastal Bangladesh. In many cases farming practices are non-sustainable and rely on diverting more saline ocean water into the inland coastal regions (Rahman et al., 2013). This further aggravates salinization. About 20 million people in the coastal areas of Bangladesh are already affected by salinity in their drinking water (Khan et al., 2011a). This is a health threat especially for pregnant women who are prone to hypertension because of the high salinity of drinking water. Salinization of soils can also have negative consequences for crop yields.

Riverbed Erosion

In Bangladesh many villages, especially those located on chars (islands in rivers), are affected by riverbed erosion, slowly leading to the disappearance of large landmasses. Sometimes the break-off occurs in a very short time frame which puts people on these lands at high risks. River erosion is a natural phenomenon and has challenged populations living in these areas for centuries. But there are also anthropogenic influences on riverbed erosion. Human activities which are directly affecting erosion and sediment transport include deforestation and the impairment of river catchments, the construction of dams and sand mining (Walling, 2009). However, "*there is a small but growing body of evidence that climate change is having a significant impact on the sediment loads of the world's rivers*" (UN Water, 2009). Also, glacier melt-offs or changes in the monsoon patterns, leading to more heavy rainfall over shorter periods of time, may affect the amount of water being carried in rivers. Therefore, the extent of riverbed-erosion may also increase. But "*in most rivers, it is likely to prove difficult to disentangle the impact of climate change or variability from changes resulting from other human impacts and existing evidence suggests that, in most cases, these human impacts are at present likely to be more significant*" (UN Water, 2009).

Thereby, migration triggered by river erosion currently cannot be clearly attributed to climate change. Nonetheless, being a widespread phenomenon in southern Bangladesh, it is included in this study, and its magnitude may be amplified by precipitation changes and glacier melts connected to climate change. The impacts of river erosion on livelihoods are in fact continuous and severe as stated in the interviews: "*First, we lost our agricultural land, then after three years, we lost our homestead land. Then we received land from the government. After two years, we lost the land given by the government*" (Interview 22, Barisal). People also explained that there were conflicts around the building of dams and embankments. Some villages were unprotected from erosion because the construction of an embankment system around the village area would lead to flooding in the nearby city.

Cyclones
Per se, the Bay of Bengal does not have an extremely high occurrence of tropical cyclones (Alam et al., 2003). Comparing the formation rates to the Pacific or Atlantic ocean basins, it is in fact relatively low (Balaguru et al., 2014). However, the coincidence of several other factors expose the populations in the Bay of Bengal to the occurrence of cyclones. One factor is that the coastal zones as well as the bay itself are relatively shallow and the basin is semi enclosed which means that "*most of the cyclones that form make landfall*" (Balaguru et al., 2014). To aggravate the situation, the human settlements in the low-lying deltaic regions of the Bay of Bengal are often densely populated and poorly built. Past tropical storms have thus caused high death tolls, although recent advancements in disaster risk reduction infrastructure such as cyclone shelters and early warning systems have decreased vulnerability. The death toll of recent storms was reduced, compared to storms of similar strength which hit the country in 1970 and 1991 (Mallick and Etzold, 2015).

Whereas the connection between cyclone genesis and climate change still needs further research, there is scientific evidence already in the literature about how rising temperatures contribute to the intensification of tropical cyclones in the Bay of Bengal. When analyzing tropical cyclones in the Bay of Bengal, one can distinguish between two seasons in which cyclones usually occur: before and after the monsoon (Balaguru et al., 2014). During the post-monsoon season (October and November) most of the strong cyclones form. Balaguru et al. (2014) have analyzed historical post-monsoon cyclone activity from 1981-2010 in the Bay and found that the intensity of strong cyclones has increased. They also established that the rise of the sea surface temperature is a reason for the intensification of cyclones: "*Increases in sea surface temperature and upper ocean heat content made the ocean more conducive to TC intensification, while enhanced convective instability made the atmosphere more favorable for the growth of TCs*" (Balaguru et al., 2014). Their findings support the evidence generated by previous research that showed an intensification and rise in frequency of tropical cyclones in the Indian Ocean. From the positive linear correlation between the changes in climatic conditions and the formation of strong cyclones Balaguru et al. (2014) derive that "*postmonsoon BoB* [Bay of Bengal] *TCs* [Tropical Cyclones] *may continue to increase in the future.*" The increase in sea surface temperatures in the Indian Ocean is among the highest globally and is attributable largely to climate (Knutson et al., 2006). This continuing warming trend will thus likely lead to an increase of strong tropical storms in the basin. However, specific and reliable studies for the Bay of Bengal remain scarce, and particularly the projection of future cyclone genesis under different warming scenarios is difficult. At the beginning of this century, the southwestern part of the country was successively hit by two storms which prompted large migratory movements; the cyclones Sidr in 2007 and Aila in 2009. These cyclones occurred in a very short sequence, therefore making it difficult for communities to rebuild capacities and resilience in between.

Cyclone Sidr

On November 15th, 2007 category 4 cyclone Sidr with top wind speeds of 250km/h made landfall on Bangladesh's southwest coast. Moving further inland, the storm affected about half of Bangladesh's districts. While 600 000 people were evacuated, 3 295 people died and more than 53 000 were reported missing (International Federation of Red Cross and Red Crescent Societies, 2010). About 15% of people exposed sought refuge in cyclone shelters; without this disaster risk reduction infrastructure the death toll would have been considerably higher (Jisan et al., 2018). Moreover, 1.5 million households were damaged, displacing several million people temporarily (International Federation of Red Cross and Red Crescent Societies, 2010). Overall, 8.7 million people were affected by damaged or destroyed houses, livestock or land. Agricultural livelihoods in the rural areas were particularly battered, as approximately 9000 km2 crop land was damaged and 1.7 million farming animals perished (International Federation of Red Cross and Red Crescent Societies, 2010).

Cyclone Aila

Just two years after cyclone Sidr, the southwest of Bangladesh was again hit by a major cyclone in 2009. Cyclone Aila, which made landfall on

Bangladesh's west coast in May of 2009, did not have the same magnitude as Sidr. About 190 people died and 4.8 million people were affected by the storm (Jisan et al., 2018). But, as it occurred in roughly the same region shortly after Sidr, many households who had struggled to recover after the previous disaster were unable to cope with yet another economic setback. Approximately 243 000 houses were destroyed and more than 373 000 damaged (International Federation of the Red Cross and Crescent Societies, 2009). Around 1 million people were rendered homeless (ICRC, 2009). Some remained in the affected villages, mostly under harsh conditions. Many people who had lost their land and livelihood decided to relocate, and five to seven years after the event groups of them were still living in the places to which they had fled. For example, the district of Khulna was strongly affected by both cyclones which displaced many people from the rural coastal areas of the district into the city of Khulna.

Although the frequency of very intense cyclones has risen in the last decades due to sea-surface temperature warming in the Indian Ocean, it cannot be conclusively documented whether these two particular storms were "caused" by climate change. But the set of two cyclones within only two years represents a threat that is projected to emerge more frequently in the future. Therefore, the case study of migration from the cyclone-affected areas will reflect the challenges that are likely to accumulate over the coming decades and also show the impacts of observed climate trends, even if the singular case of a storm may be difficult to attribute to climate change.

6.3. Future Climate Change Impacts and their Implications for Migration

Whereas significant changes have already been observed in Bangladesh, future climate impacts could result in additional challenges especially for livelihoods that are strongly dependent on intact ecosystems. To understand the results of this case study in the context of future climate change, I summarize how climate change impacts could affect Bangladesh, comparing a business-as-usual (RCP8.5) scenario which corresponds to a global mean temperature rise of 4°C by the end of the century and a Paris-

Consensus Scenario (RCP 2.6) which would limit global warming to below 2°C by the end of the century.

"Bangladesh emerges as an impact hotspot with increasing and compounding challenges occurring in the same timeframe from extreme river floods, more intense tropical cyclones, rising sea levels, extraordinarily high temperatures and declining crop yields" (Vinke et al., 2016). Likely, the region will undergo stressors, such as changes in precipitation and the monsoon pattern, plus more frequent and more intense storms and cyclones. Climate models show severe impacts on the region already under a Paris-Consensus Scenario. There is "a rapidly increasing risk for Bangladesh as warming rises towards 2°C, due to flooding, with losses plateauing as the flooded area stabilizes, at a time that Bangladesh is projected to need to increase grain production by 3% per year (historically 2% / year)" (Hare et al., 2011). This means that sustaining food production could become more challenging in a country in which malnutrition is already prevalent. Moreover, in the 5th assessment report of the IPCC it is analyzed that "by 2050 Bangladesh's at-risk population [from sea level rise] is predicted to grow to 27 million - more than double since 2008" (Olsson et al., 2014; Wheeler, 2011). In some regions, sea level rise will cause high losses of agricultural land, destabilizing livelihoods further. Such frequent setbacks caused by changes in the environment will counteract or even undo advancements of development in the poverty-ridden areas of southern Bangladesh.

The anticipated sea level rise under a 2°C scenario will also augment the impacts of cyclones, as larger areas may be affected by storm surges and the concomitant inundation. Recent modeling of storm surge inundation zones in Bangladesh show that the same storms would have more severe effects. A simulation of the category 5 cyclone Sidr following the same cyclone tracks with the same intensities shows that under a 26 cm sea level rise by 2050 the inundated area would be 31% larger. A sea level rise of 54 cm by the end of the century would lead to 53% more land under water as compared to 2007 when Sidr occurred (Jisan et al., 2018). Whereas previous studies found that the impact could be even larger for similar storms:

"*In Bangladesh* [...] *a projected 27 cm sea level rise by 2050, combined with a storm surge induced by an average 10-year return-period cyclone such as Sidr, could inundate an area 88-percent larger than the area inundated by current cyclonic storm surges*" (The World Bank, 2013).

Global mean projections indicate that if strong mitigation is implemented and global warming stays below 2°C, sea level rise could still reach 65 cm by the end of the century. However, a business-as-usual scenario could cause a sea level rise of 1.4 m by the end of the century and continued sea level rise over the following centuries (Mengel et al., 2016). The long-term implications of rising CO_2 concentrations in the atmosphere for global sea-levels strongly depend on self-reinforcing feedbacks in the earth system, which are not yet fully understood and would pose existential risks to human civilization (Steffen et al., 2018). Taking into account the modelling work on storm surges under moderate sea level rise scenarios, one can estimate that a 1.4 m higher sea level would lead to large damages of cyclonic storm surges which in turn could cause mass-outmigration from the deltaic areas. Moreover, Yu et al. (2010) found out that a sea level rise of approximately 62 cm by the 2080s may result in losses of 13% of land in the coastal regions of the country and will extend the overall area affected by perennial floods by 20% (Yu et al., 2010). For agricultural production, increased climate variability could also negatively affect crops. For example, Yu et al. (2010) also project that climate change will have a negative impact on rice yields in Bangladesh, reducing the total harvest by 80 Mt between 2005 and 2050, equaling losses of an average of 3.9% per annum. Especially the regions of Khulna and Pathuakali, which are experiencing internal migration as well as outmigration and are addressed in this case study, emerge as particularly affected by decreases in rice production (Yu et al., 2010).

There are high uncertainties around demographic, socio-economic and political developments over the course of this century and it is difficult to make projections of migration patterns under a changing climate. Rigaud et al. (2018) estimate that by 2050 there will be between 3.6 in a climate-friendly, and 13.3 million internal climate migrants in Bangladesh in a pessimistic scenario, corresponding to 2 or 7.5 percent of the country's overall population. Presently, (internal) migration monitoring is already a challenge. The Internal Displacement Monitoring Center relies for example on different sources of reporting, including national, subnational, media, UN or NGO sources (Internal Displacement Monitoring Center, 2018). The analysis of cell phone data may in the future help to make better estimates on internal migration after extreme events (Lu et al., 2016). When comparing the climate impacts under a Paris-Consensus and a business-as-usual scenario, it becomes evident that under the latter much larger areas would become unsafe for habitation because of recurring or permanent flooding by the end of the century. Moreover, intensified tropical cyclones and storm surges would continue to displace people. If the time between these events decreases, people may decide to leave and not to return to their place of origin, instead of migrating temporarily. The nature of today's climate-related movements and their implications for human wellbeing, societal peace and security could foreshadow the extensive consequences of climate impacts in the future (Edenhofer et al., 2018).

6.4. Interactions of Physical Climate Impacts with Human Systems

Cyclones and floods affect people's lives in various aspects. In the southwest of Bangladesh, the interaction of climate impacts with (housing) infrastructure, agriculture, fisheries and health are significant push factors for migration, as was identified during the interview process. This is also reflected in the literature (Ahsan et al., 2011; Kartiki, 2011). Many respondents mentioned losing their source of income, their housing, their land or experiencing threats to their health like injuries or malnutrition as decisive factors leading to their outmigration. For this reason, I focus on these variables in the following analysis. One can distinguish between the immediate and the medium to long-term effects of climate impacts on human systems. Immediate effects include loss of human life, damage and demolition of houses, loss of livestock, harvest or land. All of these may prompt households to relocate, most of them temporarily, until they have rebuilt homes and formed an income base again. While the destruction caused by high wind speed cyclones and flooding events is clearly, the long-term effects which cyclones have on livelihoods and communities must also be taken into consideration.

Agriculture & Fisheries

47% of Bangladeshis work in the agricultural sector, but generate only about 15% of the country's GDP (CIA World Factbook, 2017a). While many of those living on subsistence farming are struggling to provide for their families even under normal climate conditions, climate change poses new and additional challenges. Floods, but also droughts or increased rainfall variability can have negative effects on crops. While the projection of yields under different climate change scenarios remains a challenge and uncertainties over yield increases due to technological advancements in cropping or irrigations systems prevail, some climate impacts can be identified which negatively impact agriculture in South Asia (see an overview of the literature in: Vinke et al., 2016). For example, storm surges often cause extended periods of flooding and land loss aggravates the salinization of agricultural soils. This circumstance remains a threat to people's livelihood or even survival for weeks and months after the cyclone impact occurred. Economic losses from cyclone and flood damages can strongly impede a household's capability to re-invest in their land for agriculture or family business: "*After Aila, households that had taken on micro-credit loans to invest in shrimp farming reported taking on additional loans to counteract losses*" (Kartiki, 2011).

In Bangladesh, about 1.2 million people work in inland water fishing and approximately 0.3 million people in marine fishing (FAO, 2014b). While the effects of climate change on marine ecosystems, aquaculture and fisheries in the Bay of Bengal still have to be further researched, it is acknowledged that both sectors are strongly dependent on a stable climate: "*Bangladesh fisheries and aquaculture are very sensitive to climatic variability and climate change*" (FAO, 2014b). In the riverine and marine ecosystems climate change impacts such as temperature rise, or changes in salinity levels may affect the fish's reproductive capacity and alter their migration behavior (Ministry of Environment and Forests, 2010). Rainfall is also a crucial factor for the oxygen content in rivers which in turn could be altered by changing precipitation patterns (Moreno-Rodenas et al., 2016; Ochoa-Rodriguez et al., 2015). An increase in water temperature may also give rise to new outbreaks of diseases or facilitate the circulation of infections within fish stocks both in wildlife and in farmed fish. Moreover, after cyclones, the habitat for different species of fish could be destroyed, such as mangrove forests. As fisheries and aquaculture provide for income sources of large groups and because the availability of fish for local consumption is a key factor for food security in some regions of Bangladesh, interruptions in the productivity of these sectors may have far-reaching consequences for communities. The FAO (2014) therefore broadly describes which aspects could be negatively affected by climate impacts on fisheries in Bangladesh: "*food access, nutrition aspects, livelihoods, development gender opportunities, etc.*" In turn these can be push factors for outmigration.

Health

Apart from injuries caused by the immediate effects of the cyclone, such as the winds and the storm surge, the weeks after the cyclone can also pose high public health risks to communities. For example, when sanitary facilities such as latrines are flooded or destroyed, diseases like cholera can spread quickly. Health systems which are in many countries not sufficient to serve the population adequately without a crisis are under extreme pressure when having to handle a multitude of injuries after a natural disaster. An epidemic of diarrhea can thus become a severe threat to the population, especially in a country where large parts of the population are in high-risk groups, such as newborns and infants or people who are already malnourished. Several studies have documented diarrheal outbreaks after floods in Bangladesh and pointed out that above all children were affected (Khan et al., 2011b). Moreover, some bacteria, such as Vibrio cholera, survive for longer time periods in saline water, increasing the risk of infection in inundated coastal areas with poor sanitary facilities (Borroto, 1998).

Other factors causing health hazards are the diminished availability of drinking water and food. In the Barisal and Khulna districts, a representative study showed that already 59% and 48.2% of children under five years respectively are malnourished, meaning either they were underweight, stunted (too short for their age), or wasted (too thin for their height) (Mohsena et al., 2015). The destruction of agricultural land, stored food and livestock can be disastrous for communities, especially in remote areas where supply chains to the villages are scarce and often cut off when roads are washed out. In addition, the salinization of freshwater ponds through storm surges means that the drinking water supply is a key problem in the aftermath of cyclones. The threats to life do not end with the passing of the storm but may continue the weeks thereafter.

Insufficiently addressed mental health issues in the wake of such intense and tragic natural disasters include traumata of individuals as well as in whole communities (Udomratn, 2008). Taking into consideration that in Bangladesh large areas and often millions of people are affected by cyclonic events, one could assume that there are potentially long-lasting negative psychological effects on parts of the society, as has been found in other cases like after Hurricane Katrina in New Orleans, USA (Kessler et al., 2008). Literature on the psychological impacts of climate change has started to emerge over the last years (Bourque and Cunsolo Willox, 2014; Clayton et al., 2017; Doherty and Clayton, 2011; Gifford and Gifford, 2016), but only few focus on Bangladesh. One study for example looked at aggressive behavior and bedwetting of children in Bangladesh, both of which increased after floods, pointing to posttraumatic psychological effects of flooding events (Durkin et al., 1993). In the article of Doherty and Clayton (2011) the psychological effects of migration and displacement are in fact also categorized as psychosocial impacts of climate change. It is often difficult for the national government to provide basic housing, medical and food supplies in the aftermath of a disaster and psychological care often falls short. This is even more problematic for those who are uprooted from their communities or have lost their family in the disaster and therefore lack social support through their personal surroundings. In the chaotic situation after a natural disaster, vulnerable groups of society can also become victims of human trafficking (Kälin, 2005).

Health risks of climate impacts in the Southwest of Bangladesh are present in both the affected rural and urban areas. They can be a crucial reason for migration because people flee from areas in which they are exposed to severe threats to their life. At the same time, migration as a consequence of climate impacts can also expose people to hazards (Coutin, 2005; Guiraudon, 2003). This may be the case during migration, when people move with little resources, skipping meals, experiencing physical exhaustion and using unsafe means of transportation. As mentioned before, people often relocate to areas in the city where rental prices are low, or they settle informally on available land. These less-valued parts of the city are often also exposed to climate impacts such as flooding or extreme heat, or pose other health hazards, including violent crime and communicable diseases.

In the following table the health implications related to climate migration are summarized for sending and receiving communities as well as for migrants themselves. A division is made between short- term and long-term effects because these can vary significantly. Overall, both negative and positive effects of such migration exist, which can also depend on the groups or the individual's vulnerability. For sending and receiving communities migration can be beneficial or problematic, depending on the community's capacity of migration management and integration of migrants in the destination labor market.

	Short Term	Long Term
Migrants	- Wounding / direct physical injuries / death during migration process - Malnutrition - Shock - Insecurity during migration - Violence & crime - Respiratory diseases, - Waterborne & infectious diseases, e.g. tuberculosis - Cultural shock, anxiety and stress upon arrival	- Malnutrition - Risk of infectious diseases - Mental health & stress - Premature birth - Development of chronic diseases - Decreased capacities for managing chronic diseases - Loss of traditional health practices. Changes in the diet - Hopelessness leading to informal forms of employment such as prostitution, housework etc. Health risks associated with unregulated labor + Improved access to health care in cities compared to rural areas
Receiving Communities	- Risk of introduction of infectious or waterborne diseases - Reduced quality of care for receiving communities because health systems are under pressure - Sanitary settlement problems - Societal friction and competition for resources	- Introduction of communicable diseases - Changing local demographics - Stress on the educational system - Economic effects on employment - Decreased availability of resources - Mental health - Competition for jobs: migrants would work for less, stress associated with job loss - Overall economic effects, for instance decreased availability of adequate housing - Formation of an informal economy, black markets + Availability of informal labor could benefit receiving communities + Increase in GDP as migrants add to the economy
Sending Community	- Labour drain: increased workload for women & children who stay & do agricultural labor - Remaining locked- in population such as the elderly may receive less care	+ Improved access to medicine because of remittances + Improved nutrition because of remittances + Decrease in population pressure in exposed areas, potentially more resources for those who stay

Table 4 Climate Migration and its potential Effects on Health – Overview. Legend: "+" refers to possible positive effects, "-" refers to possible negative effects (source: own, synthesis of group discussions with health professionals at Barcelona Summer School on Global Health, University of Barcelona, July 15th, Risk of introduction of infectious or water2015 and Heidelberg Summer School on Climate Change and Health,

Despite the high relevance for adaptation planning, the connections between climate change, migration and health are not sufficiently researched yet (Schwerdtle et al., 2018). While in-depth study of such complex and interconnected risks is beyond the scope of this dissertation, I will include references to the health problems which migrants mentioned during the interviews because health is one indicator for the effectiveness of migration as adaptation (see chapter 3.4. and 6.7.).

6.5. Migration Patterns Bangladesh

The interactions between physical climate change impacts with human systems create push factors for outmigration from affected areas. However, it is crucial to acknowledge and consider that Bangladesh has large internal migratory movements and that the drivers of migration in the country are multifold. Rural to rural migration is a common practice of landless agricultural laborers and of farmers who cannot generate sufficient income from their own yields. Income disparities between rural and urban areas as well as the perception of opportunities in the urban labor market have led to rapid urbanization over the last fifty years that is characterized by the formation of large informal settlements. "*In Bangladesh the number of urban population is growing up day by day. The urban migration is motivated by rural poverty, river erosion and natural disaster forcing them to migrate to urban area. These new comers floating people in the city end up sleeping in public places such as street corners, railway station, bus stop and open places*" (Bangladesh Bureau of Statistics, 2015b). Bangladesh's integration into the global textile industry has caused an increasing number of women to migrate to the capital in order to find more profitable livelihoods in garment factories than what they could derive from the agricultural labor in their rural home communities (Mallick and Etzold, 2015). The overall share of the urban population in Bangladesh increased from 5% in 1960, when the vast majority still lived in rural areas, to 34% in 2015, which is still well below the global average and continues to rise (The World Bank, 2017a). But not only hope for a better future prompts people to migrate. Although a longstanding assumption exists that people move to receive better public services, correlation analysis carried out by UNDP delivered "*little solid evidence of any such link*" (Marshall and Rahman, 2013). This assumption, however, has been "*the justification for the de facto official response of national authorities, in not prioritizing living conditions and public services within urban slums*" (Marshall and Rahman, 2013). Rashid, Hunt, & Haider (2007) already investigated the propensity for people to migrate in exchange for aid in two slums in Dhaka heavily affected by flood events. By using a stated preference choice model they found that moderate "*economic incentives were not attractive enough for* [people] *to relocate to flood-free areas*". This points to the fact that there is a difference in motivations of economic migrants and climate change-affected households and that the nature of the movement of the latter is being forced or pushed out, rather than being pulled by the opportunities of the city. This case study confirms this assumption. Actually, many people are forced to leave and the majority of new displacements within Bangladesh occurs because of natural disasters. Between 2008 and 2016 an average of 614 000 people per year were displaced after natural disasters, mainly storms and floods (Internal Displacement Monitoring Center, 2017). Climate impacts, which trigger more intense and frequent storms and floods, are becoming a major factor in the current migration patterns. For example, income disparities between rural and urban areas, a key driver for rural-urban migration as described by the Harris-Todaro Model (see chapter 3.2.), may be fortified or even aggravated by climate change.

Overview: Climate Impacts and Migration

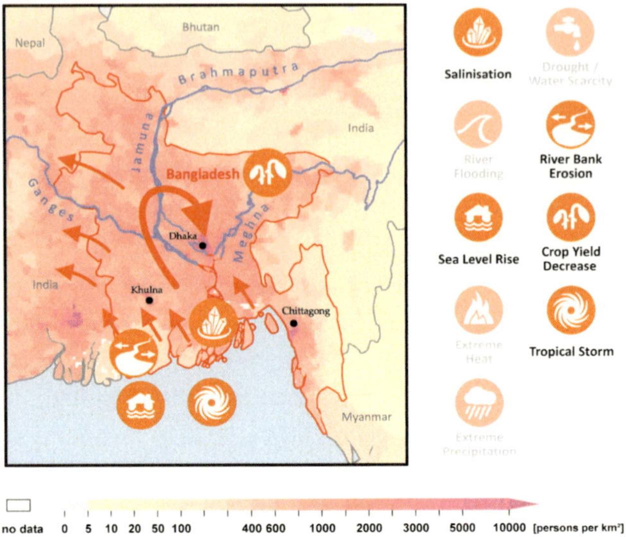

Figure 6 Possible Climate Migration Pathways in Bangladesh. (source: adapted with modification from Vinke et al., 2017)

Figure 7 Simplified Migration Pathways of Respondents to Khulna (source: own, Vinke (2014) Google Earth).

In figure 6 the most significant interactions of climate change impacts and human mobility in Bangladesh are schematically depicted. In the southern part of Bangladesh, which is an area of high food insecurity (WFP, 2005), several climate impacts coincide such as sea level rise, tropical cyclones risks, riverbank erosion and the salinization of soils. Whereas the effects of some of these impacts on human systems can be reduced through infrastructural in-situ adaptation measures or financial assistance after storms, most populations are not adequately protected and often do not have access to basic income.

Arguably, climate impacts have already contributed to the net-outmigration from southern Bangladesh. The districts with the largest negative net-migration between 2011 and 2001 are Bhola (-11.22% of the total population) Jhalokati (-10.94), Gopalganj (-10.83) and Bagerhat (-10.82) (Ionesco et al., 2017). The district of Khulna has a net migration rate of -10.02% with 11.28% of men and 8.68% of women of the total population leaving the area. Within that timeframe overall more men than women migrated out of southwestern Bangladesh. This data supports the observation that households often send men to work in cities to generate a more stable or higher income, while some women and children remain in the villages. After cyclones a rise in seasonal movements has also been observed (Bhattacharyya and Werz, 2012). What is furthermore underlined by figure 6 is that people are migrating to already densely populated areas. Most of Bangladesh, except for parts of the Chittagong Hills in the East and the protected areas of the Sundarban forest reserves in the South, is inhabited.

Cascadal Migration

Parts of the observed climate change-related movements in Bangladesh can be identified as cascadal. For instance, when storms, sea level rise, salinization of groundwater affect rural incomes by diminishing agricultural yields, they can trigger migratory movements. Some of them may be circular or seasonal, like those connected to the monsoon season. Others are permanent, either because people find adequate livelihoods in other places such as cities, or because there is no place to return to. Climate migration may in this case also constitute a push factor for other forms of migration, inducing cascadal effects. For instance, if a city takes in a lot of migrants who may work for below average incomes, other city dwellers may decide to leave and migrate to the capital. There, middle or high-income groups may decide to leave their country as informal settlements around their capital continue to grow. During our field research we identified migration patterns which led to permanent resettlement to medium-sized regional urban centers such as the city of Khulna or Satkhira in the Southwest of Bangladesh. This confirms findings of previous studies which were conducted soon after the occurrence of the cyclone Aila (Kartiki, 2011). In the 2009 field research of Kartiki (2011) it was already suggested that some people would likely not return to the villages and that displacement would be permanent. This was also the case with the respondents which were interviewed in this case study. However, these arrival cities are incapable of absorbing high numbers of incoming migrants, as there is not sufficient demand for unskilled laborers (Vinke, 2015). For example, Khulna is the third largest city in Bangladesh, with around 1.5 million inhabitants and a population growth rate of about 5%. Estimates of people living below poverty line lie at around 40% (KfW, 2011). Whereas Khulna is a point of destination for migrants from the region who resettle because of floods, erosion or cyclones, it is important to note that the city itself lies only 2.5 meters above sea level and is exposed to storms and flooding events.

Because newly arrived migrants frequently offer their workforce in unregulated markets below the local average wage, tensions between new settlers and residents possibly can arise. If the income opportunities do not grow with the increase in population in these medium-sized cities, people with better educational backgrounds who have a certain degree of mobility and resources may decide to move to the capital city of Dhaka. In Dhaka, those with financial means and family networks may decide to migrate internationally if incoming migrants from medium-sized cities underbid their wages. While these movements then cannot be labeled as climate migration, they may be connected to the initial movements which were climate-induced. It is important to note that a cascadal migration accompanied by a brain drain is not inevitable. As presented before, migrants can add to the economy and add to a country's productivity which would be a positive effect of migration. If cities are able to capitalize on incoming migrants and expand their economic base, the cascade of migration from one place to the next may not occur. However, this will only happen if migrants successfully integrate into the urban labor market and are able to do so by acquiring a set of skills, which serves the demands of employment in the city. Overall, the push and pull factors for migration need to outweigh the costs of migration, which are not limited to economic factors but also potentially include the loss of a social net or of one's own culture.

Each year up to half a million Bangladeshis migrate to Dhaka and most of them find shelter in informal settlements (German and Pyne, 2010). This expansion has contributed to the challenges the city faces which are reflected by its placement on the Economist's Intelligence Unit's livability city index, where Dhaka ranks 137 out of 140, outperforming only Lagos, Tripoli and Damascus (The Economist Intelligence Unit, 2017). Subsequently, Bangladesh's capital is among the cities with the worst living conditions in the world. The index measures indicators of various aspects of city life varying from culture and environment to education, stability, healthcare as well as the city's infrastructure (The Economist Intelligence Unit, 2017). Moreover, Dhaka is a megacity at high risk from various climate impacts, including sea level rise, salinization of freshwater sources and increasing cyclone impacts (ADB, 2012). These risks are multiplied by "poor urban planning" (ADB, 2012). Overall, it is questionable if migration to a destination such as Dhaka – already overcrowded, poor and hazardous – can be considered a good option for adaptation to climate change. Bhattacharyya & Werz (2012) point out that international migration from urban centers in Bangladesh may increase because of the failure to provide basic services in cities such as Dhaka.

Networks and Migration

Mallick and Etzold draw attention to the fact that "*People's access to migration opportunities and their choice of destinations reflects existing patterns of social inequality*" (Mallick and Etzold, 2015). For example, to extremely impoverished people migration may not be an option after a climate impact occurred because resources necessary for the move are diminished. Many landless peasants possibly migrate into urban slums to take up physical day labor, but more affluent families may be able to pay for one family member to receive university level education in a medium-sized city and therefore diversify the income sources of the family in the long term. These migration patterns heavily reflect socio economic disparities. Mallick and Etzold (2015) also stress that the reality of migration in Bangladesh is much more complex than a onetime permanent movement from one place to another. Families often have members who live and work in several different places and so can cope with risks of income losses through insecure work environments such as agricultural labor or their work in factories and sweat-shops. One man had tried to return to his home after the cyclone Aila but because of the effects of the storm on the village he could not sustain his family by operating a cycle rickshaw: "*I had come here immediately after Aila and stayed 6-7 months, then I went back. At first I came here alone and then with my family, I came here again*" (Interview 16, Satkhira). This case exemplifies another commonality in the migration patterns: often the men leave to work in the cities temporarily to increase the household income. Then, at a later point when climate impacts are too severe in the village, the entire family relocates. The same family who had been affected by Aila was later affected by river erosion and together shifted permanently to the city (Interview 16, Satkhira). A woman in Khulna recounts the reasons for eventually relocating the entire household after the cyclone Sidr had occurred:

"Interviewer: Why have you come here, because of Sidr or for looking for work?

Respondent: At first my husband came here for work. But when Sidr occurred and our house was totally damaged we all shifted here permanently"

(Interview 09, Khulna).

The translocality of households can be beneficial in financial terms, but can also cause stress due to the separation of families and because of a possibly higher workload for women and children who remain in the village and may be left with the majority of agricultural labor (Melde, S.,

Laczko, F., & Gemenne, 2017). Return migrants can also introduce new infectious diseases and sexually transmitted diseases to villages in which these were previously not present (Hugo, 2003; WHO, 2000). For communities with limited access to healthcare and basic health education, a higher disease burden can become a severe impediment to public health and well-being. The importance of social media in the perception of livelihood opportunities at potential destinations has only recently been addressed in research (Dekker et al., 2018; Dekker and Engbersen, 2014). More and more people have (indirect) access to the internet, through smart phones or internet cafés, and the influence of largely positive representations of migration experiences and opportunities elsewhere displayed in the social media on migration decision-making processes should not be underestimated.

Locked-in Populations in villages

When analyzing the migration patterns of Bangladesh, it is important not to overlook those who remain in the affected communities. Staying in a place that is impacted by climate change does not necessarily indicate successful in-situ adaptation. When one migrant was asked whether there are other people from his home village who intend to migrate he responded: *"They want to but cannot because of scarcity of land. Some rich people have lands, land they have bought in town and they start to live here*" (Interview 17, Satkhira). They may find temporary protection in cyclone shelters during a tropical storm, but may not be able to finance transport to a nearby city. It was mentioned by several respondents that people who had returned to villages immediately after cyclonic events received aid from international organizations or the government. Those who remained in the cities under poor conditions did not receive this support, pointing to the fact that government benefits or disaster aid entitlements are not necessarily transferable when a person changes their location.

Cross Border Migration

While outmigration is mostly directed at cities within Bangladesh, some people do migrate across the border to West Bengal, India, with and without documents. A man whose family had lived for three generations in the village of Mathurapur, Munshiganj/ Satkhira District explained that many people had left Mathurapur, which was affected by Aila and Sidr, also due to increasing cases of robbery in the Sundarban jungle where people collected wood or fished:

"Respondent: *People who left went to India. You can go by boat.*
Interviewer: *No paper documents requirement?*
Respondent: *No"*
(Interview 21, Satkhira).

According to other respondents people also went on foot through the Sundarban jungle in order to reach India. At the border the Indian patrol would allegedly fire guns at them. Nevertheless, they still frequently attempt to cross over. When household members in Badarghata, Shyamnagar/ Satkhira district were asked how environmental factors were affecting their lives, they responded:

"Respondent (1): *All the men and women here work to survive. During natural calamities there is no job.*
Respondent (2): *It is difficult to get job especially in [the] monsoon [season]?*
Respondent (3): *Many people from here go to city in search for job in brick field. Some people even go to India.*
Interviewer: *India?*
Respondent (3): *Yes, now about 200-300 people from this place are in India.*
Interviewer: *For how long did the people stay in the city area?*
Respondent (2): *About 6 months.*
Interviewer: *So the male go...*
Respondent (1): *Both male and female go. Some widowed female go for the job of cooking"*
(Interview 24, Satkhira).

The environmental push factors identified by this household are closely intertwined with the opportunity to generate an income. One of the pull factors for cross-border migration to India, which induces people to the hazardous illegal immigration instead of migration within the country, is the prospect of higher wages in West Bengal. The transit from Bangladesh to India is the second largest migration corridor worldwide (The World Bank, 2008). However, as Walsham (2010) points out, most migratory movements are taking place over relatively short distances; people generally move from the rural areas to the urban centers within their own district.

Governance of Climate Migration

The government of Bangladesh has acknowledged climate migration as a challenge which is likely to become more substantial as climate impacts intensify. Bangladesh's National Adaptation Programme of Action (NAPA) lists several points which target at reducing climate change- induced migration from rural areas into cities through the adaptation of agricultural systems to salinization and flash floods (Ministry of Environment and Forests Government of the People's Republic of Bangladesh, 2005). Herein migration is seen as a consequence or impact of climate change that adaptation measures seek to avoid or at least reduce. For example, project 11 in the NAPA "Promoting adaptation to coastal crop agriculture to combat salinization" lists as possible long-term outcomes: "*Affected community would not migrate to cities for job and livelihood*" and "*social consequences of mass scale migration to cities would to some extent be halted*" (Ministry of Environment and Forests Government of the People's Republic of Bangladesh, 2005). While these attempts to increase in-situ adaptation options can help to decrease migration pressure, they have so far not been scaled up in order to match the challenge. Despite the advancements in early warning systems for cyclones, the climate change impacts on society and livelihoods will intensify if no further improvements in adaptation planning are realized. Overall, migration within Bangladesh is taking place without adequate governance structures. The lack of effective management of migration flows is of course connected to limited financial government resources and prevailing general deficiencies in good governance. Governance indicators such as for corruption, rule of law, regulatory quality, stability or accountability reflect the weaknesses in all three branches of government (The World Bank, 2017b).

6.6. Migrant Household Profiles

To analyze under which circumstances migration can be considered an effective adaptation to climate change, it is necessary to find out who the people are that are migrating and whether there are commonalities between them which perhaps lead to an "effective" adaptation or hinder it. According to Kartiki (2011): "*Analysing who migrates, why, how, and where they go, can provide useful insights for development planners and practitioners aiming to support poor women, men and their families*." The assessment in this study of 'who is migrating' will furthermore contextualize the data derived from the qualitative interviews. In the following section the background of the migrants is explained, including their reasons for migration, where they had come from, which type of work they did and where they were going to. In the next chapter, their situation post-migration is analyzed as part of the evaluation of effectiveness of their migration, including patterns of employment in the migrants' arrival destinations. This chapter is based on the existing literature, interview findings and observations. The list of interview partners can be found in the Annex Bangladesh.

Vulnerability: Poor Communities in Southern Bangladesh

In terms of vulnerability, there is an urban-rural divide in Bangladesh. "All the indicators except floating population show that in 2001, rural areas were more vulnerable than urban areas which remain unchanged in 2011" (Bangladesh Bureau of Statistics, 2015b). This statement is particularly interesting in the context of this study, for the displaced rural population often ends up forming part of the 'floating population' which refers to a group of people without a permanent home, such as squatters. The economic base of the villages in the south of Bangladesh is largely small-scale agriculture. Some respondents lived or had lived directly on embankments prior to their migration. These communities generally have no financial means to prepare themselves for disaster. Furthermore, their housing was not built in a way to withstand storms, and huts are not elevated to secure their inhabitants from inundation. This was also the case in the study area (see picture 1).

Picture 1: Typical house in Bangladesh's southern coastal communities from which the respondents had migrated (source: own).

Many of the interviewees were landless or had become landless through the cyclone impacts. Generally, poor communities are disproportionately affected by climate impacts, also because their relative losses are high. Within these communities however, the propensity to migrate may vary for different groups based on gender, age, income and networks. The point has been raised that the weakest individuals in those communities often are unable to migrate (ADB, 2012; Kartiki, 2011).

During the field research different groups of migrants were encountered in different locations. In Khulna many people had settled in the aftermath of the two recent large cyclones, Sidr in 2007 and Aila in 2009. In figure 7 it can be seen how respondents came from various areas south of Khulna after the cyclones had made landfall. For the same reason, people had also moved to Satkhira. However, in the rice mills around Satkhira migrant workers reported that they had already occasionally sought temporary work in the city prior to the disaster and shifted permanently afterwards, often with their families. Also, social reasons played a significant role in the decision-making process because many migrants left behind parts of their family and social networks. Relocation to a nearby area would enable them to visit their hometown. In the city Barisal, the situation was different. At large, the migrants encountered had left their homes due to river erosion, and migrants from the surrounding villages often used inexpensive water transport to migrate directly to Dhaka via rivers, rather than trying to find employment in Barisal. Other factors which made a direct migration to Dhaka more favorable may have been existing family networks in the capital and very limited capacities in Barisal's labor market. This shows that there are many defining variables in the migration decisions and that accessibility to transportation can define migration patterns.

Generally, people who migrated from the villages did not have any substantial professional training except for their traditional knowledge of agriculture and fishery within the natural environment where they had lived, sometimes for generations. Typical occupations in the rural areas included honey and wood collection from the Sundarban forests, fishing, small-scale agriculture and livestock ownerships, as well as shrimp farming. Unlike in the city where after a disaster a rickshaw puller, baker or tailor can eventually resume his work, the assets in the villages like land, livestock or fish have been destroyed and often irreversibly so. The capability to regain the status quo ante is more limited and the path to it may be much longer for rural communities than for people hit by climate impacts in urban centers. As one household in Satkhira reports, the burden of debt after storm damages made it impossible for them to invest and rebuild their business again:

"Respondent: *My husband did business before. Now there is no business.*
Interviewer: *Why is there no business now?*
Respondent: *Because we have no money. We had to spend it all after Aila. Now we are borrower.*
Interviewer: *You came to city to earn. But now you are debtor. Why?*
Respondent: *We took loan to repair our houses in the village.*
(son) *Now we are trying to repay this loan. When we repay this loan, we go back home [village].*

Interviewer: *From whom did you take the loans?*
Respondent: *From cooperatives. One is 40,000 and another is 50,000 (husband) [total less than 1000 Euro]"*
(Interview 25, Satkhira*).*

This interview exemplifies how high the relative damage of cyclones is for households with little or no assets and how the effects of such sudden impacts can determine livelihoods for years to come through cycles of economic setbacks and debt. Because there was no need for agricultural labor in the urban areas, basically all participants in the study had changed their profession after migration (see chapter 6.7. and annex chapter 14.3. for a list of participants and their rural an urban livelihoods). Many who had previously worked as subsistence farmers became unskilled laborers in different urban professions. Furthermore, it can be derived from the body of interviews that rural migrants often left without sufficient funds to build or rent homes in the city area. While they had hoped to generate a higher income in the city, debt payments prevented them from investing in their business or education.

While the majority of respondents were of working age, the interviews covered the age group from 15 to 80-year olds. Women like men had migrated. However, only few women migrated alone, a finding that is also reflected in Kartiki's study (2011) which was conducted in the aftermath of Aila. This can be explained by the risks for women who arrive in cities without men, who often exercise protective functions. In some cases, men who had previously cultivated their own land left their families behind in the villages and worked in the city, in order to provide for sufficient food or to rebuild a damaged house. They would frequently return to the village to visit their families. However, this strategy was not always successful because there were no sufficient income opportunities in the cities.

Most people who did not flee their homes due to a sudden disaster, but made a planned decision to migrate, had previously been in contact with someone in the urban area they were going to. At large it can be said that people who knew someone in the city areas, like a relative who could provide them with work or initially with shelter, were more likely to migrate than those who did not, because it would reduce the risks and uncertainties which come with relocation. Nevertheless, many families who were now migrants had lived in the villages for generations. Because of the severity of climate impacts, possibly in connection with rising population pressure, they were forced to move for the first time. The population pressure in the rural areas was also captured in one interview. The respondent, who had to move out of his village after the cyclone Aila described his work in the village which included farming. However, he did not farm on his own land: "*My land was not suitable for cultivation. After all we are 5 brothers and it is divided among us so we got only a little land*" (Satkhira, Interview 19). As the poor are the most severely affected by disasters, they have to diversify their income in order to distribute the risk of income loss which is often not feasible in the villages. It can thus be explained why the interviewed migrants who had left their homeland for reasons of environmental degradation had a low socioeconomic status; they were prior to their migration part of the rural poor and then moved to urban (extreme) poverty.

Interactions of Exposure and Vulnerability: Disaster Risk Infrastructure and Awareness

It was observed that there were cyclone shelters in some of the villages, but for several interviewed household the location of the shelters was too far away to reach quickly during a calamity. While shelters would protect the people from loss of life, a cyclone of the magnitude such as Sidr or Aila could cause such high losses through infrastructural damages diminishing future income that threats to survival persisted even weeks after the occurrence of the event. Some respondents explained that they did not go to the shelter because previously the early warning system had frequently signaled the highest storm warnings, but an extreme storm surge had not followed. Hence, they thought it unnecessary to seek shelter. When the cyclone occurred, the family was caught by surprise since they had never experienced a cyclone of this magnitude. Because they were especially vulnerable due to their lack of knowledge about possible extreme events, they were unable to reduce their exposure by using the available risk infrastructure adequately. Another family who remained in their home village in Barguna recounts the events of cyclone Sidr and describes the dangers of the walk to the cyclone shelter:

"Respondent (1):	*We were in our house. When my elder brother's house was damaged, I came to the road and saw that water was flowing over the road. Then we started to go to the cyclone shelter. We thought we could go to the shelter as water was not that high. But by the time we reached to the sluice gate [within 5 minutes walking distance from his house] suddenly the water level was so high. The sluice gate broke down and my whole family fell down with the wave.*
Interviewer:	*How far is the shelter from here?*
Respondent (2):	*About 1 km.*
Respondent (1):	*Yes, 1 km from here.*
Interviewer:	*Okay, please continue.*
Respondent (1):	*I felt that earth beneath my feet was moved. We were into the water. The current was so strong that it was difficult to hold something.*
Interviewer:	*What time was it?*
Respondent (1):	*It was 9 at night and it was dark. When the cyclone stopped it was 1 at night. I came to home. I found dead body of my only son 3 days later. He [man standing beside him] found his daughter's dead body at night. We buried them here.*
Interviewer:	*Wasn't there any warning?*
Respondent (1):	*Yes, we knew. But we were confident about the embankment.*
Respondent (2):	*We heard a lot of number 10 signals [highest warning for cyclone]. But the surge had never come over the embankment.*
Respondent (1):	*We were frightened when water came over the embankment. We untied our cattle. But our houses were not damaged.*

Respondent (1):	*If we stayed in house, then this might not happen.*
Interviewer:	*How old was your son?*
Respondent (1):	*8 years.*
Respondent (2):	*At about 10 at night, I found no people around. Then I went to the road which was flooded. If the road [embankment] was not breached, it would not be a problem. My mother and grandfather were with me. I lost my grandfather on the same day"* (Interview 37, Barguna).

The further away cyclone shelters are, the earlier people have to evacuate in order to minimize risks. In the case mentioned above, people did not respond to the cyclone warning, but thought the embankment would be enough to protect their village. They only tried going to the shelter when the storm surge swept over the embankment. This in turn led to the death of several family members.

"Interviewer:	*Can you share the experience on the occurrence of the cyclone?*
Respondent:	*We were sleeping then. How the water flooded all thing. I could not understand. [...]*
Interviewer:	*Did you get the alert before Sidr?*
Respondent:	*Yes. But I did not take it seriously.*
Interviewer:	*Did anyone go to the cyclone shelter then?*
Respondent:	*No. None of our village people went there. We thought it wouldn't happen.*
Interviewer:	*Do you think, if you went to the cyclone shelter you would have been able to minimize the losses?*
Respondent:	*Yes"* (Interview 08, Khulna).

These interview excerpts underline that disaster risk reduction infrastructure can only reach its full efficacy if it goes hand in hand with trainings and information dissemination on safe evacuation practices as well as capacity development for correct interpretation of warning signals.

Without adequate disaster and climate risk preparedness, climate change can indirectly act as a threat multiplier. For example, although the correlation between extreme events and violent crime has not been sufficiently researched, several case studies (most of which focused on disasters in the US) point to increases in domestic and interpersonal violence, as well as in child abuse and neglect (WHO, 2005). Also, increasing temperatures, which affect people in urban slums, have been linked to higher suicide rates (Burke et al., 2018). In cases of limited disaster preparedness and response, socio-economic conditions emerge which give entry points for organized crime such as human trafficking (WHO, 2005). Moreover, climate impacts lead to a further diminishing of agricultural livelihood options and negatively affect the economy while a "*lack of economic opportunity and recessionary economies are positively correlated with terrorism*" even though many terrorists themselves often have better educational and economic backgrounds (de Mesquita, 2005). One of the effects of climate change is the increase of economic disparities and the intensification of state fragility, which can make terrorist recruitment and mobilization more successful (de Mesquita, 2005; Nett and Rüttinger, 2016).

Disaster preparedness therefore is a key element of reducing vulnerability to both direct and indirect effects of climate change. The majority of respondents had not received a formal education, or only primary school, which is in accordance with the findings of the 2011 census that only one third of slum dwellers was literate (Bangladesh Bureau of Statistics, 2015a). This explains why the migrants interviewed were not aware of climate change and the risks of unprecedented or unusual events such as extreme storm surges and high wind cyclones. During the interview process all participants were asked if they had perceived changes in their natural environment over the last years. The great majority responded with yes and listed a variety of climate impacts which are in accordance with the scientific literature on regional climate change. One person mentioned, "*There were storms before but not water. But now storms come with the surge. The height of water is also increased*" (Interview 25, Satkhira). "*Cyclone and rainfall have increased*" (Interview 13, Khulna). Another respondent reflects: "*My father, grandfather never saw this kind of things which we see now*" (Interview 23, Satkhira). In the village of Shahid Smrity Sarak in Barguna, one resident reports, "*The water level is higher now. Previously the water did not come inside house. Now it does*" (Interview 35, Barguna). These interview excerpts show that the respondents are closely observing the changes in their environment. They compare them to their own lived experiences or those of their ancestors. Even though these are of course subjective and localized experiences, they fit in with the larger picture of observed climate impacts in the south of Bangladesh.

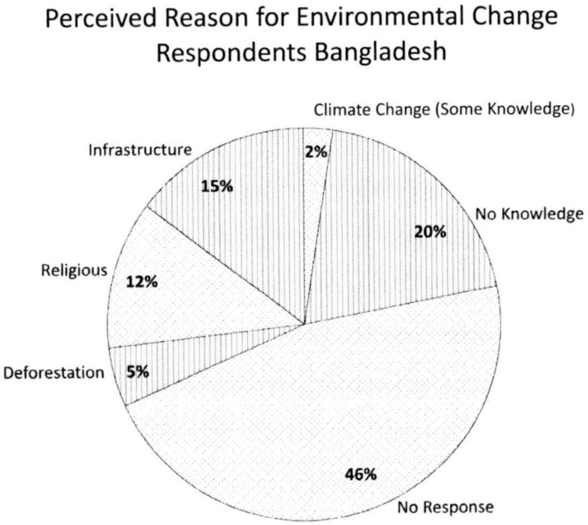

Figure 8 Perceived Reason for Environmental Change of Respondents in Bangladesh (Migrants and Sending Communities) (source: own).

When asked about the reasons for the changes in the environment which people had witnessed, most respondents did not have any explanation and only one could point to climate change. Out of the stock of interviews 20% responded they do not know, 15% referred to infrastructural problems and 5% attributed the increase in the magnitude of the storm to deforestation. One migrant who mentioned deforestation as a reason explained that because of the lack of trees, the winds could reach the villages at full speed without any obstacle (Interview 19, Satkhira). 12% of interviewees gave a response related to religious beliefs such as "God knows." One respondent elaborated: "*Sand, earth, water, human, death, all are act of God. Rain, cloud all occur by the willingness of God. Human has nothing to do*" (Interview 21, Satkhira). This finding confirms the results of a study in 14 villages in the districts of Mushiganj, Chapai Nawabganj and Satkhira which aimed at deciphering people's adaptation and migration decision-making processes when faced with floods, droughts and cyclones: "*Villagers tend to believe that the success of their household is mostly determined by factors outside their control. 'It is all in God's hands*" (Sussex Centre for Migration Research and Refugee and Migratory Movements Research Unit, 2012).

6.7. Effective or Not? Migration as Adaptation in Southwestern Bangladesh

Effectiveness of Migration as Adaptation for Migrants

If the evaluation of effectiveness of migration as adaptation were based on the simplistic comparison between the benefits of staying versus leaving the affected area, the result would be evident in the southwest of Bangladesh. In the villages I visited for the field research the climate impacts on the land and ecosystem services were so severe that they impeded the area's carrying capacity for the existing population, at least temporarily. Most in-situ adaptation options were rendered impossible, either due to the incurred costs, technological feasibility or the severity of the climate impact. The standard of living in the villages – which was often below the poverty line prior to the natural disaster – was once again decreased by the effects of the storms. It is uncontestable that a majority of the migrant interviewees had saved their lives by migrating to the city. This finding underlines the fact that even under a moderate level of global warming, the climate impacts in some of the world's regions will be so severe that some populous areas will become uninhabitable, or at least uninhabitable for the current number of households settled there. In turn, migration is the only feasible measure for people in severely affected areas, even if it results in further impoverishment.

However, in this analysis the evaluation of effectiveness goes beyond the individual's fulfillment of his or her objective of migration, whether it is to save his or her life or to stabilize the income source after a climate impact occurred (see chapter 3.4., operationalization of effectiveness). Herein adaptation would be considered effective if migrants were able to maintain or even improve their standard of living[2] compared to the situation *before* a climate impact happened, such as before cyclone Aila or Sidr, or compared to the hypothetical situation that it had not occurred. In the following sections, the migrants' responses regarding their economic situation, health and wellbeing, as well as their capacity of self-determination which emerged as an important category from this field research, and possible impediments or benefits to their social capital are analyzed through a process of coding-based text reduction (Froschauer and Lueger, 2003).

Economic Situation and Livelihoods

The economic situation of those who had migrated from the rural southwest of the Bangladeshi coastline is characterized by great financial difficulties and insecurity. On the basis of the interviews at large it can be said that many migrants were only trying to survive. "*We live by hands to mouth*" one respondent summarizes, a situation which was described by many (Interview 12, Khulna). Migrants were in general unable to make savings and often struggling to repay debts. Any additional unexpected expenditure could create existential problems. This situation was not a temporary one immediately after arrival. Even several years after their displacement, most participants did not have a reliable source of income in the cities. If they had employment, it was generally in the informal sector. While the informal sector makes up "*more than half of the global labor force and more than 90% of Micro and Small Enterprises*" (ILO, 2017), it is necessary to acknowledge the disadvantages of this form of labor which

[2] The evaluation of the standard of living includes several variables, which go beyond economic indicators (see chapter 3.4.).

ranges from income insecurity to unregulated and therefore often hazardous working conditions to the absence of social security systems for the workers. In Bangladesh, 75.5% of urban employment is in the informal sector (ADB and Bangladesh Bureau of Statistics, 2012). Some typical livelihood strategies of the migrants, most of them based on employment in the informal sector, could be identified during the course of this field research and are summarized in the following paragraphs. A table listing the interviews and an overview of interviewees' previous rural employment and urban work can be found in the Annex.

Cycle Rickshaw Conducting

Because it mostly requires physical strength and no other qualifications, rickshaw pulling became a key source of income for many migrants. Usually, the household rents the cycle rickshaw. The daily rent payments present a large burden on their livelihoods and sometimes lead to indebtedness. Furthermore, many rickshaw pullers and their families reported that during rainfall there is no demand by customers, so they do not generate a sufficient income to provide food and shelter for their families. The chief town planner of Khulna explains the extent of the increase in rickshaw conductors in the city: "*Mostly, their [the migrants'] job is driving an easy bike or rickshaw. From Khulna City Corporation side we only give out 2000 licenses for easy bikes. Now, in the city area, the easy bike number is more than 10 000. This is uncontrollable and the city cannot manage it*" (Interview Town Planner, Khulna).

This indicates that the town planner already sees a saturation point for the amount of cycle rickshaws according to the city's analysis. The choice of wording "uncontrollable" and "cannot manage" can be interpreted as signs that migrants are perceived as a burden to the city and create chaos, rather than contributing their labor force to a demand in the city. As with other physical labor, the profession of cycle rickshaw pulling may turn out to be even less economically viable in the coming years if the supply of workers continues to increase, while the need for rickshaw services may not grow accordingly. Overall, the demand for physical labor in these cities may not grow fast enough to provide opportunities for incoming migrants without other training and continuing mechanization may even decrease the demand.

Seasonal Work on Rice Mills and Brick Factories

Besides working as rickshaw pullers, migrants were also encountered working in rice mills and brick factories, mostly located on the outskirts of the cities. The migrants who were interviewed were provided with shelter and other facilities by the owners of the rice mills or brick farms as part of their reimbursement for their labor. However, this employment is seasonal as the rice mills and brick farms do not operate during the rainy season. In this time frame, people would fall into debt with owners of the enterprises, since they would continue to live on the premises of the company, but were not able to pay rent by means of their labor. One rice mill laborer who had lost his property in the village due to river erosion reports: *"Here we are good, but not like before. Because I have to rely on our mill owner. And I have to give my utmost physical labor"* (Interview 16, Satkhira). This interview therefore indicates that people were not able to keep their standard of living which they had prior to the migration.

Another person, displaced by the cyclone Aila and currently working in a rice mill, explains: "*Suppose I am in a mill but it has no work for the rainy season. So to survive, we have to borrow money from the mahajon [owner of the mill] month after month. And if we do not [feel] comfort with this mahajon, we have to go to another mahajon. But as we are indebted to that first mahajon we have to borrow money from the present mahajon to give back ex-mahajon's money. As long as we do not give back this money, they don't allow us to leave this place. For this we had to give them our national ID cards which they keep*" (Interview 20, Satkhira).

The case described by the migrant constitutes a form of debt-bondage. This in turn could be considered a contemporary type of slavery as defined by the Supplementary Convention on the Abolition of Slavery, the Slave Trade, and Institutions and Practices Similar to Slavery, in 1957. By the definition of the convention debt-bondage is "*the status or condition arising from a pledge by a debtor of his personal services or of those of a person under his control as security for a debt, if the value of those services as reasonably assessed is not applied towards the liquidation of the debt or the length and nature of those services are not respectively limited and defined*" (UN Economic and Social Council (ECOSOC), 1956). Often, the families did not know how long they had to stay to repay their debt and the off-payments through labor were defined arbitrarily.

Women's Labor Options

The majority of female migrants interviewed took care of the household's children, housekeeping, cooking and tried to improve their family's food security through micro-urban farming. Some women took temporary employment, often in construction, as described in the following section. Again others worked part-time as maids in other households in order to provide an additional income for the family. It is important to recognize that displaced women in urban areas are particularly vulnerable and often exposed to gender-based violence (UNHCR, 2012).

Day Labor

For the majority of interviewed migrants one occupation alone did not generate sufficient income to sustain their families. Therefore, they took on other employment on the side. These include hard physical labor such as brick crushing for road construction or the repair and construction of embankments. For repairs and improvements in the city infrastructure, migrants were contracted by the government or non-governmental organizations, which execute cash for work projects. Some of the day labor activities were also part of the informal sector, where private companies hire people off the road for temporary work.

Begging

When the interviewing team was approached by beggars in the city, they asked them why they were in the position of having to beg. The responses also point towards a wide prevalence of extreme events and environmental degradation severely affecting people's lives. Some women who were begging had lost their husbands during Aila or Sidr and were then exposed to existential threats to survival, since they had no income source. Others had also relocated after riverbed erosion or a cyclone and then were evicted from the slum they had first arrived at.[3]

Debt and other Economic Restraints

When people left their homeland because their basis of living was destroyed, they went to cities, in order to find food and shelter and eventually to rebuild their lives after disaster. However, all of the typical livelihood strategies outlined above indicate that migrants move to the bottom of the urban socio-economic structure when they arrive in the city and are often unable to improve their situation in the long run. For a family who migrated because of riverbed erosion the migration from their disappeared homeland to the city meant a significantly lower socio-economic status: "*We can only survive here. We were better in the village when we had our own land. Now, we are like beggars*" (Interview 28, Barisal).

Some families had to borrow money for shelter and food directly upon arrival in the city after their displacement by a disaster and were still repaying these loans several years after their displacement. One negative aspect of the work in the cities that arose through most interviews was that during the monsoon season income opportunities disappeared. As stated before, people who worked in rice mills or brick factories could not continue their labor during the rainy season because the rice and the bricks could not dry. As a result, they fell into debt.

"Respondent: *I have to go back. I cannot stay here forever.*
Interviewer: *When?*
Respondent: *It is not possible this year because of some loan from the owner of rice mill"*
(Interview 25, Satkhira).

---

[3] In one case a women was invited to do an interview and signed the informed consent after being briefed on the scope of the study. In the other cases, the findings are just based on brief personal communication.

Besides those whose debt is connected to their post-migration situation, some already were indebted because of extreme weather events and could not earn enough to repay it. Therefore, debt due to natural disasters may also be a determining factor in migration decisions. But the connections between debt and natural disasters can be hard to trace as this interview exemplifies:

"Interviewer:	*Why were you in debt?*
Respondent:	*As there were no work opportunities during calamity, we had to borrow money from others to survive. [...]*
Interviewer:	*What is the connection between Aila and this debt?*
Respondent:	*After Aila and my marriage we got into debt as we had no work.*
Interviewer:	*So you mean to say, Aila affected on your income?*
Respondent:	*Yes.*
Interviewer:	*Do you still have that debt?*
Respondent:	*Yes, and we are still paying that"* (Interview 11, Khulna).

This excerpt shows that people who live from hands to mouth immediately fall into debt if they cannot work for several days or weeks. Once they migrate to the city, seeking alternative livelihoods is also difficult because their skills and knowledge do not match any demands of more secure or profitable jobs in the city. The interviews mirror the migrants' struggle to find work and to distribute risks; but they were unable to substantially improve their lives.

The overall living conditions in the urban areas were difficult due to overcrowding, lack of sanitary facilities, lack of public schools, and lack of basic resources, such as electricity. In general, families had to pay a monthly rent for their shelter, which was overpriced for what they were receiving. In fact, many did not have land rights to the place they lived in, although they paid rent regularly. "*Problems are huge. We hardly can provide for the necessary things, we have to pay for room, drinking water.* [...] *As we have less money we can't give good facility for education, even we cannot provide a private tutor for them and also can't pay money for a good school*" (Interview 14, Focus Group Discussion, Khulna). For example, this group of households from the interview excerpt described that they did not have access to a public primary school for their children, but had to pay to send them to a private school, the quality of which was insufficient. Moreover, in some informal settlements the only schools available were religious schools (Madrasa) or schools run by a nongovernmental organization.

Picture 2 Typical urban informal settlement in South-West Bangladesh (source: own).

When respondents were asked in the concluding part of the interview whether they preferred to stay or leave the cities, the answers were mixed. Some wanted to return to the villages under the precondition of access to land which they could cultivate. When participants said that they preferred to stay in the city areas, it was often connected to the lack of work opportunities in their home village, which in turn were frequently related to environmental changes. Because many migrants described throughout the interview process that they were longing for home and would go back if they were provided with land or an income opportunity, I interpreted this last section in the context of their previous statements. Although many had stated in their last sentence that they preferred to stay in the city, one can assess this as a lock-in situation, in where the return to the village would mean an uncertain future under potentially worse conditions, instead of interpreting it as the migrant's general preference of the slum life over the village life. One interview captures the multiplicity of factors which determine the assessment of people's living situations.

"Interviewer: *As your profession is different from the work you were doing beforehand, what place is better to you [the village or the town]?*

Respondent: *I don't feel good. Living in town yet I am no capable of rearing my children: I think if I could find any quiet place I would have managed to rear my children.*

Interviewer: *Economically which place do you prefer?*

Respondent: *As working opportunity is available in the city, I prefer this on account of work"*
(Interview 17, Satkhira).

However, the same person reemphasizes towards the end of the interview: "*Here we are not happy either. Village has some tranquil environment where town is quite crowded. As we live in rent house I cannot provide my children proper education facility*" (Interview 17, Satkhira). This case is not unique. Despite the strains on the urban job markets, people continue to migrate from the villages to the city. In Khulna a migrant explains:

"Interviewer: *Do the people from your village want to migrate here?*

Respondent: *Yes, they do as they are in scarcity. There they have no opportunity of work"*
(Interview 05, Khulna).

This circumstance is also well reflected in another interview, where a migrant describes his livelihood prior to the migration:

"Interviewer: *What did you do before in your village?*

Respondent:	*Daily laborer in agriculture.*
Interviewer:	*All the year you lived by agricultural work?*
Respondent:	*Yes, there I earned one day and sit for another 5 days* without work" (Interview 11, Khulna).

In some cases the economic situation in the rural areas was in general extremely difficult and the climate impacts could have been 'only' the ultimate trigger for the outmigration, the straw that broke the camel's back. This is by no means less significant in terms of real world relevance than if the climate impacts had been the only reason for migration. There are large populations in Bangladesh and other least-developed or extremely unequal countries who may suffer greatly from any additional adverse effects and may in turn be forced out of their homelands. In other cases these difficult situations are directly connected to changes in the environment. One migrated fisher reports on the changes before and after Aila which impeded his livelihood and recounts how his relatives who remained in the village were doing:

"Respondent:	*I started fishing from my childhood on. Before Aila, we earned between 500-600 Tk per Day. But it has turned into 100-150 Tk per day now. Sometimes nothing."*
Interviewer:	*Do you know someone who is still living in the village?*
Respondent:	*My two brothers and my uncle still live there.*
Interviewer:	*Where do they live in the village now?*
Respondent:	*They live on the road.*
Interviewer:	*What is their occupation?*
Respondent:	*Fishing in the river"* (Interview 04, Khulna).

This excerpt exemplifies why people continue to move to cities despite the risks of life in the slums. Furthermore, the interview indicates that migration was an adaptation strategy of this migrant. He was confronted with a new living situation after the cyclone. His income was substantially decreased, which led him to move to the city. Later in the interview he said that his brothers and uncle who remained in the village were also planning to go to Khulna because they had lost their income source in the village (Interview 04, Khulna). Another migrant, who was working first in a rice mill in the rural area and then moved after cyclone Aila to an urban area, where he worked for another rice mill, was able to increase his salary. When comparing the two jobs, he concluded "*This one* [in the city] *is better because income rate and facility are higher than there. There I earned BDT 2000 and here I earn BDT 3000*" (Satkhira, Interview 18). However, the rice mill only operated six months per year. The rest of the year this interviewee worked as a day laborer or a rickshaw puller. He planned to return to the village once he had saved enough money to buy a home.

The scarcity of job and training opportunities migrants encounter combined with the burden of debt substantially reduce the migrants' possibilities of integrating into the urban community and labor market as equals. Rather, they form a new urban underclass. In turn, these migrants are again often rendered vulnerable to climate hazards in the urban areas. Working in the extensive shadow economy, they are by and large kept from leading dignified lives. Saroar & Routray (2012) confirm that low income and social status have a negative correlation with adaptive capacity. In this, they identified landlessness as a significant factor: "*the amount of land in possession and level of income play an overwhelmingly important role in adaptive capacity enhancement.*" Considering the population dynamics over the availability of land, this issue will continue to be problematic for parts of the Bangladeshi population. One respondent explains their vulnerability, "*Because those who have good house or building it doesn't harm them but the people or family who have house built by government or have own it from relief or from any NGOs get harmed. The roof of their house gets blown by the storm*" (Interview 14, Focus Group Discussion, Khulna). Being landless prevented people from returning to their home village and the lack of land rights or secure lease left people in fear of eviction in the urban areas. Comparing the situation before and after the climate impact, it remains difficult to say which type of poverty was worse; one characterized by food insecurity and lack of opportunities in the rural areas and the other one developed in slums without adequate housing and high risks of infectious diseases through lack of sanitation, extreme overcrowding and the danger of exposure to violence. While people in the cities were sometimes able to generate more income, it was often costly to live in the slums and they were not able to make savings or invest in their skills to improve their prospects for a better livelihood.

Health

Besides the economic indicators covered in the last sections, health is an important aspect in evaluating the situation of the migrants after relocations. Whereas none of the interviewees mentioned going to a regular medical practice, most migrants had at least theoretically access to a governmental or private hospital. One challenge was the distance to the medical facilities. In some cases the hospital was one hour or further away, depending on the mode of transportation available. Another problem was the cost of treatments. Visits were not free, the government hospital usually charged a fee of around 5-10 Bangladeshi Taka per visit while private hospitals sometimes charged 500 Bangladeshi Taka to see a doctor, one migrant explained (Interview 04, Khulna). In general, the prescription medicine had to be purchased which meant an additional financial burden to the family, as is reflected in the following excerpt:

"Interviewer:	*What do you do when you feel sick?*
Respondent:	*Go to our land owner for money and go to hospital.*
Interviewer:	*Which hospital you go?*
Respondent:	*If it is severe then go to government hospital.*
Interviewer:	*How do you manage medicine?*
Respondent:	*We get it for free. Sometimes [...] medicines are to be bought"* (Interview 20, Satkhira).

The number of medical facilities is increasing, but adequate basic healthcare for the poor remains a problem in Bangladesh. Especially in the Khulna division the situation is dramatic, the population per bed in hospitals of the public sector ratio is 33 069, compared to Dhaka with 9091 and Barisal with 8772. However, *"the Government* [...] *by constitution, is responsible not only for setting policy and regulation but also for providing comprehensive health services, including financing and employing health staff*" (Ahmed et al. 2015). While the constitution guarantees access to healthcare to all people, in many rural areas the dominant healthcare providers are in the informal sector: "*Unqualified/semi- qualified allopathic practitioners such as village doctors and Community Health Workers* [...] *are mainly concentrated in rural areas*" (Ahmed et al., 2015). There is a clear rural/urban divide in the provision of healthcare. "*The overwhelming urban bias of the distribution of qualified professionals remains a persistent phenomenon*", conclude Ahmed et al. (2015). Although the rural-urban migration may have increased the proximity to a medical facility, basic medical care remains a financial problem for migrants. Hospitals in the medium-sized urban centers have too few resources for the increasing urban population. Furthermore, it has to be taken into consideration that there is not only a rural/urban divide, but also a stark difference from city to city in terms of access to health facilities. Most medical centers are concentrated in the capital region of Dhaka, whereas other cities, while having a better health infrastructure than remote villages, are still lacking adequate medical services. As outlined in chapter 6.4., there are complex interactions between migration, health and climate change which exceed the issue of access to healthcare. While an in-depth analysis on the health of migrants and the situation in the receiving communities is beyond the scope of this study, I want to highlight a few problems which have surfaced during the course of the research. These, in turn, may be taken up in future studies for more rigid interdisciplinary assessments.

It has been already identified by previous research that internal and cross-border migration can be a concern of public health because vector-borne diseases could spread to areas which were previously not affected and may not have the respectively needed medical care available (Ahmed et al., 2015; Coker et al., 2011). This holds also true for Bangladesh, especially with regard to Malaria which is endemic in thirteen states in the northeast of the country (Ahmed et al., 2015). Migrants themselves are also exposed to health problems. For example, in the summer months, temperatures in the city can become unbearable because of extreme heat events which are reinforced by global warming and the urban heat island effect. Especially overcrowded settlements and shacks with a corrugated roof are prone to extreme interior temperatures:

"Interviewer: *How do environmental calamities affect your town life?*
Respondent: *Due to excessive temperature, I sometimes lose my senses"*
(Interview 3, Khulna).

Whereas many migrants had previously lived in larger huts with mostly thatched roofs, the housing situation in the informal settlements exposed them to extreme heat events. One respondent summarizes, "*in summer season it is difficult to live*" (Interview 11, Khulna). Often this condition was aggravated by indoor air pollution and excess heat from cooking with charcoal or wood, a fuel used both in rural and urban areas. Previous research confirms that traditional housing is often better adjusted to the local climatic conditions than new materials such as cement or scrap supplies which are used in slums (Sheuya et al., 2007).

Another problem in the slums was frequent flooding and the subsequent water logging. During the rainy season, many cities in Bangladesh are affected by severe flooding. There are no or no sufficient drainage systems installed. In the slum areas the resulting problems are amplified by the fact that the shacks are easily inundated because they are oftentimes built without any professional expertise. Some women showed us infections on their legs from constantly having to wade through the water. Also, when sanitary facilities are not present, flooding can lead to health hazards, as diseases spread easily. Respondents in Dhaka mentioned that their children often get waterborne or other infectious diseases. Furthermore, many informal settlements are built on the outskirts of the cities, often near or on embankments or floodplains. It is well reflected in the literature that slum residents are less resilient to cope with extreme events such as floods than inhabitants of formal settlements. Some settlements were even built partially in the water (see picture 3).

Picture 3 Informal Settlement in Barisal (source: own).

The fact that most migrants stayed in makeshift shelters after being displaced also caused other health risks. Largely, these shelters lacked sanitary facilities, more than half of the interviewees had only access to unimproved latrines or no latrines at all. Especially women would in turn try to avoid open defecation during the day and only did so in the after dark. This in turn exposed them to risks of violent crime such as assault. Open defecation, especially in highly populated areas, can furthermore lead to the spread of infectious diseases, for example diarrhea or cholera. Overall, the access to improved sanitation facilities is higher for the rural population of Bangladesh (62.1% of the population have access) than for the urban dwellers (57.7% of population have access) (CIA World Factbook, 2017a). In urban areas, the absence of facilities is particularly problematic because of the population and settlement density. The fact that housing can be a determining factor of health has also been addressed in the literature, for example by the WHO (WHO Kobe Centre, 2005) or in public health research (Krieger and Higgins, 2002; Sheuya et al., 2007).

Another problem was the food and water insecurity of migrants. The lack of income, especially during the monsoon season in the city, also incurred health risks connected to undernutrition. For example, one woman responds, "*Frankly, sometimes during monsoon we are used to starve*" (Interview 21, Barisal). Access to freshwater was a challenge to some migrants and became a burden especially to women. Some women had to invest several hours a day to go to a well and fetch freshwater for their families. One woman who had migrated before the storm Sidr to the city of Khulna describes how difficult it was to find access to freshwater.

"Interviewer:	*When you came in Khulna, what problem you face most?*
Respondent:	*The problem we faced was drinking water.*
Interviewer:	*Means you did not find any water at all?*
Respondent:	*No, we have had to fetch it from far, it took 30 minutes"* (Interview 13, Khulna).

Besides physical health risks, some respondents also identified psychological problems connected to their resettlement: "*We were well in the village because the environment was good. We now feel psychological depression because living here meant to leave our own home. The urban areas are more chaotic than the rural regions. Here, income is less than in my village*" (Interview 19, Satkhira). The loss of ancestral land, community, traditions and culture can have severe negative effects on people. Moreover, many had to migrate in a rush and the natural disaster as well as the migration experience itself was a traumatic event. Some research on the mental challenges of migration and of living in another social setting exist (Bhugra, 2004b). Relevant in this context is the study of Bhugra (2004) which analyzed the possible long-term effects of living in a different setting. He arrived at the hypothesis that "when sociocentric individuals from sociocentric cultures migrate to egocentric societies they may feel more alienated" (Bhugra, 2004a). This could apply to a shift from rural surroundings, including village and family structures, to an urban environment where these social ties may no longer exist. Additionally, there is evidence in other studies such as in the case of hurricane Katrina in New Orleans that "antisocial behavior [...] occurs in the immediate and longer term aftermath of disaster" which could point to impairments of mental health (Frailing et al., 2015). All in all, psychosocial wellbeing of migrants is relevant in the context of adaptation because if the individuals have good mental health it can enhance their resilience and thereby the resilience of the community.

Self-Determination

"First, I lost my land and then my house. Then I came to Barisal" (Interview 31, Barisal).

During the course of the interviews, it became more and more apparent that people who had migrated out of the vulnerable areas generally left because their livelihood base had vanished. This means that most of the migration took place as a response to climate impacts and not as a preemptive adaptation strategy, which would lessen the effect occurring climate impacts would have on communities. In a group interview in Khulna, families describe how their migration was involuntary and sudden after the cyclones had affected their village:

"Interviewer: *Why have you come here?*

Respondent: *Only to save our lives. We did not have anything. No clothes, no house. We came to Khulna with one set of wet clothes and barefooted. All three days of our journey to Khulna we wore that single wet cloth. We are not exaggerating - this is what we have experienced and saw, we are just telling about that"*

(Interview 14, Focus Group Discussion, Khulna).

For these families it was impossible to return as their land was worthless after the storm: *"We have no way to live there now because some land has gone under water, some of the land was dug up to make roads and the rest has become unsuitable for cultivation and we have no use for it"* (Interview 14, Focus Group Discussion, Khulna). These examples of climate migration stand contrary to the notion that climate migrants often fall under the category of labor or economic migration. Some people had been displaced by a storm or sea level rise and then migrated from one place to another, staying where they could survive for a few more months. They did not migrate just to improve their economic situation. One woman who had lived in several places over the last one and a half years after her house had been destroyed and her land damaged concludes: *"If we can manage some money, then we will go back to the village and repair our house. We will start our lives there"* (Interview 32, Barisal). The last sentence also highlights the perception that people's lives were put on hold during the displacement, which had lasted over a year.

Also, many respondents described situations that made it impossible for them to return, such as debt-bondage, financial insecurity, no source of livelihood and no access to shelter or land in their home village. Prior to the field research I had expected that a majority of migrants would either want to return to their home village or move on to Dhaka because the medium-sized cities were only layover settlements. However, on the whole the migrants did not have set plans to leave the respective urban areas, although many replied that there were severe problems in the city, and some preferred life in the village. Some had successfully established sources of livelihoods which were more fruitful than their agricultural labor. Sometimes, no one could return because everything was destroyed and the climate impacts, such as flooding and salinization of groundwater, would not accommodate a resettlement.

"Respondent:	*I want to stay here. I do not have any place to go and our houses have been damaged.*
Interviewer:	*Do you still have any land?*
Respondent:	*No, we once had, but it has gone into the water"* (Interview 03, Khulna).

Also the diminished livelihoods because of the storm made it impossible for some to return: "*Now that there are no fishes in the watery area of jungle we will not be able to catch fish. And since the government has forbid cutting down trees from jungle due to Aila, we are not able to get wood to sell. So when the circumstances will be suitable to live then we will think of going*" (Interview 05, Khulna). This means that the landlessness and absence of livelihood options due to the environmental change which were the reasons for the outmigration also prevented people to return several years after the storm. Other problems reported by people living in the rural Sundarban area were frequent incursions of robbers and pirates who attacked local fishers or honey collectors in the jungle. "*At present I am living in town and I prefer living there as I am getting facilities. We used to get our livelihood from the forest, but the forest itself is threatening us*" (Interview 20, Satkhira). There were also social reasons not to return. A fourteen year-old girl who migrated to Khulna after her village had been destroyed during Sidr recounts: "*Everyone has died*" (Interview 09, Khulna). Because of the death of her family she did not see a reason to return to her place of origin. It is clear that while part of the displaced population had already returned to the villages after the natural disaster, others could not. Therefore, it is important to note that locked-in populations are not only located in the affected areas but also in the places of first arrival after the migration. Consequently, it was not the migration itself that was problematic to the migrants, but that they could not return because of the burden of debt, or because they did not have access to land in their home villages anymore.

"Interviewer: How long do you wish to live here or do you have any plan to go somewhere else from here?

Respondent: As long as our debt is not resolved we cannot go there from here.

Interviewer: Under what condition do you want to go to your village?

Respondent: If our debt is resolved and an income source is ensured then we go there"

(Interview 11, Khulna).

A woman who had come from a village to Dhaka after riverbed erosion had destroyed her house explains:

"Interviewer: Do you want to live here rest of your life?

Respondent: We will stay here. But if there is any situation [possibility] to go, then we will go.

Interviewer: So under what condition you want to go?

Respondent: *If the environment is suitable"* (Interview 2, Dhaka).

In general, the migrant's financial situation and often fragile income sources did not allow them to make plans for the future. Many families also had to fear eviction from the land which they inhabited as they did not possess an official lease. They stay in a certain area as long as possible if they can generate income and find shelter. The Chief Town Planner of Khulna concludes "*Once people come to the city, they will not* [go] *back. That is the trend"* (Interview Town Planner, Khulna). However, many of the interviewees indicated they would return to the village if the government provided them with land for cultivation. But this may be a very difficult task because (fertile) land is scarce and already densely populated in Bangladesh. It can be concluded that the migrants' ability to determine their own lives is low because of their economic situation and because of the environmental and economic conditions in their places of origin.

Insights into the Migrants' Social System

Comparing the social systems from which people had originated with those they migrated into allows for more generic findings regarding what helped or hindered the effectiveness of migration as an adaptation. This in turn can serve to derive hypotheses which are not only applicable in the context of the case studies, but may apply to other settings as well.

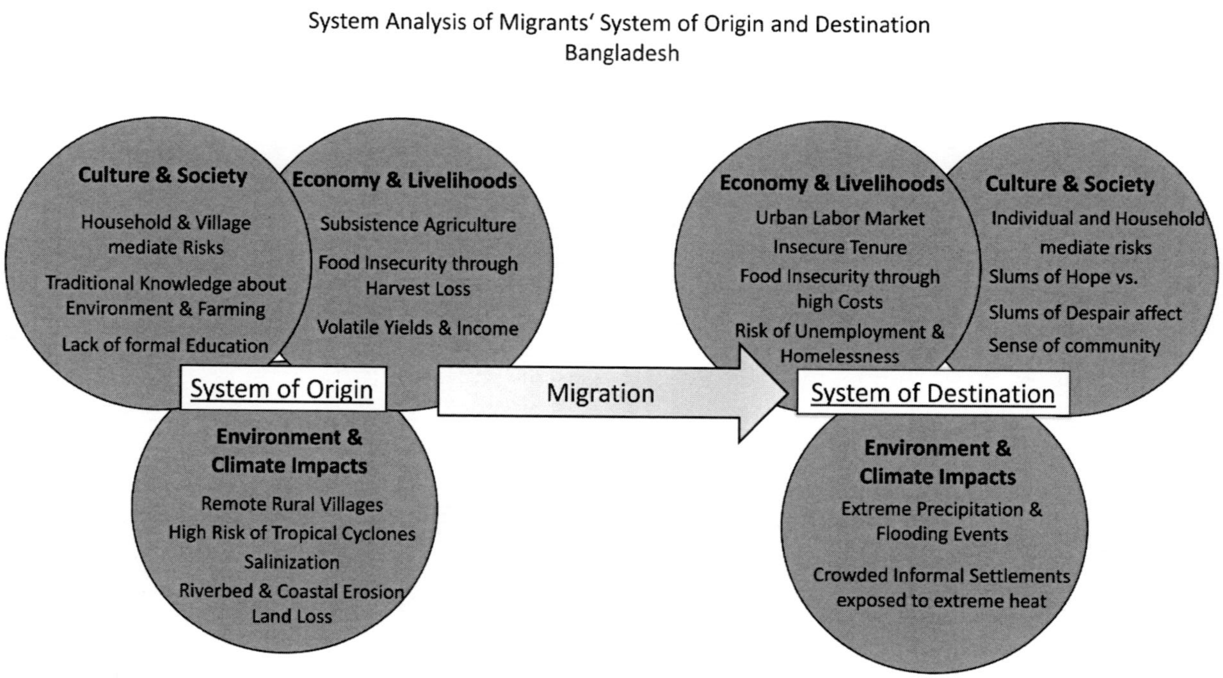

Figure 9 System Analysis of Migrants' System of Origin and Destination Bangladesh (source: own).

Social System of Origin

Based on the interview data, literature and observations it can be established that there is a system of origin that has several characteristics which apply to the social system of most participants. The migrants largely were subsistence farmers and therefore have had ties to the land on which they had lived for several generations. The family is the main entity which mediates risks. To some degree, the village serves this function as well. However, above the village level there is only limited influence from the regional or even central government. In some regions it can be said that international non-governmental organizations have a more direct sphere of influence on the villages than for example the central government.

In these villages, the people have accumulated knowledge of their natural environment over generations. This means they have a quite specialized expertise in the field of agriculture and fisheries and are generally well adapted to the difficulties connected to life in a river delta. As farmers they are particularly observant of and attentive to changes in the environment. However, they had only limited access to schooling and many of them are illiterate. Their expectations and anticipation of the future largely build upon the experiences of their parents and grandparents. These include assumptions about possible changes in the environment. Whereas this knowledge has helped them cope with past calamities, it now makes them particularly vulnerable to climate change because the current changes have been described as unprecedented. The lack of access to education and knowledge means that they are reliant on their social structures for information. Their planning horizon is determined by environmental factors and seasonal changes which govern harvest practices. Planning generally does not go beyond the next few months as many do not have the financial resources which could lead them to plan further ahead. Their daily routines are strongly shaped by the task to fulfill basic needs, such as finding enough freshwater and food.

Social System of Destination

The cities in which the migrants settled are made up of social systems very different from the rural villages. Migrants with specialized knowledge of agriculture had to adjust to a city system which requires different skill sets. Moreover, the power structures in the city are unlike those in the village. Whereas the land in the rural areas had belonged to the same families for generations, many had to settle in slum areas where they could be evicted any day, despite paying comparatively high rents. Although some cultural factors remained the same, such as religious practice and language, other aspects between the urban and the rural system were profoundly divergent. Traditional family structures in which the men generate income and the women stay at home may be altered through the need for a second income in the city. Some women worked in other households as maids, a work that was mentioned to be exploitative. The migrants' actions in the city were overall limited by their economic situation. Although many respondents stated that the city provided better sources of income, savings were impossible for most. The cost of living being higher in the urban area and without land available for cultivation, people rely on their income to buy basic food products. "*I was better in the village. Here in the city, everything has to be bought*" (Barisal, Interview 31).

While the slums of hope, slums of despair metaphor introduced by Stokes (1962) simplifies the diverse realities in different squatter settlements, it still captures the essence of how some slum communities enable upward mobility whereas others are poverty traps. This is reflected in several interviews. One indicator for this could be whether people are making plans for the future or are able to save some money from their income, as discussed in the chapter on self-determination. Another indicator could be the following observations. In a few slums functional communities existed and were open to integration of new arrivals. Some migrants spoke of good relations with the people in their neighborhood and mutual support which points to the formation of a new social network. Where conditions were particularly perilous, no such community development was observable and a sense of competition between urban residents and newly arrived migrants emerged from the interviews, often with concomitant hopelessness. Competing claims for identity and resources between new arrivals and already established residents have been researched for other communities before (Malkki, 1992).

All in all it can be concluded that people from the exposed rural areas migrated into another high risk situation in which they could not succeed with the skill sets they had. The tight social structures and safety nets which were prevalent in the villages were absent or differently constituted in the city slums. Moreover, as many of these settlements are situated in exposed areas, the migrants were again exposed to the hazards of different climate change impacts (for a differentiation between the vulnerabilities of migrants in rural and urban settings see also Michael et al., 2018).

Effectiveness of Migration as Adaptation for Sending Communities

Due to frequent floods and salinization of soils, the potential of crop failure is putting more and more stress on local subsistence farmers. In order to diversify income, some families send one family member to work in the city who eventually sends them back remittances. The higher prevalence of men in urban areas can be found in the quantitative data and could be linked to a high number of male migrants in the cities. The 2011 household census shows that more than 52.2% of urban citizens are male and only 47.7% are female, which is significantly different from the more equal rural male to female sex ratio, and the overall ratio of .97 male per female among the entire population in Bangladesh (Bangladesh Bureau of Statistics, 2014; CIA World Factbook, 2017a). The family as the decision making entity for migration has already been recognized by Stark & Bloom (1985). However, rural-urban migration does not always deliver remittances, like this case study clearly shows. All participants were asked whether or not they send money to relatives in the rural areas. The results were mixed. Some were able to support their families in the villages, while others were not. In some cases, there was no need for remittances in the village and in some cases the urban migrants even received money and food supplies from the villages, as they could not sustain themselves. For example when asked whether he and his relatives in the village help one another, one migrant who moved to the city responds: "*They sent some rice to my family. But I could not help them*" (Interview 06, Khulna). This quote shows that while the intention was for him to find work and send back money or goods to the village, this migrant was not able to fulfill this goal and in turn relied on support from his relative himself. Other families eventually relocated entirely because they did not want to stay apart or the environmental degradation was too severe to be offset by remittances. However, having a relative in an urban area can mean a disaster risk reduction strategy in itself, as can be deduced from the following interview:

"Interviewer:	*Do you have any relatives there [in your home community]?*
Respondent:	*Yes, my in-laws' house is there. They are also helpless. And I keep contact with them. [...]*
Interviewer:	*Do you support them monetarily or do they support?*
Respondent:	*No, they do not, but I support them. I give them shelter during disaster*" (Interview 17, Satkhira).

The diverse results show that the assumption of prosperity from a life in the city and consequential remittances to the village will not automatically come true. Especially when poor people migrated, the migration often did not lead to substantially better economic prospects and sometimes resulted in further impoverishment. Therefore, the sending communities did not necessarily benefit from the migration of community members. In some cases, the sending community supported the migrants by sending food even years after the migration. However, if migrants are able to provide shelter during natural disasters, the migration at least leads to a risk diversification for the sending community. It can be stipulated that with more capital, preparation and capacity to form their livelihoods in the city, many migrants could have likely avoided falling into debt soon after arrival and would have provided support to the villages. Despite the fact that the migrants sought new forms of employment, they were ultimately positioned in the urban community by their socio-economic backgrounds. In general, the respondents in the sending communities did not view migration as an adaptation strategy to shape their economic future in the face of growing hazards. Instead it was seen as a measure of last resort with potentially negative effects.

Part of the interviews in the sending communities showed that there are trapped populations in the rural areas because of lack of access to safe land, due to economic restraints and population pressure. In general, trapped populations refer to groups of people who in the face of climate impacts would want to migrate, but are unable to (Foresight, 2011); there is however an ongoing academic discussion on how to clearly define the term and identify individuals who are trapped (Ayeb-Karlsson et al., 2018). In the interviews in the sending communities several respondents were well aware of hazards but felt there was little choice for them:

"Interviewer: *So storms are common in this place and it will happen in future too. Then what is your plan? Will you stay here or move elsewhere?*

Respondent: *Where can we go?"*
(Interview 20, Satkhira).

This statement can refer to the respondent's awareness of the extremely limited options in the cities. The stronger the push factor of climate change gets in the rural areas, the more people will be forced to leave. One migrant who had moved to Satkhira after his house and land were submerged by flooding describes the conditions in the sending community:

"Interviewer: *Is this circumstance affecting your home community in the same way?*

Respondent: *Yes, it affects them in the same way. They have also lost their homes, land and working source as well. They, leaving their own places, are taking shelter in other different places"*
(Interview 17, Satkhira).

In another rural area, nearby the town of Barisal, the respondents recount that other villagers had already migrated to the city and were trying to survive:

"Respondents: *We may lose this land anytime this year. There is no security.*

Interviewer: *Other people in this area also lost their land. Some even lost their homestead land. Where did they go?*

Respondents:	*Barisal. Some also went to Dhaka. [...] They do whatever they can to survive. Some are pulling rickshaw or van, some are involved in construction works on daily basis. They are doing every sort of informal jobs.*
Interviewer:	*What is the future of this place and these surroundings?*
Respondents:	*Most probably this place will go under water. Maybe next week you cannot see this place.*
Interviewer:	*So what is your preparation?*
Respondents:	*We do not know. We do not have land. We do not know what to do. The houses you are noticing here are the last resources of the people"* (Interview 30, Barisal).

This section indicates the awareness in the sending communities about the risk of poverty in the city. The situation in the urban centers therefore does not necessarily constitute pull factors but rather push back factors. Hence the trapped populations at the destinations may not have been aware about the risks in the destination places before they moved and now are unable to return due to financial or logistical constraints. Despite the generally difficult situation in the sending communities and the fact that remittances from urban areas did not significantly contribute to adaptive capacity, it is important to consider more indirect mechanisms that lead to positive migration outcomes. One could be that the population pressure in the sending communities is reduced through outmigration. Therefore, the carrying capacity of perhaps fragile ecosystems such as the Sundarban mangrove forest is potentially put under less stress. Even if there were no remittances, the diversification of incomes in translocal households may foster resilience.

Effectiveness of Migration as Adaptation for Receiving Communities

The case of Khulna city illustrates that assessing the challenge of climate change and migration for receiving communities is difficult. It currently cannot be exactly determined how many people are migrating overall and how many of them are coming due to environmental reasons. An expert from the Khulna City Corporation planning department explains:

"Interviewer:	*Do you think climatic factors are pressuring the people to migrate?*
Town Planner:	*Yes.*
Interviewer:	*Has the migration pressure increased?*
Town Planner:	*Yes, it is increasing. [...] [But] there is no study for climate migrants. We are just feeling that people are coming. We are seeing it with our own eyes that people are coming here. But there is no study. We don't know"* (Interview 15, Town Planner, Khulna).

This lack of oversight and management of migration flows is due to limited financial and personnel capacity. It also captures why making estimates for the future can be difficult if current datasets are insufficient. The example of one city, whose administration is aware of the problem of climate change and migration, but cannot take adequate measures, represents a global problem of vulnerable cities under financial restraints and lack of capacities. "[The number of climate migrants] *are causing the growth of the informal settlements. And some people come to Khulna city for working, education and living with their relatives or sometimes rent in the slums. This is called industrial city. But 25 industries are closed now. So,* […] *people and climate migrant people, they are altogether searching for work or daily activities*" (Interview 15, Town Planner, Khulna). Because industries were closed many people also left the city between 2001 and 2011, as is reflected in the 2011 census which shows a decrease of the population in the Khulna City Cooperation (Bangladesh Bureau of Statistics, 2014). However, it could be that those who migrated out were potentially more skilled than the average worker, causing a brain drain in the city which was then followed by an immigration of unskilled labor. The perspective of the city administration carries a critical undertone towards incoming migrants, who he sees as aggravating some of the existing challenges in the city including housing and unemployment. As climate migrants have often settled in the slums and worked in the black market, the city administration views their presence as a challenge: "*They pressure on road, they pressure on sanitation facilities, they are generating waste. But they did not pay any tax to the KCC* [Khulna City Cooperation]. *And it is the prime duty of KCC to clean the road, drain. But no tax from that side. That is the gap"* (Interview 15, Town Planner, Khulna). When asked why people are settling under these conditions and why they can build without adhering to local building codes, the town planner points to the lack of oversight and capacity. The functionality of the urban labor market emerges as a crucial determinant of whether or not migration can be effective for both the migrants and the receiving communities. The town planner describes the increase of cycle rickshaw drivers, which he links to incoming migration, as "*unmanageable*" (Interview Town Planner, Khulna). There is no parallel increase in demand for labor, so the influx of migrants leads to a wage race to the bottom. Governance instruments such as licensing of rickshaws lack oversight and thus compliance. The additional workforce in the cities is not used to increase the cities' resilience either. The city itself is exposed to climate hazards such as storms and secondary impacts like migration flows, but it is not sufficiently prepared to manage disasters:

"Interviewer: *So you have mentioned before that the situation was diff cult after the cyclone? What is going to happen next time such a disaster happens? Is there a plan for that? Will the city be better prepared?*

Town Planner: *No. The city is not prepared. If there is an adverse situation for climate change effect, the city will not manage everything. The city will be under pressure. Very difficult to manage. And we have no plan for disaster. And we have no manpower in disaster sector, also"* (Interview 15, Town Planner, Khulna).

In general, migration to cities could be beneficial to the receiving communities if the migrants' skills are used or expanded and if they are able to take on formal labor which would increase tax revenues for the municipality. Because in Bangladesh the working-age population is growing and since this is the largest group migrating to cities, urban labor markets could use the benefits of this demographic dividend. This however can only be achieved if the migrants are integrated into the cities as a labor force and not pushed into the least profitable margins of the informal sector. As stated widely in the development and acknowledged by the International Labor Organization, "*The skill composition of migrant workers needs to change toward more skilled workers*" (ADB and ILO, 2016). In order to provide equal opportunities to urban slum residents and rural immigrants, vocational training and capacity building need to take place on the local level. Some policy prerequisites for this are elaborated in chapter 9.

6.8. Synergetic System Analysis

On the basis of the field research and existing literature I identified for the group of migrants the most significant climate impacts and their secondary economic effects influencing their migration decisions. Moreover, the main social and possible political effects of the degradation of livelihoods and migration were outlined. Figure 10 gives a schematic overview of these major interactions and provides a synergetic summary of the chapter. The arrow on the left hand side of the figure shows the increasing complexity of the interactions between climate impacts and economic, social and political effects. This also implies that there are other intervening variables in this process and that the interactions shown here should be seen as schematic reduction to understand the general processes of migration and climate change in the southwest of Bangladesh. The figure shows that anthropogenic greenhouse gas emissions lead to the warming of air, water and land (1). One of the major physical effects for the low-lying country Bangladesh is sea level rise. Moreover, the changed composition of the atmosphere is causing an increasing frequency of severe tropical cyclones in the Bay of Bengal. These climate impacts in turn have detrimental effects on plant growth as well as livestock and pose risks to human health (2). The disruption of ecosystem services puts pressure on agricultural livelihoods (3). People in the rural areas of southern Bangladesh are very vulnerable to these risks and some seek, shelter, food security and alternative sources for income in cities. This migration can help people to diversify their risks, but in the majority of the investigated cases the peasants fell further into poverty and had to move to urban slums (4). The tightly knit village communities once served as risk managing entities. In the cities, the migrants generally do not have access to formal or informal social protection. The change from the system of origin to the system of destination can mean that the migrants' economic bargaining power decreases which places them low in the urban social order. They often fall into debt after arrival because they do not have financial resources and cannot access a source of sufficient income (5). It has been shown in the literature that such alienation and impoverishment can increase susceptibility to extremist groups. The rural-urban climate migration contributes to the population growth dynamics of cities in Bangladesh, where migrants stand in competition with residents over job opportunities, service provisions and other resources. Urban administrations in cities such as Khulna or Barisal presently do not have the capacity to manage these complex challenges.

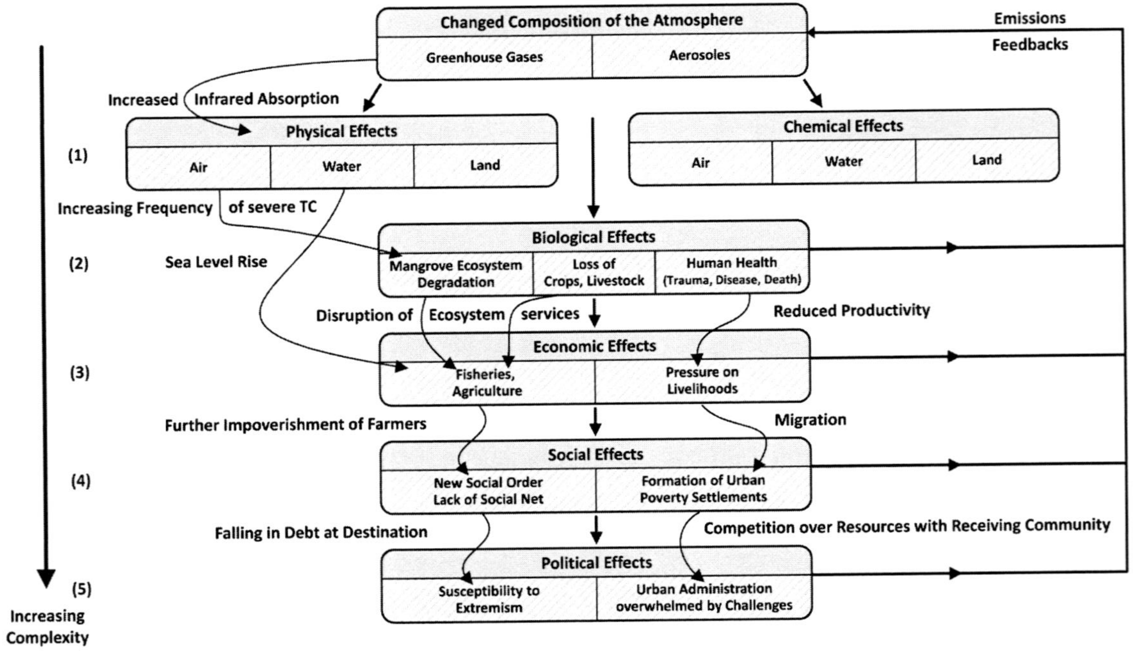

Figure 10 Synergetic System Analysis of Climate Change and Migration in Southwest Bangladesh (source: own, based on Schellnhuber, 2015).

Taking into account both the analysis of the social system of origin and destination as well as the synergetic system analysis, one particularly vulnerable social group and two subsets thereof can be identified in this case study. The major group encountered during the field research are poor subsistence farmers who are displaced from their land as a result of extreme events under the precondition of an absence of government and social welfare systems and lack of disaster risk insurance schemes. This group has no or very limited access to education and relies heavily on knowledge of the community passed on over generations. Because of these characteristics, this group is extremely vulnerable to the effects of climate change. These farmers do not have capacities to identify, finance or implement adaptation measures, which are outside of traditional farming practices. In fact, within their individual capacity many have taken various actions to try to create alternative livelihoods, but their options were quickly exhausted in the face of an unprecedented rate of change. Because their work was largely non-remunerated subsistence agriculture, they lost everything once a climate impact occurred and did not have monetary savings or portable assets to assist their relocation. Furthermore, this group can be largely characterized as conservative or traditional with strong religious believes to the degree that a common explanation for changes in the environment is the will of God. Their religious and educational reference frame and previous experiences of government inaction may even discourage them from seeking scientific explanations or information from the government.

A subgroup to this are women. They often migrated to work as housemaids, exposing them to additional threats of abuse. Women's work in the city generally did not lead to emancipation, but rather caused further dependencies on often exploitative employers. Widowed women were particularly vulnerable to the effects of climate impacts and were left with little options to make a living, other than begging. The situation of women in the context of climate migration mirrors existing gender disparities in Bangladesh. It furthermore supports the claim that climate change is a threat multiplier, which is not only true with regards to larger social dynamics, but also for the individual.

The field research and the literature provide also some evidence of the special vulnerability of children, which are identified as another subgroup. The children of the affected families often also had to work in the cities under hazardous conditions. If their parents died, they were in particularly precarious situations, at risk of human trafficking and homelessness, unless other family members or friends took over guardianship. Furthermore, the migration could also lead to either disruption or discontinuation of their education, depending on the availability and cost of schools in the cities. In some cases, the migration entailed better educational options for the children. An important insight from the Bangladesh case study is that the characteristics of the social system strongly define the vulnerability of individuals. Therefore, personal agency is limited by external constraints imposed upon individuals by the social group they belong to.

In this case study a group of highly successful migrants could not be identified from the interviews. This is likely linked to the case and site selection, as the rural exposed areas have high poverty rates. The migrants encountered in the cities whose migration was linked to observed climate impacts were largely from these areas. The findings lead to the conclusion that part of the present generation of rural poor and their children may in the future become the urban poor, pushed out of the rural areas by an intensified agrarian livelihood crisis and eventually settling on the fringes of cities, where their vulnerability continues or increases. As the city administration does not acknowledge slums as part of the city, or as "legal" housing, there is no responsibility taken for the welfare of migrants. Hence no provision of services occurs. The "*demographic dividend*", described in the World Bank study of Rigaud et al., (2018), of having a larger Bangladeshi working-age population in the future can therefore only be advantageous for development if sufficient employment opportunities are created in both rural and urban areas.

6.9. Discussion of the Bangladesh Case Study Results

In brief, the interviews with migrants showed that relocation fulfilled the migrant's objective which was often basic survival. Yet, the migration experience identified in this empirical study can largely not be categorized as strategic adaptive behavior. First of all, the migration often happened suddenly and unplanned. Several respondents stated that they left in a hurry, with only the clothes they were wearing, or remarked that they had never expected to live outside of their own village. Unless they had a family member already living in the city, they did not gather information about the destinations beforehand. Secondly, respondents also described circumstances that left them without a choice but to leave, so their migration was often involuntary. Thirdly, they had no knowledge about climate change and therefore were not in the position to make strategic decisions on adaptation to climate risks. Hence the migration often turned out to be ineffective in terms of regaining the standard of living the migrant had prior to the climate impact. In general, the migrants traded the imminent physical threat of storms or erosion for profound economic risks connected to finding work in the city.

While some people took precautionary measures to save their lives, such as going to a cyclone shelter, it was not possible for them to prepare their homes against the storms, or to plan their outmigration. After their houses, land and livestock were damaged or destroyed by storms or erosion, the respondents faced extreme food insecurity, health risks and poverty. The nature of their movements can be characterized as forced by environmental change and largely unassisted. Taking the operationalization of effectiveness into account, the effectiveness of migration has to be measured with regard to whether the person was able to restore or even improve their living standard, compared to their situation before the climate impact affected their life. Not even considering the costs and risks of the migration itself, even keeping the living standard was in many cases impossible. With regard to their financial situation, some people were able to make a higher wage than before in the village, but their standard of living in the overcrowded and strongly polluted slums was lower than before. In the cities the migrants were confronted with high costs because of the commodification of education, health, food and rent. Although the healthcare and education facilities were in general more advanced than in the rural areas, many migrants could not afford to make use of this infrastructure due to shortage of money. As described in the chapter on self-determination, the majority of respondents could not take stewardship over their lives and future. This finding is connected to the constraints of poverty and lack of opportunities for training and education that existed in the rural areas even prior to the climate impact. However, the migration did not provide them with better opportunities, but rather meant the beginning of a further economic descent. This case study confirms the assumption that climate change will increase inequality and arrives at the hypothesis that socio-economic situation of the migrant prior to departure is a determinant of climate migration outcomes.

This case study analysis leads to the conclusion that deterrence will not end migration; people will continue to migrate out of life-threatening situations and in pursuit of a secure life. The fact that people migrate to avoid severe physical harm or death and at the same time have to accept dire working and living conditions in the places of arrival, can be termed as 'survival migration' (see also Betts, 2013, who uses this term in different contexts). Unmanaged survival migration has detrimental outcomes not only for the migrants themselves, but also prevents potential benefits to sending and receiving communities. However, this could be avoided if states engaged in the protection of climate migrants and invested in their capacities. The first step to achieve this is the acknowledgement of the existence of the phenomenon, which has been recognized by town planners and migrants themselves, but continues to cause dispute in the discourses of science and policy.

In addition to the discussed findings, some methodological insights and policy implications can be gathered on the basis of the Bangladesh case study. The field research itself contributed to the knowledge on climate migration and the interactions of vulnerability and migration. Even if there had not been a correlation to climate change in the environmental events identified by the respondents as the reason for their migration, the method deployed in this case study arrives at conclusions which provide insights into the mechanisms of migration in response to climate change. The choice of categories to operationalize effectiveness (as described in chapter 3.4.) was further developed and refined in an iterative process throughout the interviews with the migrants. At large, the interviews with migrants capture in the analysis of their own migration experience that effectiveness is not merely a question of economic efficiency. This bears strong implications for the migration as adaptation discourse. If migration itself is viewed as an adaptation, it may in many cases be the economically most efficient way of adapting. For example, it can be less costly to relocate a community than to provide extensive infrastructural adaptation. However, economic considerations have to be weighed carefully against the detrimental effects of such measures (see chapter 9). The negative effects of relocations on communities have been already discussed in the literature on slum relocation or forced evacuations for development projects. For example, UNHCR emphasizes that planned relocation is "*a measure of last resort*" (UNHCR, 2014). It can furthermore be derived from the interviews that climate change may alter the dynamics of rural-urban migration. Whereas the decision-making processes which lead to rural-urban migration may be best explained by the "*New Economics of Labor Migration*", climate- driven outmigration is much more defined by the environmental push factors and questions of household resilience than labor market considerations (Stark and Bloom, 1985).

There are also some insights which are relevant for the second case study. Whereas in Bangladesh most of the interviews were conducted with migrants themselves, some thought-provoking findings came from the interviews in the sending communities and with the town planner of Khulna. During the Bangladesh study, the importance of capturing the perceptions of sending communities and local experts has emerged. Because of this, the next field study will include more of those perspectives through interviews with city administration representatives, community leaders and people who have stayed behind.

7. Case Study 2: Migration in the Marshall Islands as a Response to Sea Level Rise and related Crop Failure

The Republic of the Marshall Islands in the Western North Pacific is one of the few states whose landmass is completely based on coral atolls. Each of the 29 atolls consists of several islands. The country has an extremely limited amount of land. Subsequently, any adverse effect on the scarce resources available for agriculture can challenge food security on the less connected outer islands. The total landmass is about 181 square kilometers, roughly equal to the size of Washington D.C. (CIA World Factbook, 2017b). However, when lagoon waters are calculated in, the size of the Marshall Islands is larger, more than 11.600 square kilometers. Its exclusive economic zone extends to over more than 2.1 Million square kilometers of ocean waters. The resources of these waters as well as the registry of ships are an important economic pillar of the Marshall Islands. The average elevation of the island state is only two meters, which exposes the country to sea level rise and its consequences such as coastal erosion and flooding. As regards the climate, the Marshall Islands are characterized by regional differences between the northern and southern islands. The southern islands have substantially higher precipitation rates of an average of approximately 4000 mm per year, whereas the northern islands have an average of about 500 mm and are frequently affected by droughts and water scarcity (Embassy of the Republic of the Marshall Islands to the United States of America, 2018).

The island nation today has a relatively high population density – given the scarcity of freshwater resources – of approximately 295 people per square kilometer, compared to 237 in Germany and 35 in the United States (The World Bank, 2017a). On the main island Majuro, the population density is much higher than the national average with 2850 people per square kilometer in 2011 (Secretariat of the Pacific Community, 2012). In both urban centers, Kwajalein and Majuro, population density has been rising over the last decades, and the overall population of the Marshall Islands is still growing at a rate of 1.55. An important social issue is the high teenage pregnancy rate which has ranged between 15 and 20% over the last two decades and is the highest in the Pacific (Braun, 2012; Johnson, 2014). These early pregnancies may also be connected to low education levels since less than 25% of the total population aged 25 years or older completed a high school level education (Secretariat of the Pacific Community, 2012).

Remotely located, the Marshall Islands are heavily dependent on imports of food, fossil fuels for transportation and for the largely diesel-based on-grid electricity production. Because of rising energy and food prices, the Republic declared a state of economic emergency in 2008. The severe effects that the global financial crisis had on the Marshall Islands reflect the country's intertwinement with foreign markets. The still ongoing shift from rural traditional lifestyles and subsistence farming to largely urbanized communities and dependency on foreign investment or aid is deeply rooted in the colonial history of the islands and in its relationship with the United States. A more recent pressure which puts into question the sustention of traditional livelihoods is the impact of climate change on the small island state. Already 73.2% of the population live in urban areas and the majority of the population is located in Majuro or Ebeye (Kwajalein atoll) (CIA World Factbook, 2017b). The GDP per capita is 3400 USD. Most wage-earners are employed in the service sector. These jobs are largely located in urban areas and generate more than 85% of the country's GDP. On the outer islands livelihoods depend on agriculture. Besides subsistence farming, many islanders produce copra – dried coconut – that can be used for coconut oil production. The Marshall Islands government subsidizes the price of copra, however earnings are still volatile. The unemployment rate of the Marshall Islands is high with 36%, but there is no data available on how many people live below the poverty line (CIA World Factbook, 2017b). Because of the tightly knit communities and traditional social nets, homelessness is extremely rare.

The Marshall Islands have a complex history of foreign rule that is significant for the understanding of contemporary Marshallese society and migration patterns. In the late 19th century the Marshall Islands were slowly integrated into the German Empire and in 1906 became an official part of the colony German New Guinea. During World War I Japan annexed the islands which were not yet militarized. After the end of the First World War, the Marshall Islands were officially administered by the Japanese Empire under the South Pacific Mandate of the League of Nations. The Japanese increased their military presence in the Pacific and operated war ships and supply lines from the Marshall Islands that served attacks on the US territory in Hawaii. Towards the end of World War II the United States attacked the Japanese occupational forces and besieged them. Between 1946 and 1958, the US military used the territory for the testing of nuclear bombs. This was possible because prior to the country's independence in 1986, the Marshall Islands were a Trust Territory of the United Nations under the administration of the United States, executed by the US Navy until 1951 and then by the US Department for the Interior until 1986. The military governor of the Marshall Islands Ben Wyatt went to Bikini in 1946 to convince the Bikinians to leave their islands temporarily. He told the chief and the community that the testing of the bombs was "*for the good of mankind, and to end all wars*" (Keju-Johnson, 2003). The US Navy's strategy was to appeal to the strong Christian faith of the community. Commander Wyatt therefore visited them on a Sunday after their church service and compared them "*to the children of Israel whom God had saved from their enemy and would now lead to the Promised Land*" (Titus, 2001). Left with no conceivable option, Bikini chief Juda Kessibuki agreed and the community departed from the islands. They could never resettle in their homeland.

Today the Marshall Islands remain closely tied to the United States under the Compact of Free Association (1986) which provides financial assistance to the islands in return for exclusive military presence on their territory. Until 2023, when the Compact is set to expire, the United States provides the Marshall Islands with about 70 Million USD per annum. Although distinct cultural and political settings characterize the Republic of the Marshall Islands, the challenges connected to limited resources and land, dependency on foreign actors and few industrial opportunities, which all shape migration patterns, are similar to those of other small island states. Already, communities on low lying islands in the Pacific, such as in the

Marshall Islands, Kiribati, Tuvalu, Tokelau and the Maldives in the Indian Ocean, are affected by climate change impacts. As global temperatures rise, these impacts are certain to intensify. In turn, larger populations may be affected elsewhere in the future, too. Taking the case of the Marshall Islands for a research project and studying the effectiveness of migration as adaptation in the context of remoteness and resource scarcity is expected to deliver insights that are transferrable to other island nations and perhaps even to emerging migration flows in other regions of the world. In fact, whether international climate governance and migration policy will address and ease the problems of the small nations is a litmus test for global climate justice. For this reason, the case of the Marshall Islands is also politically relevant. It is envisioned that the assessment of effectiveness of current migration patterns as means of adaptation will help to formulate advice on holistic adaptation strategies, taking into consideration receiving and sending communities and foremost the migrants themselves.

7.1. Methods of Field Research

The case study on migration in the Marshall Islands builds upon the findings from the Bangladesh field research and the existing literature on vulnerability, migration and climate change in small island states and in particular in the Republic of the Marshall Islands. The field research took place in November and December 2017 and was carried out in collaboration with the Okeanos Foundation for the Sea. The foundation operates a wind, solar and coconut oil powered catamaran in the Marshall Islands which helps remotely located communities by delivering supplies such as rice or medicines to locations which are only irregularly serviced by cargo ships (Okeanos Foundation for the Sea, 2018). To do my research, I sailed with the crew on the catamaran (also called vaka in Polynesian and Micronesian languages) from Majuro to two other atolls from which people had already migrated and where extreme droughts, saltwater intrusion and coastal erosion were affecting livelihoods. By working in collaboration with the Okeanos Marshall Islands, it was possible to engage directly with communities and use the catamaran not only as a means of transport but also as a bridge for communication.

During the field research 32 qualitative interviews including one focus group discussion with 8 participants were held in the sending communities to capture the situation of the families who had stayed behind and who were trying to adapt in-situ with the help of migrants' remittances. Moreover, another set of eight semi-structured interviews were done with local experts and government representatives. In Majuro eight migrants (one interview per household) who had relocated to the capital were asked about their experience and migration outcomes. A detailed list of migrant and sending community interview partners can be found in the Annex Marshall Islands.

Category:	Migrants	Sending Community	Local Experts	Total
Number of Participants:	8	32 (24 individual interviews + 8 in a focus group)	8	48

Table 5 Overview of Interview Partners Republic of the Marshall Islands (source: own)

The expert interviews were conducted with community experts who had worked ten years or more with or in outer island communities, a representative of the IOM office in Majuro which also operates on the outer islands, a senator who is actively involved in a Marshallese women's organization and three representatives of the local governments.

Field of Expertise	Position / Organization	Number of People Interviewed
Community Expert	Directors of local NGOs working with Outer Island Communities	2
Migration Expert	Representative of IOM Marshall Islands	1
Policy Maker	Senator from an Outer Island	1
Traditional Leader	Representative of the Northern Islands	1
Local Government	Representative of the Mayor of Majuro, Mayors of Ailuk and Maloelap	3

Table 6 Overview of Expert Interviews (source: own).

The semi-structured interviews followed the interview guide which was discussed prior to the field research with a local community expert to identify possible problems in the dialogue with the respondents (see 15.1. Annex). With participants who only spoke Marshallese or who preferred to speak in their native tongue the interviews were held in Marshallese and simultaneously translated.

Site Selection in the Marshall Islands

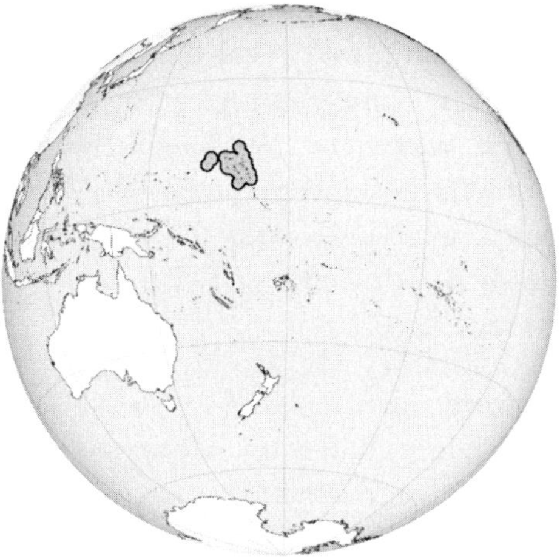

Figure 11 Location of the Republic of the Marshall Islands in the Pacific. Source: (TUBS, 2011b)

Within the Marshall Islands I wanted to reach a wide spectrum of respondents and focus on sending communities and local experts, to understand the consequences of migration for sending communities and to learn about their perspective on the migration of family and community members. This stands in contrast to the Bangladesh case study which concentrated largely on the migrants' experience. In this case study, also migrants in Majuro were interviewed to learn about their individual migration experience. The challenges of the diaspora communities of the Marshall Islands in Arkansas or Hawai'i have been already researched to a degree (Hirata, 2015; Jimeno, 2013; Mitchell-Eaton, 2016), but in-depth research on the effects within the islands has not been developed. From the existing literature insights can be gained also for this study because outmigration may depend on current family networks abroad; and people who will migrate due to climate change will mostly follow existing migration routes. Since the effects on sending communities, their adaptive capacity in the context of climate change have not been sufficiently addressed, I decided to do the data collection in the Marshall Islands and not in the diaspora communities in the United States. Therefore Majuro is both directly affected by physical impacts of climate change, such as flooding and drought, and indirectly through the secondary effects of immigration, such as increasing pressures on local resources. In Majuro, two typical working places of migrants from the outer islands, a tuna factory and a harbor for fishing boats where catches are unloaded as well as migrant neighborhoods were visited. Expert interviews were held in the city center. On Maloelap and Ailuk we first conducted expert interviews with the local traditional chiefs and elected leaders and then followed a snowball-system to select different households to interview.

Selection of Interviewees

The selection of interviewees builds upon the experience from the Bangladesh case study and on the successive selection methods of theoretical sampling. Interviews were conducted with three groups of respondents: migrants, families in sending communities and local leaders / experts. The first interviews were done with local government officials and experts on internal migration to gain an overview of the migration dynamics and connected challenges. Afterwards, migrants in the urban center of Majuro were interviewed. Migrants were selected through theoretical sampling at the sites were most of the migrants from outer islands work or live. Because this case study aimed primarily at finding out about the effectiveness of migration in the sending communities, the migrant interviews aimed at both capturing the situation of farmers in the outer islands and how it relates to climate change and migration as well as their experience after relocation.

Oftentimes, the climate factor in their migration decision surfaced only well into the interview. This stands in contrast to the Bangladesh case study and can be attributed to the nature of the climate impact. In southern Bangladesh people mainly migrated because of sudden events, and in the Marshall Islands they migrated as a more indirect effect on livelihoods through slow onset droughts and gradual sea level rise. When people explain why they migrated, a decisive factor for the attribution of causes for their migration to environmental changes is also the degree to which people normalized their natural environment, meaning which natural disasters or extreme events are perceived and accepted as normal. This can be connected to culture in terms of which timeframe people take as the baseline for their perception what a normal environment is. For example, it may be the span of their own lifetime, their parents' or grandparents', or it could be based on data which they received. Thus the nature of the changes is another important factor because slow onset changes for instance can be normalized in the perspective of the affected communities. Quantitative estimates of how many people may be pushed out due to climate change in addition to existing migration dynamics may therefore differ from people's accounts of why they migrated.

The interviews with migrants were followed by interviews on the outer atolls, where we decided to first interview the traditional chiefs and then the sending families who had remained on the islands. On Ailuk it was first intended to visit two different villages, but because of festivities both communities had joined together on one island and all interviews could be held in one community. At the end of the research stay in the Marshall Islands, we interviewed more migrants in low- income communities of Majuro and received also an appointment with the city administrator who could give insights into some of the topics which had come up during the course of the research. Through this approach of capturing different viewpoints a triangulation of sources is ensured.

Methodological Problems and Possible Bias

The migration patterns in the Marshall Islands are influenced by a variety of factors as outlined in chapter 7.5. Nevertheless, it was in general possible to make out differences between voluntary movements for education and involuntary outmigration due to the combined effects of land scarcity and climate impacts on scarce resources. The interviews in the sending communities therefore addressed environmental factors directly to find out whether or not people were migrating as a result of these changes. While by and large more private conversations than in the Bangladesh case study were possible, some interviews were held with family members present.

This may have influenced some statements, however as several interviews were carried out in the same locality, the results were cross-checked. To enter tightly knit communities as a foreign researcher in order to receive private information about the impact of a family member leaving the household could have posed significant challenges. Although the omitted variable bias which may materialize because people choose not to disclose all relevant information can never be ruled out, it was possible to establish in-depth conversations through the facilitation of a local expert who had worked in the communities beforehand in different capacities.

Structure & Application of Interview Data

This case study follows the same general structure as the Bangladesh case study (see chapter 6.1.), starting with current and future climate impacts in the Marshall Islands (chapter 7.2. and 7.3.) then elaborating the interactions of these physical impacts with agricultural livelihoods and human health (chapter 7.4.). What follows is an overview of the migration patterns in the Marshall Islands (chapter 7.5.) and an analysis of typical household profiles of migrants (chapter 7.6.). The chapter on effectiveness of migration as adaptation for migrants, sending and receiving communities forms the core of the analysis (chapter 7.7.). The case study concludes with an overview of the system's analysis (chapter 7.8.) and a discussion of the results (chapter 7.9.).

Whereas the primary application of the interview data is the analysis of the effectiveness of migration in chapter 7.7., insights from the interviews are also included as supplementary information on the interactions of climate impacts with livelihoods (chapter 7.4.). These excerpts, also derived through a coding and text reduction process, reflect people's perception of climate impacts. Moreover, excerpts are selectively included in the sections on current climate hazards (chapter 7.2.) to underline that the changes documented in the academic literature are closely observed by the residents of the Marshall Islands, even if many do not have access to scientific information. To analyze the interview data, separate coding sheets were developed for the sending community, expert and migrant interviews. As the access to schooling, sanitary facilities, secure lease etc. were quite similar among respondents, the answers were only captured in excel and not coded. Building upon the themes established in the Bangladesh case study, the coding process of the Marshall Islands interview set also generated several core themes and subthemes relevant to migration effectiveness. These themes were A the "Economic Situation" with the subthemes Access to Work Opportunities and the Social Network as a Facilitator of these opportunities; B "Migrant Health" including the subthemes Healthcare Coverage & Cost, Communicable Disease Burden in Urban Areas, Consequences of Lifestyle Change as well as Mental Health & Wellbeing; and C "Loss of Culture and Identity", referring to the subthemes of Forced Migration, Absence of traditional Agriculture and the Fragmentation of Identity (see figure 12). These themes and subthemes are guiding the analysis in chapter 7.7.

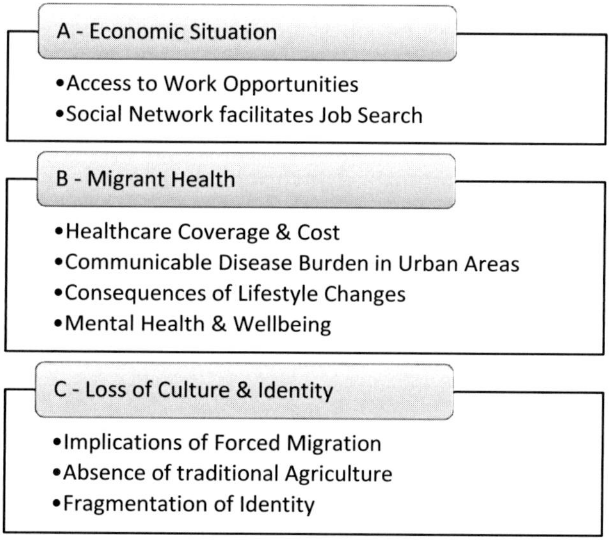

Figure 12 Themes of Effectiveness of Migration as Adaptation for Migrants Republic of the Marshall Islands (source:own).

7.2. Current Climate Hazards on the Marshall Islands

Because of their unique physical geography the Marshall Islands are already under pressures of the emerging climate change impacts. The combined effects of sea level rise and droughts are deteriorating the basis of agricultural livelihoods on the outer islands. Tropical cyclones rarely make landfall on the islands, but once they do, the damage is substantial. The remote location of the Marshall Islands and the dispersion of islets make relief efforts in case of extreme events a challenge. I observed an example of this during my field research in 2017. Only at the end of that year, food aid which had already been sent to the capital island Majuro as a relief measure for the El Niño event in 2015 could be delivered to Maloelap atoll. But shipment, which was eventually realized with the Okeanos Catamaran from Majuro to the outer atoll, had not been possible earlier because of lack of transportation options and high costs.

Sea Level Rise

It is well known that the Marshall Islands are strongly exposed to sea level rise. The following graphs in figure 13-15 show that there is a clear linear trend of rising sea levels over the past decades. Maximum, minimum and mean sea level change in the Marshall Islands show an average annual increase of 4.4 mm (maximum sea level change) to 4.7 mm (minimum / mean) between 1993 and 2017 (Pacific Sea Level Monitoring Project, 2018).

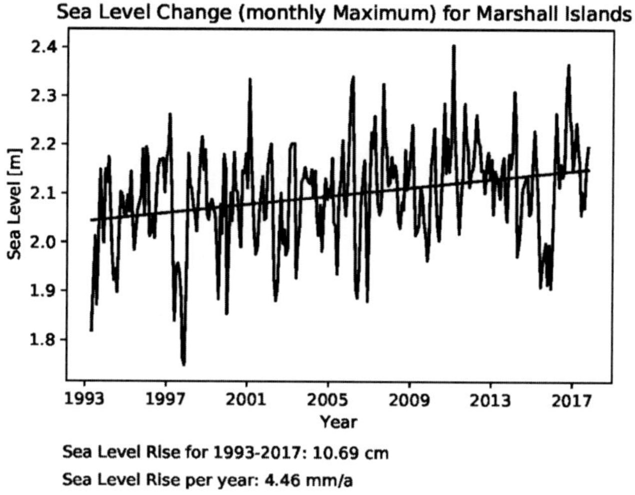

Figure 13 Observed Monthly Maximum Sea Level Change at Uliga Dock, Majuro (source: own, data: Pacific Sea Level Monitoring Project, plot: Adrian Heilmann)

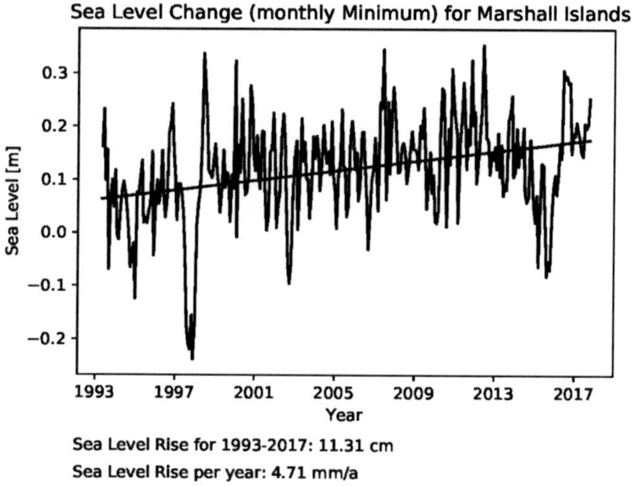

Figure 14 Observed Monthly Minimum Sea Level Change at Uliga Dock, Majuro (source: own, data: Pacific Sea Level Monitoring Project, plot: Adrian Heilmann).

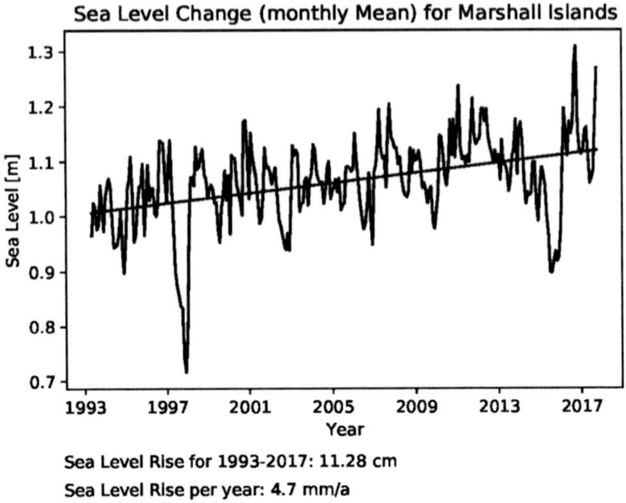

Figure 15 Observed Monthly Mean Sea Level Change at Uliga Dock, Majuro (source: own, data: Pacific Sea Level Monitoring Project, plot: Adrian Heilmann).

Rising sea levels can cause coastal erosion. However, depending on geographical factors and oscillation, shorelines are differently affected by erosion and accretion. In the Pacific, the El Niño Southern Oscillation is an important determinant for coastal erosion (Barnard et al., 2015). It should be noted that in the urban centers, reclamation of land has pushed shorelines in the past decades further into the ocean (Ford, 2013). This human interference in shoreline formation makes it hard to estimate the effect of sea level rise on erosion and accretion rates (Ford, 2013). Possibly, this reclaimed land may become particularly exposed to sea level change in the future. In a ranking of Pacific island states affected by sea level rise which weighs population, numbers of islands, type of island (coral atoll, volcanic, etc.), land area and maximum altitude, the Marshall Islands were listed as second most susceptible after Tokelau (Woodward et al., 1998).

Inundation

Besides coastal erosion connected to sea level rise, inundation during high tides is a significant problem for populations living on coral atolls. Over the past four decades, eighteen inundation events have been recorded in the urban area of the capital Majuro, affecting many people (Ford et al., 2018). Also on the outer islands, so-called king tides cause overwash which can have devastating effects on the local environment and people: "*It was mad all over because all the fishes came to the land and then they couldn't go back. And everything was so* [terrible] *because of all the rotten fish. The elderly man living there said he had never seen things like that before in his life.* [...] *It is scary*" (Expert Interview Majuro, Policy Maker). But not only rising sea levels lead to erosion and inundation. Other anthropogenic drivers i.e. sand mining along the shore (picture 7, page 189) for cement production in the construction industry, groundwater lens depletion and the resulting subsidence; the destruction of coral reefs that protect shorelines during high tides, can worsen the impacts of high tides and other inundation events, like storm surges.

Ocean Acidification and Coral Bleaching

The ph-level of the world's oceans has dropped by 0.1 since the industrial revolution because of the ocean's absorption of CO_2 from the atmosphere (Hoegh-Guldberg, 2014). This process of acidification together with increases in ocean temperatures is threatening coral reef ecosystems. These are habitats of the fish which comprise one of the key protein sources of food in the Marshallese outer island atolls. In fact, the warmer and more acidic water obstructs calcification and causes coral bleaching, the process of the coral's expulsion of its symbiotic algae which can lead to the dying of the coral. Severe bleaching occurred in the Marshallese reefs in 2014 and 2015 when a then record-breaking hot year (2014) was followed by a moderate El Niño event in 2015. "*We've seen in the last few years frequent droughts and frequent El Niño, which causes coral bleaching and which in turn causes the diminishing in the fish habitats and of the fish species as well. These are lifelines of the people in the communities* [...] *We rely mostly* [on our] *surroundings and the ocean*" (Expert Interview Community Expert 1). The area in which the damage was surveyed was limited to the Majuro, Kwajalein, Arno and Namdrik atolls, as outer island atolls are remote and the resources for a damage survey were limited (Fellenius, 2014). However, coral bleaching was reported to have occurred also on the outer islands which suffer less additional anthropogenic stress than the urbanized atolls. In the areas of the study "*three-quarters of all shallow digitate corals are dead, two-thirds of all table corals, half of all submassives other than* Porites rus, *and maybe one-quarter of all massive and encrusting corals*" died off on average by the end of 2014 (Fellenius, 2014).

Droughts and El Niño

"*We're facing an unpredictable drought every year. Before it was maybe once every few years, but now it is getting to the point where it is once or twice a year*" (Expert Interview Majuro, Community Expert 2).

A recurrent global phenomenon which determines the local climate conditions on the Marshall Islands is the El Niño Southern Oscillation. If an El Niño occurs, droughts and rising surface temperatures of the ocean water are the consequence. During El Niño events, tropical cyclones form more often in the Pacific. During La Niña events cyclones are less frequent and sea levels are higher around the Marshall Islands. Since the middle of the last century, rainfall has decreased (Pacific Climate Change Science Program, 2011). However, the various islands are differently affected and there is no monitoring of precipitation on the outer islands, where rainfall patterns can diverge greatly. For example, in Majuro precipitation during the dry season decreased. In Kwajalein both seasonal and yearly precipitation decreased (Pacific Climate Change Science Program, 2011). From most outer islands there is only anecdotal evidence of decreases in rainfall, or changes in rainfall patterns. These can have severe consequences for the residents because due to the salinization of freshwater lenses[4], people are dependent on precipitation for freshwater supply. As one respondent puts it: "*We live by rain water*" (Maloelap Interview 4). When asked whether

[4] A freshwater lense is a layer above the saline groundwater of coral atolls which is generally suitable for drinking. Sea level rise and overwash through king tides causes salinization of these lenses.

environmental factors are a problem in their home community another respondent answered: "*Yes. Drought and thirst*" (Migrant Interview 1, Majuro).

7.3. Future Climate Impacts and their Implications for Migration

The projected global sea level rise in a 2°C world of up to 65 cm (see chapter 7.3. and Mengel et al., 2016), would pose severe challenges to the Marshall Islands. In a 4°C world, in which sea levels could rise up to 1.4 meters, habitation in the Marshall Islands would no longer be possible. Even loss of some coastal areas or islets would have significant negative cultural, social but also economic effects. A long-term impact of sea level rise-induced coastal erosion may eventually be the shrinking of the exclusive economic zone of the Marshall islands, if there is no additional regulation in the Law of the Sea framework with regard to climate change-induced land loss (Holthus et al., 1992).

The challenges that come with rising sea levels are the gradual impacts of diminishing freshwater resources and soil salinization and the amplified negative effects of sudden impacts, including high tides and storm surges. The interactions of wave dynamics and sea level rise are nonlinear and can result in overwash of entire islands by the middle of the century if a high emissions pathway is followed (Storlazzi et al., 2018). Furthermore, tropical cyclones will occur 20 to 40% more often in the Pacific under El Niño events in a 4°C world[5] (Chand et al., 2017). These sudden impacts also feed back into the gradual or slow-onset impacts and may accelerate salinization or freshwater degradation. This is also the reason why Storlazzi et al. (2018) expect that most atolls could become uninhabitable by the middle of the century under a high emissions pathway, sooner than other literature suggests that analyzes sea level rise apart from other climate impacts. Overall, when estimates on sea level rise impacts on migration dynamics

---

[5] in 2070-2100 under RCP 8.5

are made, usually only the mean sea level rise is considered and the aggregate effects of sea level rise and extreme events are neglected (Barnard et al., 2015).

Even under a low emissions scenario small island states will face significant challenges. Coral reefs which are biodiversity hot spots and crucial for fish stocks will likely collapse under the temperature goals set in the Paris Agreement. To save more than 10% of global coral reefs, warming levels would have to be limited to under 1.5°C (Frieler et al., 2013). The complete dying-off of coral in the Marshall Islands could in itself be a driver for outmigration from the outer islands where people's main source of protein is fish. In a 1.5°C-world extreme El Niño events would double to one per decade even after temperature rise is halted, which in turn would bring more severe droughts to the Marshall Islands (Wang et al., 2017). As El Niño events cause coral bleaching through rising sea temperatures, this would further threaten coral ecosystems.

7.4. Interactions of Physical Climate Impacts with Human Systems on RMI

Many respondents who were working in traditional agriculture pointed to the effects of drought, salinization and coastal erosion on their land. Apart from the direct effects on agricultural livelihoods, which are summarized in the next paragraphs, there are also indirect effects, particularly with regard to people's health which have surfaced through the interviews. It is important to note that concerning some impacts women are differently affected than men.

Agriculture and Fisheries

"*It is really changing, very big change. Before I [...] lived on the Outer Islands. I grew up with my grandmother and grandfather, my mother and father stayed in Majuro capital city, but we stayed in the Outer Islands. Yes, it has really changed, I can tell. Nowadays the fruit fall down before being cut. Under the crown the fruit is very dry, the whole tree comes down ... the fruit is damaged because of less rain. It is also a [problem] for the food in the ocean. You can see less fish than before. The water is very hot.*

The water temperature is getting higher. So the fish go deeper, they go far into the ocean. The climate changed" (Expert Interview Majuro, Traditional Leader).

Picture 4 Drought and Salinity affected Pandanus Fruit and healthy Pandanus Fruit (source: own).

Marshallese traditional agriculture is largely based on farming of coconut, pandanus, taro and breadfruit (Merlin, 2005). "*The soils of the Marshall Islands are thin, sandy, alkaline, and lacking in minerals and micronutrients. Combined with poor water-retaining properties of the soil, the quantities and range of crops that can be cultivated are limited*" (Yamada et al., 2017). On the outer islands Ailuk and Maleolap salinization caused both by sea level rise and drought eroded the soil fertility, which in turn led to crop failure or decreased yields, a fact that has been closely observed by residents as the expert interview excerpt shows. When asked how people are coping with the changes in the environment one councilmen of Maloelap responds: "*They are trying their best, but they are struggling. Their resources are depleted and now income is lower. Coconut and fish are affected. The fish leave the shallow waters and go further out, so it's harder to get*" (Maloelap Interview 4). One person on Ailuk explains how this is affecting his family's food security: "*More than 50 of my trees are damaged by the tides. They are my food crops. There are no seedlings coming out of the coconut. We have less to eat now*" (Ailuk Interview 11). As one elder from Ailuk emphasizes: "*It is very hard for us growing our land and feeding our animals. It is harder than before.*" Also, shifting local climate conditions to unusual rainfall patterns and drought have led to different harvesting times according to respondents and experts. "*We see seasonal changes. Seasons are coming earlier than before*" (Ailuk Interview 13). Respondents mentioned that fruits take longer to ripe, which can also contribute to food insecurity. A councilman on Ailuk describes the changes on his island: *"There is an increasing sea level rise. The temperature is higher. Before, the coconut trees were in abundance and very healthy, but now they are very small and there is fewer food.* [...] *The dryness is much stronger. When it rains, it is only for a little while. But when it is sunny and hot, it is for a long time. The coconuts you need for copra-making you can dry only for a few hours because it is too hot"* (Ailuk Interview 12). The effect of inundation and droughts on the production of copra is important because copra is a key source of income. When asked whether the changes in the environment have affected the community the respondent replied: "*Yes. There is less food and less money*" (Ailuk Interview 12). A migrant explains the situation in his home community:

"Respondent:	*The drought damaged the food crops all over the island.*
Interviewer:	*How is it affecting the people's lives?*
Respondent:	*The number of copra is reduced significantly. You can't really earn that much to sustain the family with copra production"*
	(Migrant Interview 4, Majuro).

This impact can also be a push factor for migration: "*Another reason why I left: drought. The copra harvest is getting lower*" (Migrant Interview 1, Majuro). One expert elaborates on the interaction of climate change with harvest losses and outmigration: "*The people are affected, resources diminished. People tend to look for other sources of food because the plant life like bread fruits and coconut productions are not as in abundance as it was before.* [...] *If it is too extreme of a case, we see people just migrating out, or they get assistance from the families abroad or from Majuro. And the government also assists the communities, supplying them with food and water* [...] *during times of need especially*" (Expert Interview Community Expert). But not only food production is affected by the salinization of soils from droughts and inundation. Also the traditional way of constructing houses with wood resources is no longer feasible:

"Interviewer:	*I see many concrete houses here. Why do people use concrete?*
Respondent:	*The reason is – we used to use our own wood fromthe trees. But we can't find them any more as they died. They grow but they cannot get as tall as they used to grow and they are not as big as they used to be and we cannot utilize them. And they are very limited.*
Interviewer:	*And this is because of the changing environment orbecause of deforestation?*
Respondent:	*There was this strong impact of the droughts in the [recent] past that caused these huge trees to die. And now they are not so big as before"* (Ailuk Interview 8).

Moreover, the traditional building of canoes is becoming less frequent which may also be connected to the depletion of wood resources: "*They used the bread fruit trees to build these smaller canoes. But now the bread fruit trees are not in abundance. There are less canoes because they are only using the imported wood. There are only few people that can buy these materials*" (Ailuk Interview 8). Another aspect is the depletion of tree resources for handicraft making: "*For the women it's the actual pandanus and coconut tree leafs that they use to make handicrafts* [...] *it is a sustainable livelihood issue*" (Expert Interview Majuro, Migration Expert). These handicrafts are often sold or used for bartering. Women in the sending communities mentioned that during severe droughts it was more difficult to procure the materials which diminished their income or access to food.

While the terrestrial changes are posing challenges to livelihoods, impacts of CO_2 and temperature increase are also affecting the ocean waters. Fish from the lagoon has been the traditional source of protein, but increases in temperature especially in shallow waters around the coast together with acidification and plastic pollution are damaging coral reefs and diminishing fish stocks. The increase in temperature and decrease in ph-level are the major impacts on the outer islands, where other local anthropogenic stressors such as pollution are negligible. Several fishermen and experts recounted that the disappearance of fish and clams close to the shore have made securing their livelihood more difficult because they need to go further out to the sea. This can be both more dangerous and resource-intensive as many have abandoned traditional sailing methods in favor of diesel engines. Not only lagoon fish around coral reefs are threatened, fish stocks in the high seas of the Pacific are also under pressure because of extensive industrial fishing and to a lesser degree because of climate change. Tuna, which is an important export good of the Marshall Islands, is in a "*substantial decline*" in the Pacific (McKechnie et al., 2017). While registered fishing vessels are monitored, there are accounts of corruption and unregistered vessels which may put an additional stress on stocks (Johnson, 2017; Tsamenyi and Hanich, 2008). However, documentation of corrupt practices is hardly available. The depletion in fish stocks does not only threaten livelihoods, but also food security and so increases dependence on imported foods: "*We depend on the fish, if the fish cannot survive, we will depend mostly on processed import food. So one of the things we are facing today are non-communicable diseases: sugar-diabetes, high-blood pressure. So without the food from the land, that's what we'll get. And we already are one of the most affected islands, or countries, in the world on diabetes*" (Expert Interview Majuro, Community Expert 2).

Health

The interactions of climate change in the Marshall Islands with health are multifold: "In the Pacific Island countries, the climate-sensitive health risks of highest priority include trauma from extreme weather events, psychosocial ill-health and factors relating to mental health issues such as population pressures and health system deficiencies" (Schwerdtle et al., 2018). While especially the mental health effects of climate change require further study, some climate impacts have already been addressed as relevant to human health in the Marshall Islands. The dangers of extreme events and inundations can be especially forceful when they are unprecedented and beyond the scope of experience of people. As one respondent reports: "*When the sea level rises sometimes we have dead children who were playing in the ocean where they used to play. They are taken away by the sea. It happened nearby at the ocean side. Two children. 3 and 1 year old*" (Ailuk Interview 3). This incident happened because of an unusually high wave. Such kingtides are reported by many respondents to happen more frequently now with sometimes unprecedentedly large inundations.

Furthermore, the deterioration of agricultural land because of salinization bears implications for public health. There are limits of technical adaptation to the abovementioned challenges, such as the deployment of salt tolerant crops. This means that a revival of local food production to sustain the population is not likely (Ahlgren et al., 2014). In turn, the dependency on imported food as well as food aid will continue to increase (Ahlgren et al., 2014). One respondent in Maloelap explains: "*Food crops are decreasing. The water lenses are salinized. People have to rely on imported food*" (Maloelap Interview 2). The food intake from these imports is often processed food, high in sugar. Yamada et al. (2017) stipulate that climate effects on health may further increase the outmigration from the Marshall Islands. This is not only connected to the health hazard itself which could be interpreted as a driver, it is associated with the lack of specialized healthcare which would be needed to treat the diseases. Already, Marshallese migrate both internally and to the United States for medical help. A senator from Jaluit explains the linkages between climate impacts on agriculture, health and migration: "*They have less food, so they have to turn to the processed food that is imported from the mainland. So there are big impacts. Why more and more people are getting sick?* […] *Why we did not have this sickness before? Because we used to eat just natural food. Fish from the ocean, whatever we grow. People even move to the center because when these things happen, they want to be closer to the hospital. So there are very big impacts.* […] *Many of them, they don't want to move, they are forced to. They don't want to come here, but they are forced to*" (Expert Interview Majuro, Policy Maker).

In fact, many of the urban poverty diets based on processed foods result in obesity. At the same time, obesity is the most important risk factor for type II diabetes. Together with other risk factors – such as lack of physical activity – processed food diets have already led to a wide prevalence of type II diabetes. Dialysis which may be needed for treatment is not available on the islands. Before the Marshall Islands came under US influence which is connected to the dependency on food imports, diabetes was not a problem in the country. Now, with volatile agricultural yields and established trading lines, a return to sustainable and healthy alimentation would require significant efforts and government intervention.

On the outer islands, hunger and thirst were cited by many. "Sometimes we run out of food and people go hungry. That is one of the main problems. It has gotten worse over the years. Droughts are becoming more frequent, food crops are depleted. It does not help that shipping boats from the Marshall Islands take a long time to be here and then people go hungry" (Ailuk Interview 13). On Maloelap the conditions were also poor: "Basic needs are not always satisfied, then it is mostly food shortage" (Maloelap Interview 3). Another respondent from Ailuk elaborates: "Sometimes we get hungry and thirsty. It is lack of income and not enough resources. It is different from the past. It is just starting these days because of the drought. Many plants are dying. [There is] No water" (Ailuk Interview 3). Almost every household in the Marshall Islands has a rainwater harvesting system in order to ensure freshwater supply. However, it should be noted that in times of drought these storages often do not suffice and desalinization units for the treatment of ocean water are needed complementarily. One resident of Ailuk compares the situation to the past: "*Before it was okay, but now there are a lot of changes. Before, we used the well water, but we cannot use it now. It is very salinized*" (Ailuk Interview 4).

Picture 5 Water Desalinization Units (source: own).

In the urban centers, other anthropogenic stress such as population growth has contributed to the depletion of groundwater. Also, it should be noted that in the case of the communities from Bikini and Rongelap available freshwater was radioactively contaminated and the people were relocated to atolls with insufficient natural resources or to already inhabited islands.

Besides the effects of droughts on plant growth and local food production, temperature increase also has effects on labor productivity. One traditional chief explains: "*The environment has changed. I see the people always sleeping, from 10 in the morning until 3 when they get up to do something. It is because it is so hot, it is hotter than when I was young. The droughts are more frequent and bigger*" (Ailuk Interview 1). This anecdotal evidence of a change in productivity due to heat stress is in general supported by the scientific literature. Already, significant economic losses have been proven to occur because of decreasing productivity during heat stress for example in Australia. By the end of the century up to 40% of daylight hours could become too hot to work in some regions of the world (Kjellstrom et al., 2013, 2016; Watts et al., 2015; Zander et al., 2015). The increase in temperature not only causes productivity losses, but also affects wellbeing especially in places where there is limited access to electricity and where wooden housing has been replaced with buildings made of concrete and corrugated roof.

The 2015 / 2016 drought impacted the spread of communicable diseases: "It was found that the drought conditions caused an increase in the number of cases of diarrhea – which may have arisen because of consumption of contaminated water – influenza-like-illness caused by changing air temperature, conjunctivitis and scabies" (Leenders et al., 2017). Accordingly, healthcare expenditures increased during the drought. Also in the interviews some respondents linked the effects of drought directly to health issues:

"*Interviewer:* *Have these changes in the environment [droughts] affected your livelihood or income?*

Respondent: *Sometimes we get sick, flu, diarrhea. The drought destroys the food crops so people's income is less*"
(Ailuk Interview 13).

The health assistant on Ailuk describes: "*People have health problems during the drought seasons: diarrhea, pink eye, flu. Because dust and dirt is all over the place*"(Ailuk Interviews 14). Moreover, the remoteness of the islands can amplify difficulties in the treatment of health problems: "*If there is an outbreak of disease we are like an ark ship and there is hunger. From my point of view it is connected with the droughts*" (Ailuk Interview 6). Especially with regard to health it is important to note that climate impacts may affect women and men differently. For example, lack of freshwater availability may decrease women's access to hygiene during menstruation. There is the necessity of "*responding to female specific menstruation needs in times of drought because there are a lot of taboos around women accessing water when they are menstruating, [...]. To overlay that with a drought and the stress that comes* [with] *resource management of water in the household and the ability for how you are going to share that community water. Women aren't going to be saying: 'I need it to wash my menstruation pad'*" (Expert Interview Majuro, Migration Expert). To make matters worse, traditional medicine based on plants and trees is also put under stress. This is particularly relevant for outer island communities which at large only have access to a simple pharmacy with a pharmaceutical assistant. Another observation was that when visiting Ailuk, we were approached for the pain medication Paracetamol because the pharmaceutical facility did no longer have any medicine, due to a lack of reliable transport from the outer islands. Moreover, if a community or household is already under pressure from difficult livelihood situations, a drought can deteriorate interpersonal relationships and worsen domestic violence. The increases of (gender-based) violence and crime during sudden-onset disasters are better known than the psychosocial effects of slow-onset processes. Some incidents show that droughts may worsen already high levels of violence against women. In the Marshall Islands one expert recounts one case in which "*a woman could not access her traditional medicine and she had a miscarriage after*[wards]. *Her husband didn't believe her* [that she could not access the medicine and that her miscarriage was involuntary] *and he raped her*" (Expert Interview Majuro, Migration Expert). Research on the psychological effects of climate change on the Marshallese people is scarce, but observations during the field research and descriptions in the interviews could be linked to intense ecological grief of several interview partners, which has only recently been identified as a response to climate impacts (Albrecht et al., 2007; Cunsolo and Ellis, 2018).

Overall, the research on the interactions of climate impacts in the Pacific with human health has evolved over the past two decades. The 1998 article of Woodward et al. first measured the vulnerability of nations in the Asia Pacific regions to the effects of climate change on human health through five important factors: destructive growth, poverty, political rigidity, geographic isolation and dependency (Woodward et al., 1998). This assessment weighs key factors that are also relevant variables for the propensity of people to migrate. The push effect for outmigration could be mediated through both, the effects on human health or economic losses. For example, dependency is herein framed not only as dependency on foreign financial or food aid, but also in terms of dependency on foreign knowledge which has been identified as a factor which limits the decision-making base of people. Now the assessments of the climate impact burden on human health follow frameworks developed by the WHO for assessing vulnerability, using qualitative and quantitative methods, as can be seen in the health impact assessment of Climate Change in Pacific Island Countries (McIver et al., 2016). In this they identified direct, indirect and diffuse effects of climate impacts on health. In the Marshall Islands they found that the most important risks were "*direct health effects of extreme weather events, indirect effects of water and food security and safety, vector borne diseases, respiratory diseases, disorders of the eyes, ears, skin and other body systems and diffuse effects of disorders of mental/ psycho-social health and non-communicable diseases*" (McIver et al., 2016). This research builds upon the increase in data collection and therefore improved data base. The development of the public health research in the small island developing states provides guidance for improving both the data base and the scope of the climate migration research in the future. Better data could also help to advance the emerging field of climate change migration and health.

7.5. Foreign Imposed Migration Patterns in the Marshall Islands: Nuclear Legacy and Climate Change

"*Respondent:* *No matter how you look at it, climate change is already affecting us.*

Interviewer: *And do you think this is contributing to the migration?*

Respondent: *Eh, well, I think it is gradually. It's gradually. Right now, people can still live in the outer islands. But, you know, opportunities are less and less. So migration to the 'greener pastures' is what people are looking at right now*"

(Expert Interview Majuro, Community Expert 2).

The excerpt of the interview captures the nature of the contemporary migration flows from the outer islands which are still defined by both push and pull factors. The Republic of the Marshall Islands has a net migration rate of -4.70 per 1000 people, ranking 187th out of 221 countries, and thus is amongst the top quarter of countries with the highest outmigration rates (CIA World Factbook, 2017b). On the other hand Majuro is a destination for internal migration and for migration from other densely populated and poor atoll island states, such as Kiribati or Tuvalu. Although there are cases of circular migration, emergency evacuations, travel for visiting relatives, education and religious purposes – the dominant pattern which is related to climate change impacts is permanent rural to urban migration.

Overview: Climate Impacts and Migration

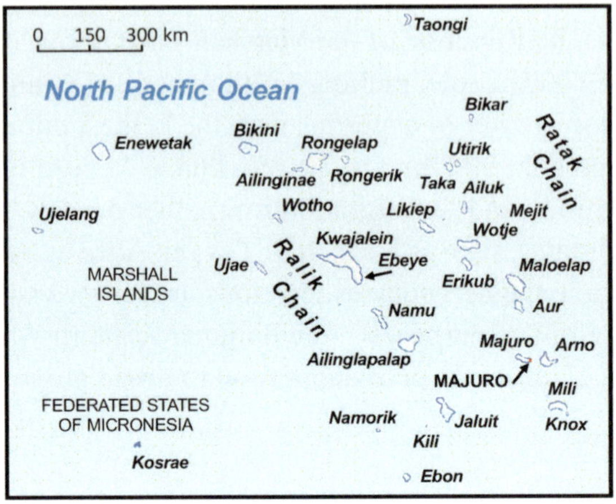

Figure 16 Map of the Marshall Islands, including Research Location Sites Majuro, Ailuk, Maloelap (source: https://en.wikipedia.org/wiki/Marshall_Islands).

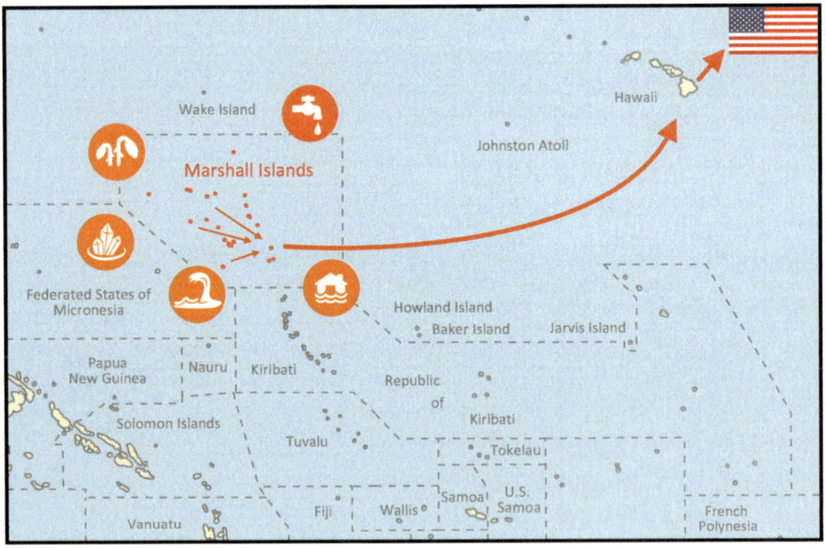

Figure 17 Possible Climate Migration Pathways in the Marshall Islands (source: own, style from Vinke et al., 2017)

Picture 6 Okeanos Marshall Islands anchored in Majuro with solar panels in the back (source: own).

Picture 7 Sand Exploitation for Cement Construction on Majuro (source: own).

Picture 8 Ailuk Atoll (source: own).

Picture 9 Maloelap Atoll (source: own).

The climate change-related migration flows originate from the outer islands and are first directed at the capital Majuro, where many try to find better employment opportunities. Figure 17 gives an overview of the main climate impacts, salinization droughts, king tides, seal level rise and freshwater scarcity and the dominant related migration pathways. A common internal migration pattern that emerged from the migrant and expert interviews was that people had only planned a temporary visit in Majuro and then decided to stay because their perceived livelihood opportunities were better in the urban area than in the outer islands where resources are diminishing. For a large part of the internal migrants Majuro is merely an intermediary stop as many wait to gain or receive enough money to go to the US, or they relocate due to a lack of better options:

"Respondent: *Well, many they come here [Majuro] and when they cannot find jobs, they move to the States. And when they move there, they are doing laborer work, that's what they usually find.*

Interviewer: *So, low-paid work?*

Respondent: *Yes, sometimes very low-paid"*
(Expert Interview Majuro, Policy Maker).

One expert who trains high school dropout youth who have come from the outer islands explains: "I work with a lot of these kids. When I ask them what the problem is, [they say] there is pretty much nothing available in the outer islands. And now with climate change there is less and less opportunities for these people" (Expert Interview Majuro, Community Expert 2). This assessment is also reflected in the interviews in the outer islands. While the overall outmigration is of course multi-causal, the additional pressure of climate change impacts in recent years contributes to increasing migration rates:

"Interviewer: *Are there other people from this island who are planning to migrate as well?*

Respondent: *Plenty of people migrate.*

Interviewer: *Why are they leaving?*

Respondent: *It has to do with the changes in the environment. Everything is less now, like copra*"
(Ailuk Interview 11).

A councilman on Ailuk explains: "*The main reason why people are leaving is because their resources are depleted. The drought leads to a decrease in the copra production. Before, the families earned enough from copra-making, but now with fewer coconuts the families can't really sustain themselves. Some people go to Majuro, others to their relatives in the US. From what I hear, the migrants are doing much better abroad; they can provide for themselves, they have jobs. The life here is really getting very hard because of these droughts and the sea level rise*" (Ailuk Interview 12). Another shop owner and councilman was asked whether the environmental changes are causing people to migrate. He replied: "*Yes. Maybe it is one of the reasons why they are leaving. There is not enough water, there are not enough food supplies. Life is not very good*" (Ailuk Interview 13). When asked the same question, one respondent summarizes: "*Yes. They are running away from these challenges*" (Ailuk Interview 8). Population pressure is not the reason why people are leaving the outer islands according to one respondent: "*[They migrate] due to lack of food resources on the island, for example, breadfruits are only enough to provide and share just for families and are not enough in the next few years. It's not because of the family growth in numbers/population, but because of frequent drought*" (Ailuk Interview 16). In fact, recent increases in migration flows from the outer islands cannot be explained by population pressure and the resulting resource scarcity because the population on most outer islands has decreased over the last decades. The replies display how climate change drives migration. The climate change-related push factors – impacts on agricultural livelihoods and health – are described in depth in chapter 7.4.

Nuclear Testing and Migration

A key determinant of present day migration routes in the Marshall Islands is the military and nuclear legacy of the United States in the small island state (Keown, 2017). In the time period of twelve years (1946-1958) the United States tested 67 nuclear bombs on the Bikini and Eniwetok atolls.

In 1950 US President Harry S. Truman decided in favor of the development of the hydrogen bomb which was in turn tested in the Marshall Islands in 1954 and proved to be 1000 times more powerful than the atomic bomb dropped on Hiroshima, Japan. As a consequence of the testing, three other atolls, Rongelap, Rongerik and Utirik, had to be evacuated in an emergency operation after the radioactive fallout from the so-called "Bravo bomb" affected 665 islanders (Kunkle and Ristvet, 2013). Contrary to popular belief, the fallout on Rongelap, Rongerik and Utirik did not occur due to an unexpected shift of the winds. The winds were roughly in line with the short term predictions of the US military. Ailuk, the atoll which is under investigation in this case study, is in relative close proximity to Utirik. However, residents of Ailuk were not evacuated, although they were exposed to radiation lifetime doses of 20 000 mR, including internal radiation from local food supplies. "*The infinity dose exposure at Ailuk certainly was known to be larger than that permitted* [for] *task force personnel";* and the US Defense Threat Reduction Intelligence Analysis Center recognizes "*It can be argued that the decision not to evacuate Ailuk was incorrect*" (Kunkle and Ristvet, 2013). Furthermore, two US military vessels would have been readily available to evacuate Ailuk (Kunkle and Ristvet, 2013). The nuclear testing resulted in the permanent forced displacement from several atolls, including Bikini, Rongelap and Rongerik to other places like Kili, Ejit and Majuro. This migration wave may have had wider long-term consequences "*generating internal processes of migration from the northern to southern Marshall Islands, but also, in the longer term, precipitating Marshall Islanders into the large-scale international migrant flows of the late twentieth century and beyond*" (Keown, 2017). These flows in turn are now also influenced by climatic factors.

Nuclear Legacy and Planned Relocation

For some Marshallese, the effects of climate change on the islands are another example of damages through foreign powers: "*Hopefully they can see what happening to us little people, [...] I consider the impact of climate change as no different from when the US came and tested nuclear [bombs] in our area. We were peaceful, happy people and we didn't bother anybody and we were just content with what we had. But then they tested nuclear and then what happened to…you know…we have so many sick people. […] the money they gave us couldn't help us, it is exhausted. It is just the same. We were happy and now, […] these big people are doing the same thing and who is affected? It is us! The small people. And they are living in luxury and enjoying their lives*" (Expert Interview Majuro, Policy Maker). A similar sentiment is reflected in another expert interview: "*[…] for all the Marshallese, the hands that feed you are the same hands that you want to slap. So 1946 we were relocated [from] Bikini for the good of mankind*[6] *and to bring peace to the world. Our kids are still fighting in the military for that same peace. From then to now, the big countries created another source that affects the world [climate change]. But this time it is not the radiation problem, but it's a problem that affects our life, that is related to the Mother Nature. […] We created [this problem] for the good of mankind we bring resource to the rich and big countries. So right now, if we will be relocated again, it's not from our island, it will be from our country*" (Expert Interview Majuro, Community Expert 2).

Because of the history of forced migration tied to the nuclear testing, planned relocation as an adaptation strategy to sea level rise is politically controversial. This approach has been taken by the government of the low-lying island country Kiribati in purchasing land on Fiji to relocate to. Tony de Brum, former Foreign Minister of the Marshall Islands, explained the Marshallese position: "*Our forced relocations have made the Marshall Islands extremely suspicious of relocations*" (Johnson, 2015). But the exiled Bikinian community which resides on the islands of Kili and Ejit is at the forefront of climate impacts, and in the face of crop failures and salinization the community leadership has raised concerns whether they could sustain themselves on their assigned land. Kili has been repeatedly flooded by king tides so that the former mayor of Bikini Nishma Jamore already

---

[6] The remark "for the good of mankind" herein refers to what the US military representative said to the Bikinians, to appeal to their Christian values and convince them to leave their island.

pleaded for relocation to the United States in 2015 (Kili/ Bikini / Ejit Local Government Council, 2015; Sinha, 2015).

Western Influences and the Relationship with the US under COFA

The Compact of Free Association (COFA, 1986) between the United States and the three Pacific countries, Federated States of Micronesia, Palau and the Marshall Islands, grants the citizens of these states permission to live and work in the United States. This special status also draws migrants from Kiribati and Tuvalu to the Marshall Islands, who hope to be able to relocate to the US eventually, for example by obtaining Marshallese citizenship. The compact has influenced the choice of destination for migrants significantly. In the US there are several large diaspora communities including in Arkansas, Hawai'i, Missouri, Oklahoma, Washington State and California. About 22 000 Marshallese now live in the United States, almost one third of the total population. However, the possibility to relocate to the United States under the compact is strongly dependent on the financial resources available to the household (Constable, 2017). Often a larger family network in the sending or receiving communities funds a household or a family member for relocation: "*Perhaps it is their plan to send all their family to the US. He left already, first he goes to Hawaii, then to US mainland. You know how he got the ticket? He got it from the sister. She left four or five years before*" (Expert Interview Majuro, Traditional Leader).

The influence of Western lifestyles and cultural change within the Marshallese society is also shaping migration behavior: "*They're migrating from the outer islands, where they could grow more, [...] they have more space to go fish, they could utilize a lot of stuff, but I guess it is not just climate change, but it is also changing of mentality. Our attitude towards life is changing because of westernization, colonisation. So it is not just the climate, but it is also life itself*" (Expert Interview Majuro, Community Expert 2). In the same interview, it was mentioned that through the influence of what is described as "western mentality," young people tend to value less what they have on the Marshall Islands. This would include for example natural resources, a tightly knit community and still pristine outer islands. I interpret the mentioning of western culture and mentality also to be linked to consumerism, which is effectively marketed through television and internet on the urbanized atolls, mostly coming from the United States and to a lesser degree from China and parts of East Asia. In the outer island communities, isolation and the sense of alienation from their own culture in favor of the perceived advantages of modernity are push factors for often permanent outmigration. "*When kids in the outer islands think about McDonald's and Burger King, they are not thinking about what they have is actually what can be utilized and be sustainable in this climate changing world. They feel that they have been left out. That all they can do is making copras and go fish and they don't even know that people actually pay thousands of dollars to stand where they stand, to do what they do*" (Expert Interview Majuro, Community Expert 2).

Security Implications of Climate Impacts in the Pacific Region

Besides analyzing current push factors for migration patterns originating from the Marshall Islands, the secondary and tertiary effects of climate change on the island and the region need to be considered from a macro perspective. "*In addition to "multiplier" issues such as the ability to preserve social order, or intensified competition for increasingly scarce resources, these impacts also serve as a threat to national survival.* […] *the potential "vanishing" of a sovereign nation, without a successor state, is not only a security implication but may rise to the level of a threat to international peace and security*" (Muller, 2009). In the future indirect, transboundary effects of local climate impacts may accumulate to immense challenges. Apart from the migration patterns which are now evolving because of climate impacts on small island states, larger (temporary) displacements have already taken place, for example in the Philippines after the tropical cyclone Haiyan (Yolanda), causing more than 6300 deaths and forcing 4.1 million people from their homes (Lagmay et al., 2015; Yonetani, 2014). US admiral Samuel Locklear III who was formerly in command of the 300 000 person strong American military presence in the Pacific remarked that "*Significant upheaval related to the warming planet is probably the thing most likely to happen… and that will cripple the security environment. Probably that will be more likely than the other scenarios we often talk about*" (Baron, 2013; Bender, 2013). Such regional stability would very likely have implications for the Republic of the Marshall Islands, too, as they are hosting an important US military base. On Kawajalein Atoll, the US operates the Anti-Ballistic Missile Defense Testing Program since 1964. At the same, a submergence of the Marshall Islands in the long term could bear implications for the security architecture in the Pacific, as the United States would lose their base in the Republic.

Human Trafficking
One issue of concern that was mentioned during the expert interviews is human trafficking. Especially women and children are trafficked for sexual abuse, often recruited under promises of profitable labor possibilities abroad. Besides forced prostitution, there are other work schemes which are linked to trafficking and conditions of modern slavery, such as the confiscation of identification cards and passports (U.S. Department of State, 2017). Climate change impacts on livelihoods can be one of the factors which make people more vulnerable to become victims of trafficking for their economic situation may press them to take greater risks. So far, however, there is no comprehensive assessment of the vulnerability factors which push certain groups into trafficking schemes in the Marshall Islands. In recent years, under the government of President Hilda Heine, some policy improvements have been made, including the launch of a National Action Plan to Combat Trafficking. Nevertheless, as of 2017 the country still "*does not fully meet the minimum standards for the elimination of trafficking*" (U.S. Department of State, 2017).

7.6. Household Profiles

Vulnerability: Poverty and Remoteness on Outer Island Communities
Generally, the households of migrants who migrate from the outer islands to Majuro and then potentially to the US are typical outer islands households. The outer island communities are quite homogeneous. Most families rely heavily on copra production for income and small-scale subsistence agriculture. Some hold other positions in the community, being members of the council or police. Largely, women are responsible for household chores such as cooking and child rearing, but also participate in agricultural

work. The standard of living is low. While the communities have access to primary school on their islands, many do not finish high school. Housing structures are basic (see picture 10) because of limited resources available on the islands and traditional building techniques of thatched roof housing have been abandoned in favor imported materials including corrugated roofs, cement and plywood. On the outer islands housing units are often assembled without training and can be susceptible to damages of extreme weather events. Medical care, especially in emergencies, is hardly available on the outer islands.

Most families do not own land, but live on land that is owned by royal families, *Iroij*. Those who own land and have financial assets often send their children for university education abroad, which can be categorized as a different type of migration than migration driven by climate impacts. During the course of the interviews with the sending communities, the majority of respondents emphasized that there is not a specific group amongst them that is migrating, rather it is the average person, who is feeling the pressure to move out: *"It is anybody. Last week there came a family who wanted to stay at my house for two weeks to wait for a ticket from their son* [who was already in the United States]. *They were not really rich"* (Expert Interview Majuro, Traditional Leader). Some respondents replied that it is especially those who have fewer assets who migrate:

"*Interviewer:* *Who is migrating?*

Respondent: *Everyone at every age level. Mostly people or families who don't have enough land to produce enough resources to provide and sustain their livelihood especially for their families and those who find it hard to cope due to climate change*"

(Ailuk Interview 16).

Picture 10 Typical housing and residential water harvesting unit on Maleolap Atoll (source: own).

Interactions of Exposure and Vulnerability: Climate Information and Awareness

On the outer islands people are largely dependent on the radio for information. The remoteness of the Outer Islands leads to substantial knowledge gaps on the issue of climate change which is already affecting people's life. As in the previous case, some respondents knew the term climate change, but had no further information as the example of one church leader on the outer islands shows:

"Interviewer: Are environmental factors in your home community a problem?
Respondent: Yes. Coastal erosion.
Interviewer: Has it increased over the past decade?
Respondent: It seems like it is increasing.
Interviewer: Why has it increased?

Respondent: *Climate change. We don't know why the climate is changing*"
(Ailuk Interview 10).

One school teacher tried to explain why the environmental damages in their community have increased: "*It has to do with climate change. The high tides are more frequent, the sky is really warm. Climate change is perhaps caused by the sun*" (Ailuk, Interview 11). This statement reflects the limited access to education and science. The lack of knowledge about climate change falls together with a lack of education and training to improve infrastructural in-situ adaptation: "*People are thinking about protecting the coast, but we don't know how we can defend ourselves*" (Ailuk Interview 1). The set of questions for sending communities and migrants were designed to first ask about whether there were environmental problems in the sending community / community of origin. Then it was asked, whether these problems had increased or intensified. Following this, the question was posed why these changes were occurring (see Annex Marshall Islands, chapter 14.4.). The overall results of the perceived reason for the environmental change are summarized in figure 18. "Mentioned the Term Climate Change" refers to the respondents who answered to the question "Why have the environmental impacts increased or intensified?" with the term "climate change", but could not explain why the climate is changing. "Climate Change (Some Knowledge)" refers to those who mentioned the mechanisms behind climate change such as melting glaciers. The figure shows that more than half of the respondents either had no knowledge why these changes occurred, or only knew about the term climate change, but had no further information.

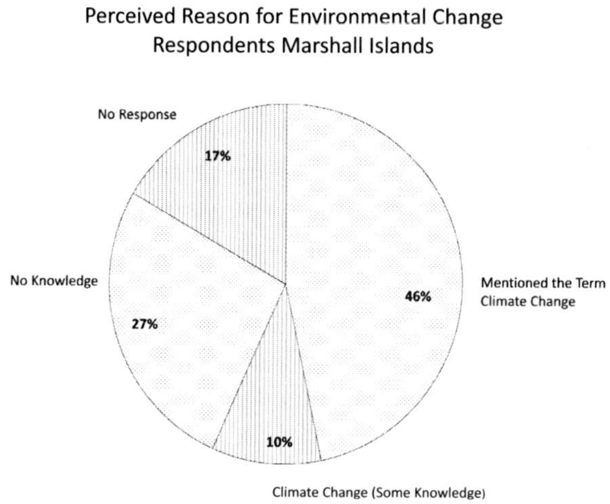

Figure 18 Perceived Reason for Environmental Change from Respondents on the Outer Islands and Migrants Interviewed in Majuro (source: own).

The lack of knowledge about climate change makes informed-decision making impossible and prevents the general population to demand from their leaders climate action on mitigation and adaptation.

7.7. Effective or Not? Migration as Adaptation on the Marshall Islands

Effectiveness of Migration as Adaptation for Migrants

From the data of the expert interviews and the interviews with internal migrants I identified factors that limit and factors which enable effectiveness of migration as adaptation. Like in the Bangladesh case study, the economic situation and skill or education level prior to the migration as well as the migrant's social networks in the destination strongly influenced their migration outcome. The investigation of health as an indicator for effectiveness brought to light a complex situation of higher health risks for certain types of diseases in the urban center of Majuro, but on the other hand better access to healthcare than on the outer islands. Self-determination, which was hindered by a lack of knowledge about the employment opportunities and the rule of law in the places of destination, appeared to be relevant, too. Furthermore, the loss of identity and or culture emerged as factors which have to be evaluated as detrimental for migration effectiveness as it has been defined in this research. Overall, the migrants weighed the possibility of economic benefits of urban employment against the loss of access to their homeland and culture, a situation that often left them torn.

Economic Situation

From the literature on the Marshallese diaspora in the United States it can be derived that there are many types of migrations serving various purposes and leading to different economic outcomes. For example, Yamada et al. (2017) point to the fact that sea level rise has induced an outmigration from the Marshall Islands directed at destinations with jobs in the American food industry, like chicken processing. Of course, migration for education is also a common pattern, but this type of migration is not the focus here. In the investigated cases on Majuro, climate change was a push factor for migration, as the respondents had previously worked in traditional subsistence farming on the outer islands that had become less and less profitable due to harvest losses. The interviewed experts were also specifically asked about climate change-related migration and its outcomes. Although the sample size of the interviews is small, through the triangulation of sources (comparison of the data from migrants, sending communities and experts) and sites (two neighborhoods and the typical working places of migrants were visited), the study still captures important issues which are complementary insights into the study of the overall Marshallese diaspora in the United States.

In general, the data analysis showed that the pull factor of perceived economic opportunities does not always match the actual circumstances in the destinations Majuro or the US: "*They* [the migrants] *think they go to the US for greener pastures. But they go and find out that they have to work. And so they have to work three jobs.* […] *It's convenient for the students that go to school and* […] *find jobs, but people that come straight from the outer island to Majuro* [and the US eventually] *it is very hard for them*"

(Expert Interview Majuro, Community Expert 2). This points to the fact that those who come from (largely urban) backgrounds and have family members who already attained higher levels of education and income can seize the opportunities of a better education abroad. Whereas migrants from poor agricultural backgrounds with only basic education, who experience the push factors of climate change, often end up in low-paid labor with little upward mobility or access to higher education. A common problem is that migrants who went to the US often underestimated the much higher living costs as one expert explained: "*Here in the Marshalls, you build a house, that's it!* [...] *You don't have to lease it, you don't have to pay any fees. It will be your house and just bring in your water source and everything else. But out there they have to deal with electricity, housing bills, so many kinds of other bills and all these other regulations they have to go through. And being aliens out there is another story*" (Expert Interview Majuro, Community Expert 1). On the Marshall Islands there are no rental costs for Marshallese. Those who own the land have to grant permission to use the land, but no costs occur. Also, facilities are generally low cost compared to the US. This is why those who do not have all the relevant information at hand before their migration may not be able to foresee whether their relocation will be economically so beneficial that it would outweigh the costs of relocation, such as the potential loss of culture. The perception on the outer islands of the migrant's situation in the US in some cases reflects this limited view, but at the same time brings to light how difficult the living situation is on the outer islands:

"*Some find it hard to cope because they don't know how to live and deal their life in the States compared to how they were here. But overall, they're living a happy yet pleasing and easy life. They find good resources with very good benefits in the States. For instance, they find good jobs with very good earnings (much more than they usually earn), food stamps, free housing and much more. In a best way to describe this, they find it hard to cope but, in some way, they're living a good life comparing to here*" (Ailuk Interview 16). A contributing factor to the positive image of Marshallese migrants living in the US could be that the migrants in the US may not want to share their problems with their friends or family back home. Another interpretation could be that living on social welfare may actually be a better option than facing the increasing food and water scarcities on the outer islands.

This migration outcome nevertheless does not prove migration to be an effective adaptation strategy because it was not possible for migrants to re-establish the status quo they had prior to migration. A councilman on Maloelap gives his assessment of the migrants' situation: "*They have not really good jobs, fishing, construction work. Their situation is pretty much the same like here but they don't know where to go else*" (Maloelap Interview 4). The majority of the first generation Marshallese abroad is employed in low-skilled jobs, like in the food processing industry. However, on the outer islands, where there are few opportunities for work, people do not have the same reference frame like in the US for what would be a good job with sufficient upward mobility. So one woman on the outer islands describes how her migrated family members are doing: "*Their work is good. They are working at a chicken factory in Arkansas*" (Maloelap Interview 3). In the most common destinations, such as Springdale, Arkansas, the Marshallese diaspora community helps new arrivals to establish their lives there (Jimeno, 2013). While the "*ethnic concentration*" of tightly knit diaspora communities serves initial integration, it also reinforces limitations: "*This concentration makes it difficult to improve one's income and educational attainment in the short run; socioeconomic improvement must frequently wait until the second or third generation*" (Jimeno, 2013).

Improving socio-economic conditions over several generations in the future is not sufficient for the people living now. Moreover, possible advancements for migrants' offspring may never materialize, depending on the socio-economic development in the destinations over the course of the century. Nevertheless, in the survey of the Marshallese community in Springdale, where the majority works in the poultry industry, many were content with their economic situation as it was (Jimeno, 2013). While in this study the new data was gathered on internal migration to Majuro, it is important to gain an understanding of the situation of the diaspora community in the US. Many migrants from the outer islands only go to Majuro to save enough money to eventually migrate to the US. Majuro is already densely populated and offers limited work opportunities; these are factors potentially causing further cascadal migration in the future.

As in the case of Bangladesh, those who migrated internally to the city (Majuro) did not necessarily avoid climate risks by relocating. Especially for low-income groups droughts can have severe consequences, even if imported food is available on the main island. The additional burden on the household income of having to purchase water during times of water scarcity can be significant: "[…] *there is a lot of urban poverty here. Even to pay for the taxi with your five gallons* [of water] *can be quite a stress,*" even though a taxi ride only costs between 0.5 and 1 USD (Expert Interview Majuro, Migration Expert). Moreover, in the urban centers Majuro and Kwajalein electricity consumption increases in times of drought which could be linked to the use of fans and air condition necessary in overcrowded concrete buildings. In a study of the 2015/2016 drought impacts it was found that "*a modest increase in per capita expenditure arising from the drought may coincide with declining levels of income arising from the same drought, and may result in a decline in overall personal well-being or quality of life*" (Leenders et al., 2017).

Migrant Livelihoods in Majuro

The type of jobs internal migrants could do in Majuro varied and often depended on the family connections they had. These family networks in the capital frequently provided them with a place to stay and a recommendation for employment, mostly in low-skilled labor. Often, people worked in the tuna industry, either at the tuna unloading station at the dock, or at the tuna factory where the fish was prepared for export. Within the tuna industry, there were different types of jobs like manual labor, cleaning and security tasks. Other migrants did not have a stable income and just did whatever temporary work they could find. Some could barely make a living and their overall economic situation worsened after their migration, as is described by this cleaner working at the tuna unloading factory: "*I earned more on the outer island, now I learn less.* […] [I work] *from eight in the morning until 10 p.m. No days off.* […] *Sometimes it is hard to put food on the table because of low income*" (Migrant Interview 1, Majuro). This person had no access to electricity and no access to improved sanitation such as toilets in his home.

Another cleaner working at the dock of the shipyard recounted: "*For working two weeks I get 280 US dollars. I work every day. I start between seven and eight and finish at night, eight or ten, depending on the work. Working in copra-making I earned more. This working here is much more physically harder*" (Migrant Interview 5, Majuro). This family had difficulties in finding employment in Majuro and was happy that one person had gotten a job as a cleaner, a job which supported a household of three. Although they wanted to go back to their place of origin, they evaluated the scope of opportunities in the urban area as more promising than the return to their home island from which people were moving away "because it is getting hot". Although there were other significant climate impacts on the place of origin of this migrant, he did not identify them as relevant.

It is important to take into account that in the small sample size some migrants also fared better after the migration compared to the strongly decreased economic opportunities of subsistence agriculture and copra- making in the outer islands. The juxtaposition of the cleaners with migrants who had found slightly more profitable jobs shows how livelihood opportunities strongly determine the migrants' evaluation of their migration outcome. It furthermore hints at general problems in the fishing business and in the case of the Marshall Islands the tuna industry which serves mostly industrialized countries and offers highly praised but often extremely low-paid jobs under difficult working conditions. It is not clear how people's working hours and conditions were determined and which agencies provided their contracts or were responsible for the labor standards. A 2018 study found that fishing in the high seas, which includes tuna fishing, is only viable economically because of heavy government subsidies (Sala et al., 2018). More than half of the industry would not operate without these subsidies, a fact which in combination with decreasing fish stocks points to the need of further research as well as improved governance and policy reform of the sector. Moreover, it has to be expected that there will be less work opportunities in the fishing industry, either due to urgently needed regulation of overfishing or because stocks will collapse in the future. Therefore, there will be fewer work options for migrants in Majuro if no alternative sources of livelihoods are created.

One migrant who had relocated to Majuro several years ago and now worked as a security guard explains: "*The living situation here is better than on the outer islands. The work here is less, we have good medical facilities, there are many places – you can never run out of food supplies. I have no problems here*" (Migrant Interview 2, Majuro). This excerpt again points to the fact that food security was a significant problem on the outer islands, resulting from the combined effects of climate impacts and seldom and unreliable sea transport. When asked whether environmental factors affected his home community on the outer island Wotje he replied:

"Respondent:	*Yes. Drought, less rainfall. I think that is the most severe effect on the community. It is really bad for agriculture, the plants die when the drought is around. But it is also good in a way that the disaster team comes in and the government brings in supplies and food for the people during the drought.*
Interviewer:	*Is this disaster relief now more often needed, have the droughts gotten worse?*
Respondent:	*Yes, it has increased.*
Interviewer:	*Why have they increased?*
Respondent:	*I have no information on that"* (Migrant Interview 2, Majuro).

Here the emphasis on the positive side of disaster relief can also be understood in the context of lacking support when there is no state of disaster. This is both connected to financial constraints and aid dependency of the Marshallese government and remoteness of the outer islands. Another migrant who had come from Ailuk atoll had found a job as packer in the fishing venture. His working conditions were significantly better than those of the cleaners working in the same environment. He had regulated hours, working from nine to five with one day off per week:

"Interviewer: *Which work is better?*
Respondent: *This current work. It is physically lighter.*
Interviewer: *How much money do you make compared to the copra production?*
Respondent: *Here I make more money.*
Interviewer: *Do you have to spend more money here or are the living-costs about the same?*
Respondent: *We spend more here than on the island.*
Interviewer: *But still you can save more?*
Respondent: *Yes"*
(Migrant Interview 7, Majuro).

However, even this person who evaluated his own economic situation as improved did not want to stay in Majuro:

"Interviewer: *For how long are you planning to stay here?*
Respondent: *I want to go back. It is better there. We have food, we have crops, we don't spend much money. We can live on the land"*
(Migrant Interview 7, Majuro).

The topic of living on the land is one that arose from several interviews and according to my interpretation the wish to return did not only refer to economic considerations. The Marshallese culture and tradition have formed around living from scarce land of a unique ecosystem. Leaving this land and abandoning the livelihood of agriculture means losing an important part of communal living. Another migrant also evaluated his living situation after the migration as positive because of an improved access to income:

"Interviewer: *What sort of work do you prefer, this type of work here as a carpenter, or back there in the copra production?*
Respondent: *It's better here.*
Interviewer: *Is this why you are staying now?*
Respondent: *Yes.*
Interviewer: *Because of more income?*

Respondent: *Yes, there is more earning here"* (Migrant Interview 4, Majuro).

This person did not have a stable income, but was working temporary jobs. However, because the income from copra- making had decreased significantly due to the effects of drought on the outer island Wotje, it was more economically rewarding for him to be in Majuro and take on temporary work. Nevertheless, it was clear that the household members were also longing for their homeland: "*Life is better on the island, on Wotje. The air is much cleaner and we can eat fish whenever you want, you can catch your own fish. Unlike on this island* [Majuro], *you don't fish a lot here*" (Migrant Interview 4, Majuro). Fishing herein not only refers to a livelihood or pass time, but is an important part of the Marshallese traditions and simply a 'way of life'. Loosing such activities means not only an economic but also a cultural crisis. Later in the interview, it became clear that the family was planning to migrate to Seattle (USA) where their son was already working on a fishing boat.

"Respondent: *The plan is for everyone to go.*
Interviewer: *Why?*
Respondent: *Life is difficult out here [in Majuro]"* (Migrant Interview 4, Majuro).

In many interviews, it is apparent that the situation in which migrants find themselves is conflicting. On the one hand, they want to return to their islands because even after years of absence it is still their home and the center of their culture. On the other hand, they do not see a feasible livelihood strategy for themselves and their family on the outer islands.

Loss of Culture

The challenges of land scarcity and natural disasters have always affected the Marshallese nation. Mobility and adaptation to the forces of nature are deeply engrained in their culture, a fact that is also captured in the poetry of the contemporary Marshallese lyric Kathy Jetñil-Kijiner. The daughter of Marshall Islands president Hilda Heine reflects in many of her writings about the Marshallese culture on the confluence of the two major outside pressures, the US nuclear legacy and the challenge of climate change. "S*everal of the poems in the collection celebrate Marshallese navigatory and seafaring traditions, signalling that migration and adaptation are central to Marshallese culture"* (Keown, 2017). However, it is clear that the character of today's outmigration is different from the migratory movements of the past. The anthropogenic changes in the atoll environment are happening at a much faster pace and affect more people than before. Even cultures that are generally well-positioned to innovate and cope with environmental stress, are unable to overcome technological and financial limits of in-situ adaptation. Already, Marshallese culture is under outside pressures and outmigration is not directed towards similar island settings, but rather imposes a complete shift to urban and nontraditional lifestyles. "*In addition, the migration of many Marshallese to the urban population centers of Majuro and Ebeye, and the consequent increased exposure to non-marshallese values and culture, have helped weaken the traditional cultural norms and organization that have been central to the society*" (Sharp et al., 2009). Climate change-driven migration, too, is a topic in Jetñil-Kijiner's poetry. As she writes in a poem to her daughter:

"They say you, your daughter
and your granddaughter, too
will wander rootless
with only a passport to call home
[…]
no one's drowning, baby
no one's moving
no one's losing
their homeland
no one's gonna become
a climate change refugee
or should i say
no one else
[…]" (Jetñil-Kijiner, 2014).

These lines of the poem which Jetnil-Kijiner performed at the UN Climate Summit in 2014 signal the danger of cultural loss associated with forced outmigration. One of the aspects which threaten the maintenance of cultural heritage is the degradation and disappearance of land. Land holds an important value in Marshallese culture and traditions: *Land tenure in the Marshall Islands is customary; land is not viewed as interchangeable real estate, but instead as a foundation of national, cultural and personal identity and spirit*" (Muller, 2009). Relocation severs the immediate ties with the land, an issue that has also been addressed by the migrants who had relocated to Majuro:

"Interviewer: *When you plan your future where do you want to live, here or in Namu [the migrant's home island]?*
Respondent: *Namu. It's my place and I have to go back to look over my land"*
(Migrant Interview 8, Majuro).

Another migrant described the need to return to his homeland:

"Respondent: *I don't think that the people need to move away from their islands. For myself, I am moving in here to work, but I always hope to go back to my island.*
Interviewer: *To visit or you want to go back permanently?*
Respondent: *As a Marshallese I will always end up on my own island"*
(Migrant Interview 5, Majuro).

While it is clear that even internal migration from the outer islands to the urbanized atolls can mean significant change and impede the continuation of cultural practices, relocation to the United States amounts to more drastic lifestyle changes. The ambassador and permanent representative of the Marshall Island's permanent mission to the United Nations wrote in his statement on climate change and security to the UN General Assembly: "*Outmigration to the United States (under the Compact of Free Association) has, as a general trend, brought some negative cultural impacts, although many migrants take advantage of positive economic and education opportunities in the US*" (Muller, 2009). This assessment is also reflected in the expert interviews. Many experts saw community disintegration and cultural loss as negative effects of migration as a response to climate change: "[…] *people are losing their culture out there. Their own culture and the custom of togetherness*" (Expert Interview Majuro, Community Expert 1). The issue of shifting from family networks and a strong sense of community to a society where this loyalty is often restrained to the nuclear family can pose significant challenges. One is the absence of the social net combined with cultural loss: "[On the Marshall Islands] *you don't have to worry too much because you know your family will be there for you.* […] *How is it there? It's one man for himself. Some families do help each other out, but it doesn't look like culture is practiced well out there with regards to helping each other. All the other culture and customs they don't know anymore. Those that are born and raised out there because of the migration. They don't know anymore*" (Expert Interview Majuro, Community Expert 1).

The other issue is that the new arrivals from the outer islands may be accustomed to a social setting where crime rates are low and people trust one another. This attitude may be misleading in foreign countries when migrants do not question dubious business proposals or ill-intentioned offers of support from strangers. Some become dependent on social welfare systems. Assimilating into an entirely different culture can be a challenge in itself: *"They have to adjust to the livelihood out there, the environment in the US. And some of them, they cope, and some of them, they don't cope really well"* (Expert Interview Majuro, Community Expert 1). Many continue to want to return to their homeland: "*Even if they're over in the US, they still feel like they belong to the Marshall Islands* […] *that is really special.* […] *Even if some people are moving, it might be because they think this is the best option for them and their family at that time, but not necessarily because they want to, per se* […]. *They are not necessarily happy*" (Expert Interview Majuro, Migration Expert).

Additional stress comes from the fact that once people relocate, it is very difficult for those who do not earn high wages to visit relatives back home. This holds true even for those who relocated to Hawai'i. There is only one commercial airline operating between the US (Hawai'i) and the Marshall Islands, hence the airfare costs are high. In many cases, people are unable to return, or visit only for very special family occasions. Many Marshallese respondents indicated the detrimental effects of outmigration on their ability to practice culture or to pass it on to their offspring. Some who had relocated did not have sufficient information about their destination to oversee the implications of their migration. It also became clear that many would have preferred to stay. An involuntary outmigration because of climate change impacts would therefore violate the cultural rights of the Marshallese. One woman on the outer islands describes her fears in connection with the possible relocation to the United States: "*Look at our handicrafts, I will lose these skills, because all the raw materials, they don't have them there! They don't have coconut trees out there, palm trees are different from ours. There they don't have Pandanus trees* [...]. *I will lose my skills. And then I will lose my food. It is part of my culture. Everything is the culture.* [...] *I will never be an American*" (Expert Interview Majuro, Policy Maker).

Loss of Identity

"I am not scared to go down the sea. I am scared to move there and be nobody" (Expert reports a woman's story on the outer islands. Expert Interview Majuro, Policy Maker).

Connected with the effects of migration on the practice of culture is the individual's identity. The potential fragmentation of identity through the relocation has emerged as a factor which people consider detrimental to the effectiveness of outmigration. One expert recounted a meeting with women on the outer islands who had received information about the decision of the government of Kiribati to purchase land in Fiji for future resettlement in response to rising sea levels. They were asked whether they would want to migrate in the long term because many Marshallese were already moving. "*They looked so sad. One of them said: No way, I don't care if I go under the sea! But I'll remain here! [...] I said: 'Why?' She said: If I moved to US - Who would I be? They don't have coconut trees! They don't have Pandanus trees! They don't have our fish! They have theirs but they don't taste like ours. I would... I will have no identity.*" (Expert Interview Majuro, Policy Maker). For those women the factor of identity and belonging outweighed possible economic benefits of relocation: "*We don't care about air condition, we don't care about luxury cars, those are not ours. We enjoy our clean trees, our environment. All we need sometimes, is just a little piece of soap to clean ourselves, we have what we need: Our breadfruit, pandanus trees and the fish, the food from the ocean*" (Expert Interview Majuro, Policy Maker). The topic not only emerged from the expert interviews, but also from the interviews with migrants who had only relocated within the Marshall Islands. One migrant who had moved to Majuro explains the necessary separation from his children:

"*Respondent:*	*The plan is that the children will go back to Ailinglaplap and I will work here to provide for them. The children will be staying with their aunties and my sisters.*
Interviewer:	*Why do you want to send them back?*
Respondent:	*They need to learn how to live as Marshallese Islanders, our livelihood there, culture and customs. And the best way to do it is to bring them back to the island*" (Migrant Interview 5, Majuro).

Herein the emphasis on "living as Marshallese Islanders" is significant and links back to the issue of identity. The person wants to provide his children with a sense of belonging to his home island and to become familiar with traditions, in order to strengthen the part of their identity as Marshallese Islanders. To achieve this, he is willing to accept the separation from his children and perhaps even dismiss better formal schooling for them.

Health

While migrants had better access to healthcare after relocation to Majuro, they also experienced new health risks of both communicable and non-communicable diseases. When asked about her living situation, one migrant reported that they do not face real problems in Majuro. She explained that in Majuro access to quality education for her children and access to medical care were much better than on Arno. Nevertheless the woman remarked:

"*Respondent:* *Life is better in Arno. Life is good, you don't get sick a lot.*
Interviewer: *Here you get sick a lot?*
Respondent: *Yes.*
Interviewer: *And what sort of sickness?*
Respondent: *Coughing, pink eye. It's dirty and just too many people*" (Migrant Interview 3, Majuro).

In the overcrowded urban centers, outbreaks of communicable diseases are a risk, especially when access to freshwater for sanitation is limited in times of drought. For example, in 2000 / 2001 there was a severe cholera outbreak in Ebeye which then spread to Lae. The population on Ebeye and Majuro continues to grow and water stress could get more severe due to more frequent droughts and overuse. This in turn could enhance the risk of outbreaks of communicable diseases. Non-communicable diseases, such as diabetes, hypertension or obesity, can also be health risk factors of migrants who relocate from rural to urban settings and from traditionally more physically active to sedentary lifestyles. In Majuro, integrating physical activity into commuting routines is difficult because of a lack of walkways and cycle paths alongside the major road. Increasing levels of coastal pollution make swimming less attractive. A study in Fiji, Kiribati and Vanuatu showed that "*Rural subjects were leaner, suffered less from diabetes and hypertension, and had greater total energy intakes than urban dwellers*" (Taylor et al., 1992). The Republic of the Marshall Islands has the fourth highest obesity rate worldwide with more than half of the population suffering from a body mass index[7] equal or larger than 30 (CIA World Factbook, 2017b). This high rate is a consequence of the loss of local food production, heavy reliance on processed food imports, changes in lifestyles and increasing urbanization. One migrant addressed the issue of food quality when asked about health problems:
"*Interviewer:* *Do you have health problems here?*

[7] An adult with a body mass index between 18.5 to 24.9 is considered to be normal weight, whereas a body mass index of 30 indicates obesity (WHO, 2018).

Respondent: *The food is not so good here, I get sick.*
Interviewer: *How was the food in Namu?*
Respondent: *Very good*"
(Migrant Interview 8, Majuro).

Also relocation to the United States does not necessarily mean an improvement in the overall health of the individual, although much better healthcare is available to those who can afford it. While the data collection of migrant interviews was limited to internal migration in this research, there is literature on the health situation of the general Marshallese diaspora in the United States. For example, in a study of the Marshallese diaspora in Hawai'i it was found that the group is particularly vulnerable to "dual epidemics" of both communicable and non-communicable diseases (Choi, 2008). Hirata (2015) concludes: "*Despite moving to the United States for better healthcare, among other benefits, Marshallese Compact of Free Association (COFA) migrants residing in Springdale, Arkansas continue to face similar acute health problems as Marshallese living in the Republic of the Marshall Islands (RMI), and often without access to health services.*"

In fact, those migrating internationally to the US with insufficient financial resources have difficulties in seeking healthcare as there are restrictions to access of Medicaid healthcare programs (Hirata, 2015). Unlike other legal immigrants, Marshallese who migrated under the Compact of Free Association, including children and elderly, cannot access Medicaid, unless they meet certain requirements in their employment history. This is due to their special immigrant status as "lawfully present," which is different from other immigrant statuses. But they can purchase the government healthcare. They qualify to receive medical insurance under the affordable care act (Obamacare), a government healthcare program that has been put into question by the current US administration of President Donald Trump. As an example of the healthcare situation of the Marshallese diaspora, the report on the Marshallese community in Springdale, Arkansas, found that 63% of the community had health insurance and less than half of that group was satisfied with it, partially due to high costs (Jimeno, 2013).

Overall, the assessment of the aspect of health with regard to migration effectiveness underlines the complexity of the causal networks linking the three elements of climate change, migration and health. Climate change effects on health can be a push factor for outmigration because migrants seek a better health care system than that found in the Marshall Islands, or try to avoid health risks like malnutrition. Concurrently, while migration was discussed as improving migrant's health care options at times, it simultaneously increased exposure or vulnerability to both communicable and non-communicable diseases.

Self-Determination & Knowledge

The internal migration in the Marshall Islands is influenced by a variety of push and pull factors, such as climate change impacts on natural resources and therefore livelihoods as well as opportunities in the urban areas. Insofar, the topic of self-determination relates to the question of whether migration is voluntary and if people want to stay in the places of destination. There is some evidence that suggests that part of the population is trapped at their destination. One expert explains: "*They go out there and find out that it is hard and some of them want to come back, but the airline ticket is not getting cheaper. It gets very expensive. To save money for that is very hard because you work a full job just to feed your family, not to make extra money.* [...] *And most of the time it is one way out*" (Expert Interview Majuro, Community Expert 2). Besides the costs for return, increasing climate impacts and the further deterioration of ecosystem services on the outer islands can also be factors which prevent or at least deter people from going back. As already mentioned in the subchapters on cultural loss, many feel conflicted between having to stay in order to make a living on the one hand and returning to their homeland and place of culture on the other hand:

"*Respondent:* *We want to go back.*
Interviewer: *Why do you stay now?*
Respondent: *I am working and trying to sustain the livelihood of my family here*"
(Migrant Interview 1, Majuro).

Another family exclaimed: "*We are waiting for an opportunity to go back*" (Migrant Interview 4, Majuro).

The topic of knowledge about rule of law in the destination places in order to avoid detrimental migration outcomes arose from several interviews and conversations. One expert explains: "*Those families that are migrating have so many issues. When they go they're running through so many problems.* [...] *I see so many people with so many issues, when they move they didn't understand. They don't understand the system. And they, from the way I see them, they are really not living well. They are not happy. Many of our people, they get into trouble and put in jail*" (Expert Interview Majuro, Policy Maker). The last sentence refers to the problem of people not adhering to the law in the US. This may happen without ill-intentions. Some crimes are hardly persecuted in the Marshall Islands such as driving under the influence, whereas in the United States this offence can amount to a felony if it happens repeatedly or causes harm to another person. Moreover, resulting from a shift from rural settings on a remote island to urban settings and high teenage pregnancy rates, the issue of child neglect arose. While it may be normal to leave children not closely attended on a rural island where a tightly knit community watches over the village children, the same parental absence in an urban setting can be viewed – and persecuted – as child neglect. This example again highlights that the relocation from one social system to another can pose significant challenges. Some of these challenges could be overcome if people were given information and trainings prior to departure, so that they could determine the outcome of their migration.

Insights into the Migrants' Social System

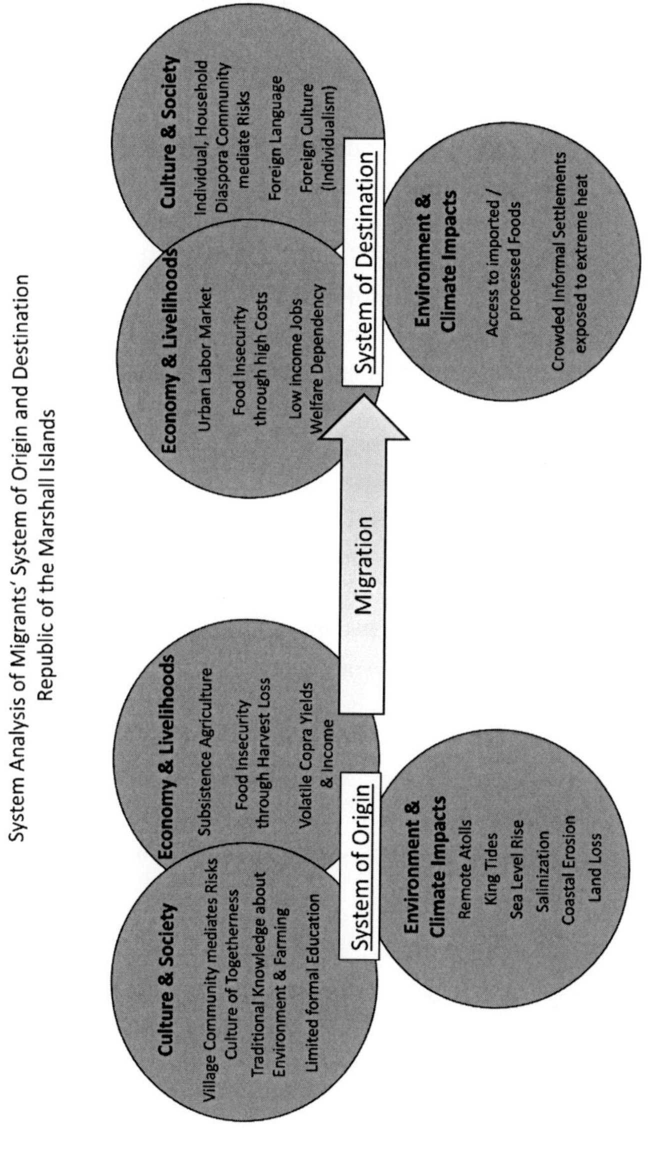

Figure 19 System Analysis of Migrants' System of Origin and Destination, Marshall Islands (source: own).

System of Origin

From the analysis of the data from the Marshall Islands also surfaces the composition of the system of origin from which the individuals migrate to another system. Maybe even stronger than in the case of Bangladesh are the people's ties to the land. As mentioned above, land is not only important for agricultural use, but is a reference point of traditions and culture. This is amplified by the scarcity and therefore high value of land and by the unique geographical setting of the Marshall Islands. On the outer islands people work in traditional agriculture. The community is an important entity to mediate risks, a social net, providing assistance to those in need. This finding was emphasized in many interviews. As in Bangladesh, people have accumulated knowledge about the land and about agriculture over generations. However, through outside influences and climate change impacts the dependency on foreign goods, such as imported food and concrete, is increasing. This development has already edged out traditional practices like weaving or wood construction, although some people and associations are trying to revive them. Due to the remoteness of the outer islands from trade and transport lines and its basic isolation from telephone and internet services, the access to knowledge is limited to radio services and infrequent visits of outside agencies and relatives. It is unquestionable that the effects of climate change on soils and coral reefs cannot be managed with the set of traditional knowledge because these rapid environmental degradations are beyond people's experience or the delivered knowledge of what has occurred before. The social system on the outer islands is still largely governed by a traditional system of chiefs, complemented by elected mayors who usually spend most of the year in Majuro and not on the respective outer island.

System of Destination

From the described system of origin people migrate first to Majuro and then often to the United States. Even the internal migration is a shift from rural to urban settings and many are not well prepared for it. They often do not have the skills or education to find good work opportunities. Another problem, especially for migrants who only have basic education from the outer islands, is learning a foreign language. Their chances in the job market are therefore limited to what their social network can provide. Moreover, in the urban settings, particularly when moving abroad, family and community may play less of a central role than before in the rural areas. Also, the social and cultural norms that the migrants are familiar with, such as deep responsibility for one another and a forgiving approach to misdemeanors, do not necessarily apply in the community of destination. This in turn may create friction and even cause some people to get into conflict with the law. Correspondingly, the identity of the people may not be recognized at the place of destination. For example, the skills of a handicraft producer or a lagoon fisherman may be very difficult to transfer into settings in Oklahoma or Arkansas and hence also recognition for being a fisherman or handicraft producer would lack. The system of destination in the United States is one of a free market economy, where there is little governmental social security for those in need. Services have to be bought and wages for those who have only a basic education and are working in production lines are quite low. Both transitions from internal and international migration are occurring relatively smoothly because of the social networks in the places of destination which provide assistance to new arrivals. But during this transition to the system of destination the fragmentation of identities, the destruction of culture through foreign influences and the lack of agency to counteract these processes negatively affect wellbeing. These challenges may only be overcome in second or third generations, which then in turn may no longer have deep cultural ties to the Marshall Islands.

Effectiveness of Migration as Adaptation for Sending Communities

On the outer islands outmigration due to climate impacts has led to negative effects, such as the shrinking of the work force and interlinked challenges for the community, as well as some limited positive effects, like moderate remittances and the reduction of pressure on resources. It is important to understand that the outer island communities are faced with different socio-economic and climate-related challenges than those on the urbanized atolls of Majuro or Kwajalein. Ailuk and Maloelap, where interviews were held, are remotely located atolls of the Northern Islands / Ratak Chain. During World War II, Maloelap was one of the headquarters of the

Japanese occupation force in the Marshall Islands and the physical remains of bunkers, supply ships and war machinery can still be found. Maloelap consists of 71 islands of which five are inhabited. Ailuk atoll consists of 57 islands and was a trading post of the German Empire in the late 19th century. The population on the two outer islands has been shrinking in the last decades, with an average growth rate of -3.5% per annum in Ailuk, the highest decline within the Marshall Islands and -1.9% per annum in Maloelap. Whereas the population grew in both locations between 1988 and 1999, it fell in the period from 1999 to 2011 (Secretariat of the Pacific Community, 2012). This pattern is representative of the population change in other outer islands in the Republic. In 2011 Ailuk had a population of 339 and Maloelap of 682. Migration contributes to this dynamic of a shrinking population. For example, between 2006 and 2011, 132 people left Ailuk while only 44 migrated there. In this time period Maloelap received slightly more people than had left the island; however, in most outer islands outmigration was higher than immigration. During the course of the interviews, people had suggested there was an increased outmigration over the period from 2012 to 2017, but there is no recent census data available which would cover this period.

Remittances

Taking an economic perspective, some families in sending communities benefited from the migration of their relatives because they received remittances. Remittances are often used for special occasions, festivities or funerals, but also just to buy food. Especially in times of drought and scarcity remittances can be an important enabler to secure sufficient amounts of alimentation. The sum of remittances sent varies strongly between families. For some it is a regular substantial source of finance: "*The migrants support the community. Each month or every second month they send between 100 to 200 dollars. It goes to the families to buy food and supplies. The islands in the north don't produce a lot of copra. On the average a copra maker earns about 100 dollar per month*" (Ailuk Interview 10). Others only received occasional support. The difficult economic situation of many migrants in Majuro and the US is reflected in the often limited remittances they can provide: "*They do send assistance but very rarely. If they* [the sending community] *ask for it they are sending money. But it is no great help"* (Maloelap Interview 2). One expert explains the different financial effects of migration: *"Usually they* [the migrants] *apply for a job as helper to feed their families or they are in the copra business, some run for office in the government, some who go to the US they come back, but some never think back, think about their family or friend or other copra makers"* (Expert Interview Majuro, Traditional Leader). Overall, personal remittances make out 14.76% of the country's GDP (The World Bank, 2017a). This is a substantial share; however, much of the non-environmentally driven migration, such as migration for education, may lead to more prosperous employment opportunities and therefore can generate more remittances. Based on the interviews, I interpret that climate migration often leads into low-skilled labor and therefore is a source of only moderate remittances.

While remittances can certainly help communities to become more resilient, they need to be used efficiently to foster a sustainable development. Otherwise, remittances from increased outmigration may also contribute to the increase of a community's dependency. Such financial flows can even be detrimental to long-term development. With regard to dependency on government and foreign aid one expert remarked that the focus should lie on improved self-sufficiency: *"Outside aid has caused people to become so ineffective in sustaining themselves. Planting more food sources and to maintaining the resources from the ocean, we can stop overfishing and* [practice] *more conservation"* (Expert Interview Majuro, Community Expert 1). One respondent on Ailuk summarizes the situation as follows: "*The good thing is if we need assistance they can always provide us from abroad. The bad thing is there are less people here to work*" (Ailuk Interview 14).

Reduction of Pressure on the Land & Shrinking Workforce

An outmigration from the outer islands reduces the pressure on the terrestrial resources of these atolls. This was mentioned as a positive aspect of migration by several respondents: *"More people will be migrating. In a way it's good, land and spaces open up for people to use. On the other hand it is sad that people are leaving the islands to live abroad, there are already empty houses"* (Ailuk Interview 12). However, as indicated in this interview excerpt, too, the increased outmigration during the past five to ten years is posing challenges to the community: "*I see problems with the migration. When people are going there is nobody to look after their place. There are not enough people to help each other*" (Ailuk Interview 10). This view was also shared by other respondents: *"Migration is a huge problem. There are not enough people to work together on huge tasks, communal tasks"* (Ailuk Interview 13). Overall, the diminishment of the workforce through increased outmigration is already negatively affecting agricultural production: "*The migration has a huge impact on the community. In terms when we need to do some communal projects we need people. There are areas where we need to plant food crops, but there are not many people to help and that does affect the people in the community*" (Maloelap Interview 2). At the same time, it can be assumed that moderate outmigration leads to less pressure on scarce land. However, if resources continue to diminish because of climate change, more people may decide to move out for both push and pull factors. In turn too few people of working age will foster the agricultural production generating even less food crops. If there is no management of the cumulative effects of climate change driven resource depletion and outmigration this dynamic could lead to an accelerated complete outmigration, already before the islands become technically uninhabitable.

Social Effects

The shrinking of the workforce is also viewed to cause fragmentation of the community. Several perceptions arose from the interviews linking migration to unspecified negative effects on the community: "*We worked together and helped each other. This is affected now*" (Ailuk Interview 8). I interpret this statement to hint at how the increased outmigration has started to challenge the culture of togetherness. The combination of a shrinking workforce, limited remittances and increasing climate impacts can create a living situation that poses overwhelming tasks to the village. One community expert explains different behaviors of migrants: *"I can see two types of people, one who thinks, maybe this is the way of life, other people who see what is happening. They come and search for answers from the government, NGOs, any advisors. So they go back and help their people. Some of them run away. They move from there completely, they are migrating from this country to find a better place where they can enjoy* [life]*"* (Expert Interview, Chief of the Northern Islands). We observed that in many cases men migrated from the outer islands to find alternative sources of income when the copra harvest was low. One expert working with the women's organization WUTMI (Women United Together Marshall Islands) explains the effects of migration on women in the sending communities:

"*Respondent:* *So many men, fathers, left, they moved to the States...so they can go and find jobs. And leave the mother and the children. [...]*

Interviewer: *And how are the families doing? The woman, children, elderly who are left there?*

Respondent: *More problem for them. [...] Because when the parents left, the father left to the US, the mother moved here [to Majuro]. [...] And then the kids live with the grandparents*"
(Expert Interview Majuro, Policy Maker).

The population reduction on the outer islands may also lead to secondary negative consequences, namely more foreign influence, as some leaders in the outer islands fear:

"*Respondent:* *Perhaps people from outside will come and buy the land which the migrants left behind.*

Interviewer: *Has this happened before?*

Respondent: *I have heard from other places where they have sold their lands to foreigners from a different country. I feel this will have a negative influence on tradition, livelihood and culture. [...] They are not here [on Ailuk] yet but. in Majuro and some other islands. I think that in 20 years it may be the same case everywhere else.*

Interviewer: *Can anything be done to avoid this?*

Respondent: *I am very concerned about people coming in and utilize this land for their own benefits and not for the communities. To avoid this there should be some platforms for local governments to constrict buying ownership of lands, especially for tourists coming in who do not believe in God. The culture and customs here are very well tied to spirituality, to God [...] they might invest into something totally different that might have negative impacts on the community. For example a casino... then they would not co-exist with the community very well. The moral of the people will suffer*"
(Ailuk Interview 12, councilman).

Considering existing problems with human trafficking and organized crime in the Marshall Islands, in addition to practices of land grabbing by countries like China, the concerns of this councilman are not unaccounted for.

Self-Determination

Also in the sending communities the climate change-related obstacles to self-determination became apparent. One respondent describes this: "*Some would like to stay here, but they would need some assistance to maintain their livelihood*" (Ailuk Interview 10). In fact, many people emphasized that they preferred to stay on the outer islands:

"*Interviewer:* *Do you want to stay here?*
Respondent: *Yes. People want to stay, but sometimes they are forced to move*"
(Ailuk Interview 13).

Leaders in the villages anticipated further involuntary outmigration in the coming decades due to climate change impacts if in-situ adaptation is not adequately financed and improved. "*If it continues to be like this in the future with no possible changes, then yes, people will have to consider migration as their best option. I believe more people will have to move, especially those living near the coastal areas because of erosions. As for me, I still have enough food resources. I even provide foods to those living near the coastal areas when their food crops have been damaged*" (Ailuk Interview 16). To achieve self-determination, the ability to stay in the face of climate impacts should be considered a positive freedom (Berlin, 2006), meaning it may require active outside measures, for example by a government. In the case of the Marshall Islands, the ability to stay could be enhanced by providing sufficient funds to enable people to adapt to changing climate conditions: "*If we really help them, people will stay*" (Expert Interview Majuro, Policy Maker).

Knowledge

In many interviews the topic of knowledge arose. Although more interviewees than in the Bangladesh interviews had heard about the term climate change, many respondents from the migrant and sending community groups could explain why the climate is changing. The lack of knowledge about climate change puts many local leaders on the outer islands in the difficult position of having to make decisions for their people without knowing the reasons behind climate change and the projections of its future impacts on their islands. As one local leader describes: "*It* [coastal erosion and inundation] *has intensified and is causing major damages to coastal areas due to the occurrence of recent but frequent king tides. Thing is I do not know why this is happening; I, too, need help to understand why this is happening*" (Ailuk Interview 16). The situation of leaders on the outer islands, trying to manage foreign influences without access to information on the state of affairs, bears resemblance to the situation of the Bikinian Chief being forced to agree to the outmigration of his people, without fully understanding the circumstances.

However, with regard to knowledge, there is also hope among leaders that migration may increase the availability and accessibility of knowledge and skills. Some mentioned the possible positive effects of return migration which could bring people with higher education and skills back to the islands. The chief of the northern islands responded when asked how he felt about the migration: "*There is no problem with* [the migration] *because life is getting hard. For me as a leader I cannot lead everybody perfectly, I cannot provide what they need...I never ask people why they leave the area* […]. *We as leaders are not really holding them, keep them, we give them freedom. Perhaps one day they will come back* […] *and bring back what they know, what they learned, how they lived there and then invest* [/share] *it with other local people*" (Expert Interview Majuro, Traditional Leader).

Effectiveness of Migration as Adaptation for Receiving Communities

While the effects of migration on the receiving communities were not the focus of this field research, it is important to mention possible limits of resettlement as an adaptation strategy with regard to the situation in the receiving communities. Although the culture of hospitality and family networks prevails, it is clear that the city of Majuro is already under population pressure. The urban growth has both negative and positive aspects: "*More people* [means] *more money for the shops.* […] *For Majuro people it is good. For the local government and the national government it is not so good. They have to accommodate us, accommodate all these people coming in.* […] *There is limited space and limited resources*" (Expert Interview Majuro, Community Expert 1). Already today, providing adequate housing, sanitation and health facilities is a challenge. The city administrator of Majuro elaborates this point: "*We are having a lot of problems. As I said, there are good things and there are bad things... Good things are, people are migrating here, not from the Outer Islands only, but from the other countries and bring might for the economy. But some bring more problems. We don't have enough money to take care of everyone here*" (Expert Interview City Administrator). However, the migration to the urban centers in the Marshall Islands is likely to continue. Some atolls already have only small aging populations and the degradation may push more people out. This would pose significant challenges to Majuro since the island is also affected by droughts and sea level rise.

"*Respondent:* *I don't think the government will be able to accommodate the rest of the population [...] in the future. Like ten years from now. With all these limited resources, withall these constraints to livelihood and to better living, health care, schooling, better schooling, and especially to sustain the livelihoods of our culture and customs, people would be more inclined to go out, I think. [...]*

Interviewer: *How do you think environmental factors will play into this?*

Respondent: *Environmental factors will expedite the process. Because everything is depleting, all our waters are being, ground water is being salinized and we used to use our ground water very abundantly [...]. Today [...] we have to bring in desalinization systems because [the freshwater] is not drinkable anymore*"
(Expert Interview Majuro, Community Expert 1).

Currently, the urbanization and economic progress on the Marshall Islands is concentrated on few islands. Instead of a polycentric development, in which the outer islands were well-connected through sea transport, a further concentration of resources, opportunities and people is occurring. There are no ambitious counterincentives to this direction of development, except for subsidies of the price of copra. An acceleration process of outmigration could put an extreme stress on the city of Majuro and further a cascadal outmigration to the United States. This again could be detrimental to the preservation of traditions, language and the 'culture of togetherness'.

7.8. Synergetic System Analysis

On the basis of the field research and the pertinent literature (figure 20) an overview of the most important impacts of climate change with regard to migration and the resulting cultural and political effects can also be made for the Marshall Islands like in the case study of Bangladesh. The schematic summary shows the following dynamics. The accumulation of CO_2 in the atmosphere leads not only to an increase in mean temperature and sea level rise but also to ocean acidification, which are all affecting the Marshall Islands (1). Ocean acidification and warming are causing the degradation of the coral reef ecosystem. Inundations which are driven further inland by sea level rise and frequent droughts salinize the soils and limit plant growth, decreasing biodiversity. Heat stress too is a problem on the islands with their limited access to electricity (2). Droughts affect agricultural productivity and the degradation of coral reefs disrupts food networks in the ocean, leading to fewer catches in proximity of the atolls. This process threatens food and water security, with negative repercussions for human livelihoods and health (3). Pressure on livelihoods together with the prospect of better employment opportunities contribute to the outmigration from outer island atolls to the capital Majuro and the United States. The transition from the system of origin to the system of destination can cause a fragmentation of the migrants' identities. In the remaining communities on the outer islands traditional agriculture and fishery that are at the core of Marshallese culture, no longer provide sufficient alimentation (4). This in turn increases the dependency on aid and food imports. In the destinations alienation of migrants from the receiving community and culture may foster seclusion of this community from other parts of society (5). While the social capital of the diaspora community can help with the orientation at the destination and provide assistance in finding employment, seclusion from other parts of society may in the long term limit opportunities for upward mobility.

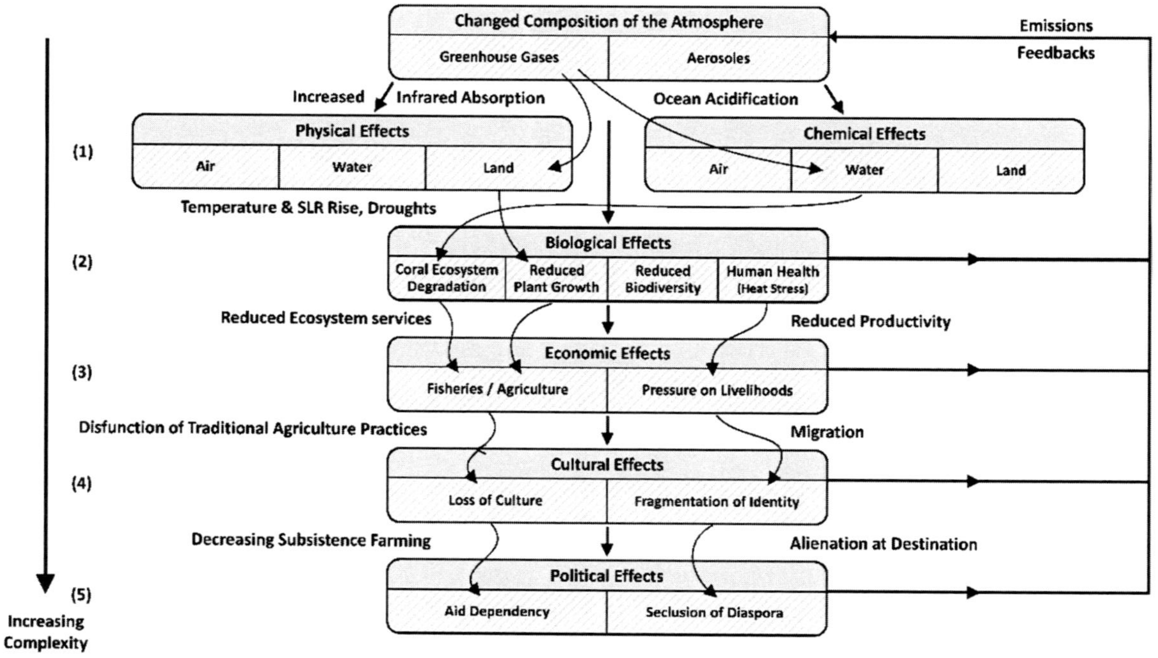

Figure 20 Synergetic System Analysis of Climate Change and Migration in the Republic of the Marshall Islands (source: own, based on Schellnhuber, 2015)

The social group identified in the Bangladesh case study of subsistence farmers who carry over their structurally-determined vulnerability to the places of destination was also found in the Marshall Islands case study. This group included traditional fishermen and subsistence farmers. As their agriculture and water security are dependent on rain, these farmers do not have many options to cope with extreme and even multi-year droughts or coral bleaching events leading to diminishing fish stocks in lagoons. Besides subsistence farming, many residents on the outer islands produced copra for export and therefore already formed part of global value chains. Because the price for copra fluctuates at a very low level, they were dependent on price subsidies by the government and did not benefit substantially from being part of a globalized market.

The factor of remoteness on the outer islands strongly limits access to information both on climate change and migration options. Even if people had access to information, they generally did not have the knowledge to process and evaluate the information for effective decision-making. The group of traditional farmers on the Marshall Islands bears the characteristic of having good basic education levels, but constrained access to (English-based) information and higher education. When people of the group of subsistence farmers or fishermen migrated internationally to the United States, their educational levels and language barriers prevented them from taking up skilled labor.

Again women form a subgroup to this, as their social status may be relegated by relocation. Without a larger family network, women can particularly suffer from alienation if they cannot work outside their own homes. Moreover, different types of stressors can increase domestic violence, to which women are particularly exposed. Moreover, if a large group of working-age individuals leaves the outer islands, women may have to take on more physical labor than before in the sending communities.

Also children were particularly affected by relocations. A change from rural to urban surroundings often meant that their usual social circle did no longer exist in the urban settings. The outer islands provided a safe space for children to be on their own, whereas children without parental supervision in urban settings could be exposed to exploitation. Moreover, children on the outer islands built up agency by obtaining traditional knowledge and taking on responsibilities in caring for the land or participating in practices of fishing and sailing. These types of agency-building activities are not transferable to other geographic and cultural contexts.

Because much of the fieldwork took place in the sending communities, another social group was identified in the research. This group is made up of people who were part of the middle or upper class and had family members who had a college education and / or mid- to high level government jobs. People in this group migrated internationally for educational purposes or improved employment opportunities. Members of this group, who lived in Majuro, also observed the changes in the environment and the shrinking possibility of continuing traditional lifestyles on the outer islands. At the same time, this group was not being directly pushed out by the effects of climate change, which is why the investigation of this group was not the focus of this study. Nevertheless, the observations and interviews suggest that this group is able to succeed after their relocation in finding better income opportunities and receiving good access to education and healthcare.

While the climate migration patterns of the Marshall Islands occur in completely different contexts than in Bangladesh, the previous finding that the vulnerability of certain groups continues in the destination places is confirmed in this case. Moreover, there is further supporting evidence of the effect of structural disparities limiting human agency of vulnerable groups in the face of climate change. This case study underlines that the effects of migration are not only economic, but also social or cultural. When people migrate, their immediate social capital is lost and a destruction of the social system takes place both in the sending communities as well as for the migrants in the receiving community.

7.9. Discussion of Results

"*We believe the more informed we are the more empowered we are*" (Expert Interview Majuro, Policy Maker).

In brief, the migration from the outer islands to the urbanized capital Majuro and the United States, has brought moderate economic relief to some migrants and sending communities, but is causing systemic problems of disintegration from and of Marshallese culture and traditions, as well as a perpetuation of food insecurity and dependency in the outer islands. To expand on this, the economic situation of migrants was in general more stable than that of the sending communities in the outer islands. Those migrants interviewed were able to receive a more regular income, compared to the volatile earnings in the climate change-affected copra production and traditional agriculture. Moreover, many sending communities reported that migrants had found work in the United States and had sent moderate amounts of remittances, a fact also reflected in the literature. However, at the same time, these jobs were often low-wage work with little upward mobility. It is problematic to fully assess the economic situation in the climate change-affected communities before the impact occurred because the outer islands are based on a subsistence farming economy. Therefore, it is difficult to ground the assessment of effectiveness on the comparison of the economic situation of places of origin and destination, as the self-sustenance of the outer islands economy cannot be valued in financial terms. Thus the loss of traditional farming practices and the fragmentation of identity have to be taken into consideration, too. Through the interviews it came out that the migration is causing a substantial shift in the migrants' life from the system of origin, a tightly knit rural village community with traditions based on the land and natural environment that has developed relatively isolated, to a system of destination that is urban, globalized and marked by a culture of individualism and a free market economy. Often, migrants are ill-equipped to manage these substantial shifts in the culture and the social system because they do not have the skills or knowledge needed in the places of destination. This shift also means that some traditions, especially those tied to the land itself, cannot be continued after relocation. On the side of the sending communities the aid dependency is increased by the decline of the agricultural workforce, together with more severe climate impacts and foreign influence. The growing outmigration is viewed as a problem by many and is causing cultural disruptions, as is described in chapter 7.7.

The case of the Marshall Islands must be seen in the context of forced migration because the climate impacts may become so severe already by the middle of the century that complete outmigration may be the only adaptation strategy (Storlazzi et al., 2018). Under this scenario, researching the question on effectiveness of migration is even more important in order to identify how the ongoing climate migration and potential future migrations may be shaped to turn out to be more effective. Since forced and sudden migration as adaptation or survival strategies seem to be the least effective forms of migration, communities and individuals need to be agents of change. In the interviews two problems surfaced which have so far limited the agency of the climate impact-affected communities. The first reason is a lack of knowledge about climate change, which was also identified as a vulnerability factor in the Bangladesh case study. The research on the Marshall Islands shows that it is very difficult to manage the slow-onset environmental degradation on the outer islands if the drivers are not known. The lack of in-situ adaptation options and alternative livelihoods in turn lead to involuntary outmigration. Knowledge about the reasons for migration, including climate change impacts, is still missing: "*We need to make people more aware of the impacts and why they are leaving*" (Expert Interview Community Expert 1). There is a small, but growing body of research on climate impacts on small islands in the Pacific. A key problem is the lack of local climate research in many of the small island states. When most of the research is done in foreign countries, it can create less of an impact within communities than information which comes from local researchers who could communicate findings more effectively. As Woodward et al. describe: "*When problems are defined by outsiders in foreign and inaccessible terms, those directly affected cannot participate in seeking solutions*" (Woodward et al., 1998). Often, there are obstacles to the dissemination of knowledge and information does not reach outer island communities. "*Climate change is really in the mind of the Marshallese people. But we don't know how to deal with it because we don't have the skills and knowledge to deal with it. But we know it is affecting the Marshall Islands. We need people who have the skill and the knowledge so we can achieve risk reduction*" (Expert Interview, Majuro City Administrator). Saroar & Routray (2010) furthermore find that climate awareness can positively influence in-situ adaptation efficacy. Therefore, expanding the knowledge base on local climate impacts would help people stay in their communities.

The second limitation is the historical dependency of the Marshall Islands, particularly on the United States since the middle of the last century, but also generally on external help. In some expert interviews a sentiment of waiting for foreign actors to propose and implement solutions has been described. A sense of helplessness, due to a lack of opportunities and knowledge, is reflected in some of the interviews in the sending communities. The influence of foreign powers can also alter traditional family networks and the organization of communities. In one interview it was expressed that there may be a shift from the perception of large family to more of a nuclear family, as present in many western cultures. The uncertainty of responsibility over common pool resources in this transition may be detrimental to community or individual agency. Also, the climate-related diminishing of natural resources is increasing dependencies of communities on government aid or foreign assistance. "*It has become very extreme these days and frequent droughts, sea level rise. External disturbances are becoming* [so] *very frequent that people are just becoming very dependent on their government to assist them. And the dependency is increased* [it is] *very, very, very high*" (Expert Interview Majuro, Community Expert 1). When asked about whether dependency on government has changed this expert responded: "*Before, people in the olden days wouldn't rely on their government or national government or local government to assist them.*" He concludes: [If] *the dependency is not going to be resolved, then we are in for a very rough, a very rough situation in the future*" (Expert Interview Majuro, Community Expert 1). I interpret the problem of increasing dependency because of climate impacts, together with the frequently notion of an influence of American culture on Marshallese society also to be push factors for migration. If people are deprived of cultural pride and traditions tied to the land, pull factors such as the perception of a better life abroad can have a greater appeal. This movement eventually loops back into the perpetuation of climate change as people migrate to participate in a culture of consumerism which in turn fosters the disappearance of their homeland.

It became clear that only through coordinated efforts and adequate financing of local non-governmental organizations participatory adaptation solutions could be developed. Otherwise, there may be further outmigration. When asked about the future migration patterns, the majority of respondents said they expected a further increase if there is no substantial government intervention:

"*Interviewer:* *Will more people be coming here to [Majuro]?*

Respondent: *I think they will, if we don't find any kind of equivalent work for them to do. This is a time the government need to also focus not just on the center [Majuro] but on the outer island to keep the people in the outer island*" (Expert Interview Majuro, Policy Maker).

This is also reflected in the interviews in the outer islands: "*For us who stayed on island, we managed to accommodate and share local food, for now. But we don't know if the problem worsens in the future or the next few years from now, who knows maybe more will decide to migrate as well*" (Ailuk Interview 16).

From the multilevel analysis it can be concluded that the decisive factors besides the necessary economic integration are provision of knowledge both on climate change and the realities of relocation; the preservation of culture and community; the sustenance of self-determination and agency; and adequate provision of healthcare and higher education. To protect the local culture from the effects of climate change is already difficult. Even if trade and transport to the outer islands were improved, the question remains whether under the 1.5°C to 2°C pathway the right to culture could be exercised on the outer islands, where traditions are tied to the land and to livelihoods which are based on functioning ecosystems. Although more research is needed, this dissertation points to health issues of distress, ecological grief (Cunsolo and Ellis, 2018) and the loss of the sense of place and belonging, which have been addressed in the literature for other indigenous communities (Berry et al., 2010).

The question arises: when communities stay on desolate islands with degraded land, and are artificially sustained there through foreign aid, foreign food and therefore ultimately forced to embrace incorporate foreign value systems of the global economic system, can this be considered effective adaptation? Furthermore, when evaluating the feasibility of technological and physical adaptation options, the financial capacity of countries to carry these out have to be taken into account. In the case of the Marshall Islands, like in other small island nations, this is a particular concern because there is only limited tax revenue, due to the small population size. Therefore, the government's adaptation planning is strongly dependent on non-tax revenue, such as foreign aid.

Part III: Settling Unsettlements

8. Conclusions: Risk Exchange through Migration

The Bangladesh and Marshall Islands case studies reflect the complexity of the nexus of migration and climate change and demonstrate the limits of current migration options as means of adaptation. When comparing the two cases it should first be emphasized that the nature of the migration flows are highly dependent on local contexts. In fact, the challenges faced by migrants, sending- and receiving communities can vary greatly. This in itself bears implications for the discourse over climate migrants. They are not a homogenous group of people, but rightly define themselves as individuals. Their interests cannot be addressed or represented as one, but are diverse and specific to the historical, political and economic realities in which these individuals move. This diversity and the absence of a legal definition of climate migration are part of the reasons behind the difficulties in identifying climate migrants in surveys or questionnaires. It can also be a result of the fact that there is no source for identity in being a climate migrant, or worse, a displaced person. In contrast, the agency that is associated with searching for new employment and broadly a better future, can serve as a positive development of identity. This may be why respondents first point to the pull factors which drew them to the city, rather than the push factors which made them leave their homes.

Despite the actions people take to secure their future, their migration can lead to a fragmentation or loss of their previous identity, for instance from being a traditional farmer in a tightly knit village community to being a day laborer living in a makeshift house on the fringes of an urban informal settlement. The often involuntary relocation to cities cannot include the transfer of livelihoods, natural and social environments, but those were defining elements for identity formation. These identities are now altered or disrupted, leading sometimes to integration problems or feelings of discontent in new settings. Moreover, many aspects of culture are tied to traditional practices of agriculture and to village communities themselves. An involuntary relocation can therefore impede the ability to exercise culture. In developing countries, like Bangladesh and the Marshall Islands, the financial and governance capacities often do not suffice to ensure progress in realizing cultural rights for migrants. Likewise, the Guiding Principles on Internal Displacement (OCHA, 2004) are not fully applied. Principle 9 states a "*particular obligation to protect against the displacement of indigenous peoples, minorities, peasants, pastoralists and other groups with a special dependency on and attachment to their land*" (OCHA, 2004). The involuntary migration identified in these case studies constitutes already a non-fulfillment of the guiding principles. The principles also call for special protection of displaced children, pregnant women and the elderly (Principle 4) which could not be observed in the case studies. Besides, in Bangladesh migrants in the cities faced eviction and displacement anew because they had no access to secure lease.

For migrants and sending communities the migration had various economic outcomes. Some were able to improve their living situation after migration and sent back remittances to the sending communities. This social group largely consisted of people who had sufficient means to relocate or knew someone in the urban centers who could provide them with employment. Also education levels played a role because people who had the level of education required to enter a university at their destination also benefited from their migration, though these movements were largely unrelated to climate impacts. In many cases the circumstances under which the migration occurred and the low level of knowledge and skills prevented people from fully benefiting from their migration. This was generally the case for people with very low income from subsistence farming, little to no savings before the migration and low educational levels. In the two case studies the absence of government was evident. Migrants largely relied on family networks and sometimes NGOs for support. Without a living wage and in the absence of cost-free training or educational programs, people are largely unable to improve their living situation if there is no demand for their work in the labor market. The migrants' children or grandchildren may benefit from their migration by having better access to education and therefore upward mobility. But if integration of migrants in urban centers fails, this is not an automatism. Many slums are home to several generations of people who may have experienced only incremental improvements of their situation over time or none at all. Even if there is substantial betterment for the next generation, migration could still not be seen as effective adaptation because the adaptation should aim at improving or maintaining the standard of living of the affected group. It should not be postponed under great uncertainties to another generation. For migration to be considered adaptation it has to be of a preventative character and not a response to already-occurred or imminent damage. Apart from the multiplicity of forms of climate migration, some patterns evolved from both case studies which can be used for building hypotheses. By analyzing similarities, the variable Q in the most different case study design, strong hypotheses can be formulated (see chapter 8.2.).

One pattern that evolved is that climate migrants are engaging in a risk exchange. They trade the risks to their life, such as food and water security, for more indirect risks related to an uncertain future in the urban areas. In the cities the migrants are confronted with new challenges that they could not foresee. One observation is that the climate impact had mostly negative effects on the economic bargaining power of those affected. Both migrants and sending communities were by and large unable to regain their previous status quo. The climate-related push factors for migration, like livelihood loss, financial problems or health issues, are generally not completely resolved, but rather the climate risks in their area of origin are replaced by other risks. In the interviews, educational opportunities in the cities did also not outweigh these risks, as they were hardly accessible to them because of structural economic inequalities. Another example of the risk exchange can be health. Climate change may affect the health of Marshallese on the outer islands through crop failure-induced food insecurity or food import dependency, causing problems like hunger or diabetes. Migration to Majuro or the United States may be the means by which people can access adequate healthcare for diabetes and find food security. However, this relocation may in turn also have negative consequences for people's health, such as increased exposure to communicable diseases, continued lack of healthcare due to high costs or mental stress because of alienation at the destination. A similar example could be given for the climate migration in Bangladesh, where many migrated because of the threats of communicable diseases and food insecurity in the aftermath of cyclones and were faced again with food insecurity because of commodification of food sources and lack of income in the cities and a high disease burden in overcrowded slums. It can therefore be concluded that while migration was effective in adverting immediate danger of physical climate impacts on livelihoods or health, it was from their perspective ineffective in re-establishing the status quo ante before the climate impact had occurred.

The vulnerability factors which had put migrants especially at risk of climate impact-induced livelihood loss or health threats were carried over to the places of destination. In fact, vulnerability factors shaped by structural inequalities, such as the socio-economic situation, physical health, education and knowledge, did not improve for the majority of interviewees through the migration. Often, migrants were even more disadvantaged than before, hence socio-economic inequalities widened through this measure of adaptation. The situation was often aggravated by the fact that unless there was a social network available to them in the destination places, they did not have access to locality-specific, contextual knowledge. This may be a barrier to access certain goods and services. In turn, if another climate impact occurs, many who were especially vulnerable in the sending communities would be as vulnerable as before or even more vulnerable after their migration.

8.1. Effectiveness of Migration in Reducing Risks

The aim of adaptation is to minimize risk, referring to both climate risks and individual or household-based socio-economic or health risks – which can in turn also be influenced by climate impacts. Although truly effective adaptation may have to go beyond risk reduction and take into consideration cultural rights of people or self-determination (see chapter 3.4.), capturing effectiveness of migration in reducing these risks is an important basis for the generation of hypotheses.

Because in the field research it became apparent that the structurally-determined vulnerability of particular social groups is a key determinant for the individual migration outcomes, the previous function (1) which was used to identify cases in which the risk of climate displacement or other climate risks was high, needs to be adjusted when researching the risks for an individual (2) and when evaluating migration as an adaptation (3). It was stipulated in function (1) (compare chapter 4.3.) that:

$$\text{Risk}_x = f_x(\text{Hazard, Exposure, Vulnerability}) \qquad (1)$$

The difference between the general risk of an occurrence x and relative risk of an occurrence x for an individual belonging to a particular social group can be explained by the following example: The risk of a tropical cyclone-related damage is defined by the hazard, the size and type of the cyclone; the exposure, which is the quantity of people and assets located in the areas where the cyclone occurs and the vulnerability of that population. The individual risk of experiencing a cyclone-related damage is also defined by the hazard, the cyclone, but the exposure herein refers to the geographic location of the individual and their assets and not the overall sum of individuals and assets in the affected region. Moreover, the structurally-determined vulnerability of a particular social group herein shapes the risk for the individual, meaning that this vulnerability defines the extent to which hazard and exposure will constitute an actual risk to an individual.

$$\text{Individual Risk}_x = f_x^{\text{Vulnerability}}(\text{Hazard, Exposure}) \qquad (2)$$

This implies that groups of people with the same type of vulnerability experience similar individual risks if exposure and hazard are the same. For instance, if a social group A has a high vulnerability because their earnings are non-monetary and their assets are located in a shack and they are female, their relative risk will be higher than that of a group B whose vulnerability is low because they live in fortified brick houses and have a high stable income and are male, even if the amount of assets exposed are larger of this group B than that of group A. Whereas in function (1) a risk for an occurrence x was defined through a function of hazard, exposure and vulnerability, in contrast to that in function (2) the individual risk of x is defined through a function of hazard and exposure. The function itself, meaning the type of dependence of risk on hazard and exposure, is shaped by the social group's particular vulnerability. This also implies that by identifying elements of structural vulnerability, such as access to education or income, the risks for social groups could be assessed for certain constellations of hazard and exposure.

When considering adaptation and its effects on the risks for particular social groups, the function again is altered:

$$\text{Individual Risk}_{x}^{A} = f_{x}^{A(\text{Vulnerability})}(\text{Hazard}, A(\text{Exposure})) \qquad (3)$$

When the aim of adaptation is to minimize risks, migration as adaptation should be effective in either decreasing the level of exposure or vulnerability, or both. A decrease in the level of vulnerability could include for example an improvement in key areas of human development such as in the areas of health, education and income. A decrease in exposure means that the migrant has moved out of harms' way. However, for many migrants in the case studies it only changed the type of climate hazards they were exposed to and often increased their vulnerability through the absence of the rural social net and the presence of extreme urban poverty.

8.2. Generation of Hypotheses

Based on the analysis of the migrants' system of origin and system of destination in both case studies, it can be said that presently the strong differences between the two systems prevent an effective adaptation because the migrants' capacity to navigate these differences is limited. Bearing in mind the effect of adaptation on individual risk and the multilevel analysis of the two case studies, several hypotheses can be formulated:

1) **Structural conditions of socio-economic exclusion limit individual agency in migration decision-making and in shaping migration outcomes.**

The nature of movements encountered in the two case studies could often be characterized as involuntary. This was not only due to the magnitude of the climate hazard, but defined by the degree of vulnerability of the affected groups before the impact occurred. In turn, some involuntary movements could have been avoided had the vulnerability of the affected groups been lower. There were similar vulnerabilities across certain groups, for example the group of subsistence farmers, women and children, as well as the relative advantage of those who had a better education. These vulnerabilities were shaped by structural conditions of an exclusionary global and national economy which has fortified patterns of unequal access to opportunities. The individual's role in first deciding whether to migrate or stay and second in determining the effectiveness of their migration was dominated by the structural limitations of their social class, profession or gender.

2) **Without outside intervention, the socio-economic situation of the migrant prior to departure predetermines migration effectiveness.**

The migrant's situation herein refers to their economic and social capital as well as their level of education. This means that if climate change severely depleted the economic resources of a person before they migrated, their migration may be less effective in re-establishing their status quo antes, and are more likely to end up in a downward cycle of poverty, unless there is a policy intervention, or a provision of aid services through non-governmental or governmental institutions. These findings confirm that education and skill trainings are essential pillars of resilience prevailing over economic losses through climate impacts. It also means that migration does not automatically translate into social upward mobility; on the contrary, socio-economic inequalities may lead to very different migration outcomes for groups that have divergent vulnerability profiles. If this hypothesis holds – and many poor people remain in very exposed areas –, a forced, sudden outmigration due to disruptive climate impacts would continue to cause humanitarian disasters in countries with strong financial limits to adaptation. It also links up to the next hypothesis because a planned outmigration before all assets are lost would more likely lead to desirable migration outcomes rather than a survival migration.

3) **Migration as strategic behavior can be effective, whereas migration as a response to an impact is ineffective as a means of adaptation.**

Drawing generalizations from the research findings, migration as an action of last-resort cannot be considered effective adaptation. It is the mere reaction to a climate impact. Strategic adaptive behavior, categorized by the IPCC as social behavioral adaptation, implies an individual's agency in the decision-making process, which many respondents in the two case studies did not have. Those who had a real choice to migrate or to stay often described a more positive experience of migration. The better in-situ adaptation measures are implemented, preventing poverty after climate impacts and thus avoiding survival migration, the more effective strategic migration can be as a means of adaptation. To characterize survival migration as (effective) adaptation is in the end a euphemism for the realities faced by the migrants. Even unintentionally, it serves to justify inaction on both mitigation and effective adaptation including in-situ adaptation options and managed outmigration from exposed areas. Moreover, from a climate justice perspective, if unassisted survival migration is viewed to be in the same group of adaptation options as for example infrastructural adaptation, it shifts the responsibility for action from the society and the polluters to the affected individual.

Besides this general analysis, some hypotheses can be formulated specifically for the individual migrants, the sending and receiving communities. The issue of the migrant's agency in the decision-making process, reflective on which side of the spectrum – from voluntary to enforced – the migration occurred, leads to a hypothesis for the effectiveness of migration for the individual:

4) **As adaptation to climate change migration is the more effective, the more agency the individual has in determining his livelihood.**

The ability to determine which work to pursue or where to live had a strong impact on how people viewed their own migration experience, linking back to the issue of survival migration. In many cases, respondents had very few options because of economic restraints. Upon arrival in the city, they had to take any job available to them to generate income. Even if there were several courses of actions that could have been taken, limits in education and access to information prevented people from making informed decisions. Tying into the lack of agency in making decisions and taking stewardship, another issue that arose was the ability to practice one's own culture.

5) **Migration is the more effective as adaptation, the more the individual is able to engage in their culture and traditions after relocation.**

This hypothesis developed from the interviews with the migrants and with community experts. Even if migration leads to economic benefits, the alienation from the home cultural traditions can still heavily affect an individual's wellbeing and their assessment of the outcome of the migration. Therefore, the active protection especially of indigenous cultures under intensifying climate impacts is crucial and links back to the effectiveness of migration for sending communities for which I arrive at the following hypothesis:

6) **Migration is the more effective as adaptation, the more it supports in-situ adaptation in the community of origin.**

Support can herein be the provision of financial help such as remittances or food supplies, but it can also be non-material goods: bringing back knowledge by returning; providing outside information; access to education and research. Indirectly, moving away can also translate into reduced population pressure and therefore less competition for resources. Otherwise, migration may also take away resources from the sending communities, such as workforce, and thus limit effectiveness. An overall increase in human capital through the positive effects of migration can outweigh this effect.

For the receiving communities the migration as adaptation from exposed rural areas can pose both challenges and opportunities, as shown in the research. A key determinant for the migration outcome to the receiving community, but also to sending communities and migrants, is the capacity of the urban labor market.

7) **Effectiveness of rural-urban climate migration is dependent on employment opportunities in the urban labor markets.**

If migrants are able to integrate into urban labor markets and use their workforce to foster urban development, their economic integration can foster social integration, too. However, the interviews with the migrants showed that their skills generally do not match the demands of the urban labor market. City administrations are under financial constraints, preventing them from investing in strongly needed infrastructure or providing other public employment opportunities.

Overall, by providing insights into the relevant variables making a migration effective or ineffective, the hypotheses highlight factors that are relevant for formulating migration and adaptation policies. While there are limitations to the scope of this study and its findings, the research design developed here can be used in the future to continue theory building on interactions of climate change with human systems. Moreover, the hypotheses generated in this research should be applied to and tested in other cases of climate migration.

Limitations of the Study
This study was designed to generate new hypotheses that would support theory building around the climate change migration and adaptation nexus. In the two case studies I only collected sufficient data to build hypotheses, not to prove them. To test some of these hypotheses in the future, a mix of both quantitative and qualitative methods could be used to verify the findings of this research. The concepts developed here cannot reflect the full reality of the climate migrants in Bangladesh or the Marshall Islands, but the hypotheses are developed through scientific methods and by reducing complexity they help understand the phenomenon. The two case studies

are transferrable to other occurrences of climate migration, but are not representative of all types of climate change-related movements. Therefore, other case studies in different economic, cultural and social contexts could further the understanding of the phenomenon and generate and test other hypotheses.

8.3. Implications for the Adaptation Discourse

Building on the research results, which represent diverse reasons, patterns and outcomes of climate migration, it is necessary to refine the use of adaptation in the context of migration. The scientific and the political discussion on climate migration has shifted from migration as an impact of climate change to being an adaptation to climate change, but it is crucial to acknowledge fundamental differences in the types of adaptation strategies. For example, structural adaptation such as building a dike to protect a home (physical adaptation) is different from merely insuring it (institutional adaptation). Planned migration in anticipation of further degradation as strategic social behavioral adaptation is again different from physical in-situ adaptation. A sole adjustment to a given situation under new conditions of climate change, such as impromptu migration after an impact has occurred, would in this connection not be defined as adaptation, but as an impact response. Because the term adaptation implies a successful mediation of harm, considering ineffective migration – which fails to secure people's livelihood, physical health and dignity – as adaptation would consequentially be a misleading euphemism. At the same time, considering effective migration, which helps people to reduce their vulnerability, an impact of climate change that is to be avoided, is also erroneous.

For example, rebuilding a house after a storm or involuntarily switching one's source of income if agricultural labor is no longer profitable due to unpredictable weather patterns, can be considered impact responses, as the effects of climate change already occurred and have been experienced by the individual. If the objective is not an anticipatory risk minimization and the individual first experiences the hazard and then migrates, the migration should be regarded an impact response. Impact responses thus take place when mitigation and adaptation were unsuccessful or not (effectively) implemented.

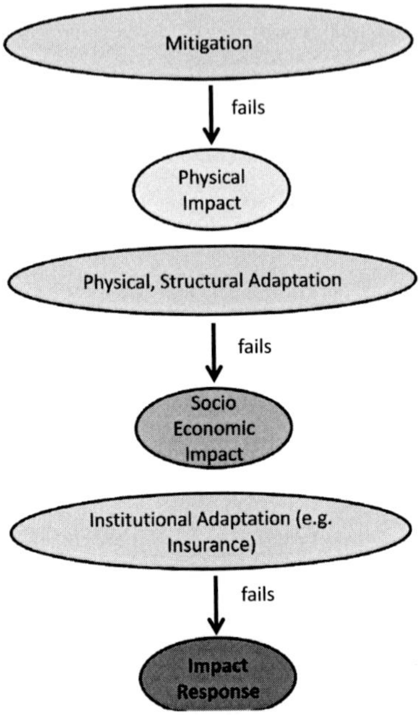

Figure 21 Conceptualization of Impact Response (source: own).

Thus, if migration fails to avoid experiencing the negative effects of climate change, including indirect or secondary effects of physical impacts such as loss of income, it is first ineffective and second it can be seen as an impact response that has not been amended through adequate adaptation measures (figure 21).

In order to distinguish adaptation from impact responses I arrive at a typology of different migratory movements (figure 22). For migration to be considered adaptation it has to be of a preventative nature and occur in anticipation of a hazard or risk. It can then be either effective or ineffective in minimizing risk by avoiding exposure or decreasing vulnerability. Depending on this, the migration should be categorized as adaptation or maladaptation. The (mal-)adaptation includes both social behavioral adaptation, such as a household deciding to diversify their income through migration in expectation of harvest loss; or institutional, such as planned relocations by the government out of high-risk areas. If the migration is a reaction to an impact which has occurred after other adaptation measures have failed to reduce risks (figure 22), it is an impact response. This impact response has a different objective than adaptation. Impact responses aim to ensure survival or "*to exploit beneficial opportunities*" (IPCC, 2012) in the face of a hazard. In achieving this, the impact response can also be either effective or ineffective.

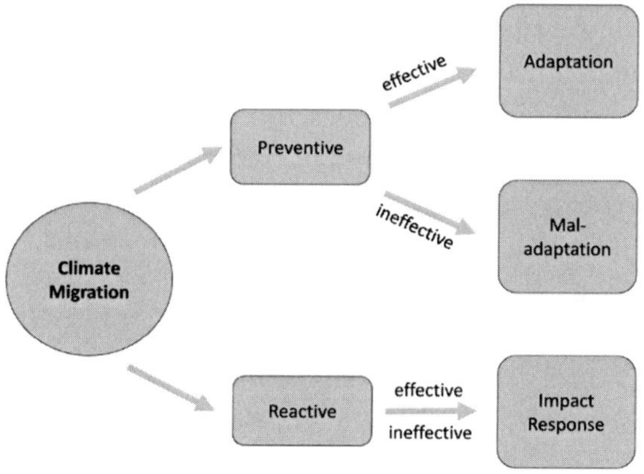

Figure 22 Typology of Climate Migration (source: own).

This differentiation aims at supporting a clearer terminology in the discourse on climate migration that reflects the diverse settings in which decision-making for migration occurs while at the same time reducing complexity.

8.4. Climate Migration in the Context of Divisive Urbanization

Overall, the often precarious situation of climate migrants reflects the wider societal degradation and economic disintegration of low-skilled and forced migrants. The climate-related migratory movements described herein can result in the dissolution of rural societies and traditions and the assimilation of individuals into urban societies. This transformation of subsistence farmers into urban laborers is demanded of individuals who have little or no formal education. It places them at the bottom of the urban socio-economic class, with little upward mobility because of limited access to education and training, constraints of debt and the obligations of sending remittances if finances are available. By migrating they do not only lose their social capital. The entire societal system in which they had previously lived in is being replaced with another one. Subsistence farmers are especially affected because they do not generate a substantial monetary income and are reliant on their own production for food security. Once their natural assets are destroyed by a climate impact, they do not have savings or access to an alternative source of income to recover their losses, meaning that they are in fact incapable to use migration as an effective adaptation strategy. While there are individual responses to climatic impacts, structural inequalities heavily constrain the range of options available to specific social groups. Vulnerability is thus not a strictly individual quality, but a characteristic of social systems. The structural conditions limiting human agency are linked to the global political economy. The wider literature on rural-urban migration suggests at least a moderate increase of opportunity and income and upward mobility through migration (de Brauw et al., 2014; Taylor & Martin, 2001); however, judging from the case studies, this is only possible for migrants who had the opportunity to obtain a solid education, or arrive in urban settings with a high demand for unskilled labor and strong economic growth.

Current nationalistic and populist discourses driven by class and identity are perpetuating exclusionary policies, creating an “us versus them” division between “insiders” or “locals” and newcomers. This populist discourse aims at identifying migrants as the cause for social or economic problems, including crime rates, wage-levels or unemployment. This also applies to many discourses on internal migrations in countries with high urbanization rates. It serves as a platform to gain votes from groups which are socio-economically disadvantaged themselves, but can be persuaded to define their identity in contrast to "them", the migrants. Votes can thus be gained by formulating exclusionary policies which seek to fend off newcomers and preserve locals' relative advantages over them, while not addressing wider structural inequalities. Hence, climate migration today is part of a pattern of divisive urbanization. The majority of migrants who were moving out of exposed areas in the two case studies did not have access to inclusive and resilient urban spaces and markets. On the contrary, besides the climate stressors in the cities, they were also exposed to hazardous and exploitative labor conditions and additional health hazards. Through the relocation from rural to urban areas vulnerable migrants thus become an important part of producing goods and services for global value chains, serving international economic elites and involuntarily the perpetuation of structural inequalities. For countries in transition from predominantly rural to urban societies there is a need for a social contract between urban socio-economic elites and rural populations which aims at reducing the structural vulnerabilities of rural populations and therefore also increasing national food security.

While the migrations in the two case studies occurred in very different national contexts, there are insights that can be applied to other cases of interactions of climate impacts with migration patterns and could therefore also serve quantitative analysis. This way, research on future characteristics of migratory movements because of different climate impacts could be improved. Poor subsistence farmers with little formal education were particularly at risk of forced displacement as an impact response, negative migration outcomes and a further spiraling into poverty on the one side, and being trapped in rural climate change affected areas without economic opportunities for alternative livelihoods on the other. The group of impoverished subsistence farmers without adequate education exists in many countries with limited reach or capacity of governmental social security programs and also in regions strongly exposed to current and future climate impacts. The identified interactions of climate change with human migration and the effectiveness of these migration decisions will not be fundamentally different for subsistence farmers in exposed areas i.e. of Peru or

Burkina Faso. This could give some hints at upcoming challenges. If reliable data can be acquired for vulnerability indicators such as education or farm-size, mixed-method approaches could further the understanding on risks of involuntary outmigration as an impact response in future research. For example, of Peru's 2.2 million people employed in agriculture almost three quarters are subsistence farmers (Morris et al., 2017). In some areas of the country these farmers will also face more frequent and intense extreme events (Reyer et al., 2017) and in many cases do not have access to training that would prepare them to compete in urban labor markets if they migrate. In Burkina Faso 90 % of people living below the poverty line are in the countryside (International Monetary Fund, 2018). Most farmers are subsistence farmers, dependent on rainfall for irrigation (FAO, 2014a). While there are still large uncertainties about future climate change impacts in the Sahel region, some evidence suggest that Burkinabe farmers may have to manage crop yield-declines amidst a growing population (Roudier et al., 2011; Waha et al., 2013). Taking just these general insights from two other countries into account, several questions arise. How will climate impacts materialize in rural livelihoods and how can science address conceptual problems and knowledge gaps in linking these effects with migration-decision making? Do governments have the capacity to provide training, social services and create better urban labor markets? Can adaptation funds serve the provision of social security and insurance to subsistence farmers? What is the role of urban elites and how does their (non-)identification with rural populations shape national decision-making? The science on climate migration needs to move forward in strengthening multidisciplinary research and providing evidence-based policy advice to answer these questions.

9. Recommendations for Addressing Climate Migration

As shown in the two case studies, already today climate migrants face very difficult situations. With mounting pressures from climate change impacts, decision-makers on the national and local levels need to aim at turning migration from a reoccurring crisis into a long-term policy subject, so that future migration flows can lead to successful and effective outcomes. From the hypotheses identified in chapter 8, several recommendations can be made to overcome obstacles to effective adaptation, addressing all three groups, migrants, sending and receiving communities. There is one group that emerged as particularly at risk of having to resort to migration as an impact response or a maladaptation: subsistence agricultural laborers (including fishermen) with little or no education. This group should be in the focus of adaptation policies. Because the reach of national governments into these areas of society is limited, new approaches have to be identified to serve those affected the most. Managing migration requires a polycentric governance structure, following a subsidiary principle of responsibility. Therefore, actions have to be taken on the international, national, regional and local levels, in order to enable in-situ adaptation where it is possible and provide opportunities to migrants at destinations. Many of these recommendations are expansions of existing development programs, tailored to the needs of climate migrants. The listed measures below should not be seen as exhaustive, but as spotlights on fields of action. These recommendations build upon the face-to-face interactions with the community members as well as the existing initiatives and literature that aim at building a framework for those who migrate in response to climate change, or who plan their outmigration as an adaptation strategy.

9.1. International Level

Increasing migration flows from the African continent across the Mediterranean to Europe since 2015 and the Rohingya refugee crisis of migration from Myanmar to Bangladesh in 2017 have demonstrated that the protection of human dignity and wellbeing is a core global challenge in migration management and human development. Although climate migration will mostly occur within countries, it still has to be addressed on the international level, as it is an adaptation or response to the effects of the industrialized nations' cumulative emissions. Countries such as Bangladesh or the Marshall Islands do not have the financial adaptive capacity, including credit-worthiness for accessing funds for adequate relief, to carry out their full obligations in protecting their citizens from harm. This is why the topic needs to be viewed from a perspective of global climate justice.

The movements analyzed in the case studies would largely be categorized as social behavioral adaptation, or responses to impacts. However, it can be argued that a more institutional approach of this adaptation strategy should be taken (for the different categories see chapter 2.3. and Noble et al., 2015). This is not limited to top down measures like planned relocations, but could favor an institutionalized facilitation of the freedom of movement for affected individuals. As of today, there is an institutional void and a lack of mandate as to which intergovernmental institution should be working specifically on the topic of climate migration. While both UNHCR and IOM have working groups on the issue, insights are so far not mainstreamed into the policies at the country office level and are often only used on a project base. Whereas many operations are designed in response to existing crises, climate migration could be addressed much more effectively at an early stage, especially as projections of regional climate impacts are becoming more refined and robust. Especially countries which will become more affected by climate impacts under the 1.5-°C temperature limits of the Paris Agreement should start to plan adaptation policies and migration accordingly. However, for this to happen, a clear mandate and adequate funding need to be given to institutions. Organizations already working with migrants and refugees have the necessary experience and institutional capacity to design potent interventions. Such could be done jointly with applied research and based on the state of the art climate research.

Many scholars have voiced concern about the gap in existing legal protection frameworks on the subject of climate migration (Biermann and Boas,

2008; McAdam and Saul, 2010). Also the United Nations Special Representative of the Secretary-General on Migration Peter Sutherland expressed that protecting vulnerable migrants who do not fall under the Geneva Convention is an urgent matter (Sutherland, 2017). An expansion of existing legal protection regimes, regarding internal displacement as well as cross border movements, could help to ensure safe and dignified migration. For internal movements, the Guiding Principles on Internal Displacement (OCHA, 2004) should be fully applied and explicitly include people who are migrating because of slow onset disasters. Regarding cross-border movements, many fear that an alteration of the Geneva Convention would pose further limitations on the right to asylum, rather than offer a widening of the eligible groups. Some researchers therefore suggested a treaty through the UNFCCC (Biermann and Boas, 2008). Through the soft power approach of the Global Compact for Safe, Orderly and Regular Migration, nation states are establishing "*non-binding principles and voluntary guidelines*" (International Organization for Migration, 2018). In the future, these could function as a reference frame for binding bilateral or multilateral agreements on migration. However, already the governments of Australia, Austria, Hungary and the United States announced their withdrawal from the compact on the grounds that it would lead to a human right to migration, which was refuted by UN special representative for international migration Louise Arbour (Rankin, 2018). The EU commission criticized the administrations of Austria and Hungary for not signing the agreement that aims to improve the management of future migration flows. In the absence of a binding global protection regime, nations like New Zealand have started discussing special humanitarian visas for climate migrants (Anderson, 2017).

As climate migration will increasingly have to occur across borders in order for people to find fertile land, a bottom-up approach granting individuals the freedom to move is preferable to top-down resettlement schemes that would limit the agency of people. Therefore, the idea of a Nansen Passport for climate migrants as introduced in the German Advisory Council report (WBGU, 2018) should be institutionalized. With this document, those displaced by climate change who cannot resettle within their own country would receive a passport that would grant them entry and permission to work in the countries that contributed more than 2% to global emissions. Such a passport however, would only work in favor of the most vulnerable if it is realized together with financial assistance, trainings and educational opportunities and the goal to help people stay as long as possible in their homeland.

9.2. National Level

So far, the issue of migration as both a response and a strategy to cope with climate change has not been sufficiently addressed on the level of national governments. However, to raise awareness of the issue and to acknowledge and manage already existing migration flows it would be beneficial to integrate migration policies into national adaptation plans. For example, migration is mentioned in the national adaptation plan of Bangladesh, but is not thoroughly assessed. Here the already existing research should be made accessible to policy makers, for example through the use of policy briefs or fact sheets. As climate migration is a relatively new phenomenon, there is an institutional void because it may require different types of support than for example labor migration. Moreover, adaptation measures should be tailored to the social realities. If adaptation practices are integrated into the culture and society, they can enhance effectiveness greatly and even enhance communal wellbeing (Berry et al., 2010).

In developing countries like the Marshall Islands and Bangladesh, the ability to manage internal migration and implement resilience-building measures in the affected regions will greatly depend on the financial adaptive capacity of the national governments. This includes both the ability to invest in long-term disaster risk reduction infrastructure, as well as the credit worthiness of countries in need of additional financing sources after disasters. While the former may be enabled through multilateral funding mechanisms like the Green Climate Fund, the latter is strongly tied to issues of national debt. In both the Marshall Islands and Bangladesh external debt is substantial (Fenton et al., 2014; Salgado et al., 2016) and future disasters may put further financial strains on the countries. This is why some researchers have already called for swapping debt repayments of indebted developing countries to industrialized creditors for financing mitigation and adaptation actions (Fenton et al., 2014). This form of debt transformation into local climate protection and resilience building could also be useful to support both the prevention of survival migration and displacement and the integration of migration in urban labor markets. Creating more government-funded adaptation and mitigation measures would also result in job creation for which migrants could receive training. Public employment schemes in rural areas for off-season agricultural laborers or in the aftermath of natural disasters have already proven to be successful in securing livelihoods and thereby decreasing seasonal migration to cities as well as increase urban wages for short term employments (Imbert and Papp, 2016). Another policy worth exploring may be the provision of an independent basic income paid to the most vulnerable people in exposed areas and funded through an international mechanism such as the Green Climate Fund. This approach could support traditional farmers and reduce uncertainty over being able to secure sufficient amounts of food during bad harvests.

9.3. Regional Level

As most policies on climate migration could affect both sending and receiving communities, regional-scale policies can produce tailored solutions which match the challenges on the ground more closely than national initiatives. Also, they have more territorial flexibility than traditional urban or rural administrative divisions. Task-oriented regional organizations could take several measures to address climate migration. Broadly, regional development should aim at a polycentric formation of cities (WBGU, 2016). A polycentric structure composited of small and medium sized cities could better provide services and housing to incoming groups of migrants, whereas very large cities may not even have sufficient land available to quickly accommodate more people. Moreover, it can be difficult to govern very large urban agglomerations, especially if government revenue is low. The strengthening of urban labor markets could target especially medium-sized cities that are geographically close to vulnerable rural areas.

Another approach that can be taken regionally is the introduction of insurance schemes for smallholder farmers that can reduce vulnerabilities of people in rural areas (Linnerooth-Bayer and Mechler, 2006). Crop and disaster insurance could prevent debt caused by droughts, floods or storms and therefore avert survival migration. Formal insurance schemes may be needed more and more as "*informal arrangements for mutual insurance are not very effective when it comes to dealing with collective risks*" (Dreze and Sen, 1989) and climate impacts will likely intensify.

9.4. City / Village Level

Both in the receiving cities and in the rural sending communities the topic of adaptation to climate change, including migration, needs to be mainstreamed into development planning. Already in many rural areas people are planting different crops and are seeking other forms of livelihoods to diversify their risks. However, without adequate information on local climate change impacts and financial aid they cannot fully exploit in-situ adaptation options. Therefore, it is necessary to provide educational services about climate change and adaptation measures. As Saroar & Routray (2010) have pointed out in their study on in-situ adaptation to rising sea levels, climate awareness helps people to increase their adaptive capacity. The use of radio or phone-based weather information may increase disaster risk preparedness and decrease displacements. For example, in Bangladesh, "*people having regular access to radio as sources of climate/weather information are more likely than those who do not have such access to prefer in situ adaptation over evacuation for both the scenarios of SLR*" (Saroar & Routray, 2010). While people who have access to the radio can prepare better, this study found that the correct understanding of weather information and the capability to assess risks are essential for reducing the vulnerability of people. A first step towards a better knowledge base in the communities would be to offer educational programs to village leaders, including religious leaders, elected officials and traditional leaders as well as to school teachers who could function as multipliers in the dissemination. Disaster risk reduction should also aim at poor migrant communities in destination places, since many cities are exposed to climate impacts. The strong detrimental effects of tropical cyclones on already displaced populations could be observed in the aftermath of cyclone Mora which damaged and destroyed thousands of houses of Rohingya refugees in Bangladesh in 2017 (UNHCR, 2017).

In addition, in the rural areas information should be disseminated on the option of migration. This could include pre-departure courses to disseminate knowledge about destinations and options in the respective labor markets as well as cultural orientations at destinations (Pillinger, 2015). An obstacle to effectiveness of internal climate migration is the lack of opportunities in many of the urban labor markets and the low capacities to absorb and use the incoming workforce. Especially in strongly exposed areas where there is a high probability that more people will chose to migrate out, trainings in skills relevant to the destination labor market should be provided. Such vocational schools would also provide opportunities in urban centers. It has been stressed that "*Unless a sufficient number of decent jobs are created, climate migrants could become a permanent underclass*" (Schellnhuber and Susantono, 2017). This can only be effectively achieved if city administrations, that can provide services and solutions directly, receive more funding. By directing more financial resources at local actors, bureaucratic processes and therefore the potential for corruption could be reduced. However, the objective of service provision is tied to the recognition of migrants as legal residents and a formalization of land ownership or tenure, which many city administrations have so far neglected.

Furthermore, in cities the commodification of goods and services requires access to finance for individuals, too (Mitlin et al., 2018), which many migrants are struggling with. Access to income could be achieved for example through cash for work programs. Moreover, to provide adequate housing for incoming migrants new forms of low-cost architectural solutions have to be found for the increasing need in cities. There are already novel modular systems providing housing to refugees (Better Shelter, 2018; WBGU, 2016). Some of these could also be used to create interim housing for migrants in urban centers. Low-cost construction techniques such as

Earthbag Building can provide sustainable and adequate housing (Barnes et al., 2009).

Overall, the degree to which climate migration can be managed in a way that protects the rights and dignity of people and addresses the needs of sending and receiving communities will depend on the amount of resources allocated to find and realize solutions. The industrialized nations, responsible for the overwhelming share of cumulative emissions, are in the position to bear the costs for these actions. For good policy to be developed, research also needs to be strengthened. While there is a push to use big data such as geographic information systems, crowdsourcing or cellphone metadata to study migration and informal settlements, it is crucial to also expand field research that focuses on the subject itself: the people. If there is no understanding of the situation of those who have to move out of the affected areas, their concerns and decision-making processes, then the rural-urban system of climate migration cannot be properly understood. At worst, the analysis of large quantitative data sets may be made under erroneous assumptions. Both case studies were carried out in countries where the capacity to conduct research is strongly limited due to a lack of finance. While some international institutes have analyzed regional climate change impacts and to some degree the respective effects on migration, it is important that the international community invests locally in research capacities, such as university level courses, training of PhDs and the transfer of knowledge from science to society.

Part IV: Arrival

10. Outlook: Migration as Adaptation in this Century

This thesis accumulated evidence across disciplines, taking into account the state of the art knowledge of climate impact research, and identified political implications of migration as adaptation. It arrived at several conclusions that can help to inform effective policy while assessing the ethical implications of the findings. The field research confirms that even the current warming level of 1°C above pre-industrial temperature levels has caused climate impacts so severe that vulnerable people's livelihoods were diminished, contributing to further outmigration. The temperature limits set in the Paris Agreement of 1.5 to 2°C above pre-industrial levels will require many additional adaptation measures. However, based on the existing knowledge of climate impacts, it can be said that a warming of 4° C or more by the end of the century under the current emissions pathway would result in humanitarian disasters pertaining to both trapped populations in exposed areas and unprecedented migration flows of people trying to survive. Under intensifying climate impacts there could be in fact a regime shift in migration patterns from less strategic behavior to more reactive behavior. Thus, for a chance of future climate migration as a means of adaptation to be effective, the goals set in the Paris Agreement must be pursued urgently.

As of today, the mounting challenge of climate migration is by no means sufficiently addressed. Taking stock of current policies, institutional bodies and governance instruments, it becomes clear that the same institutions and instruments which have in many cases failed to prevent or manage previous migration crises will fail to manage upcoming migration crises of possibly larger magnitudes if no ambitious reforms are implemented. With regard to ensuring effectiveness of migration as an adaptation measure the questions arise what are the duties of the nation state? Have these duties been performed? The rejection of the Global Compact on Migration by several states (see chapter 9) can be interpreted as a rejection of the norms established in several other documents of international law, such as the Universal Declaration of Human Rights. To accept the compromising and relativizing of cultural and human rights for migrants could eventually result in the overall erosion of these legal frameworks. Managing climate migration is a multi-level governance challenge. It has to be confronted both on the international level through clear mandates to UNHCR by the United Nations General Assembly for transboundary migration due to climate change, as well as on the national and subnational level, addressing the lack of capacity and adequate finance in city administrations and for rural development. Chapter 9 outlined some recommendations pertaining to this.

The political and scientific debates on the protection of climate migrants is halted because of challenges in the definition and our imperfect knowledge on the interactions of climate change with migration patterns, as discussed in chapter 3. However, the burden of proof of whether or not a person has been displaced by a climate impact should not lay with the displaced person, unlike in the case of political persecution as it is the practice in most asylum procedures. On the one hand, many people do not have the knowledge to articulate or prove such connections, and even some countries do not have the capacity to produce regional climate science. On the other hand, there are gaps in our knowledge about climate impacts that currently cannot be resolved. Nevertheless, we see that the changing climate is already affecting many vulnerable people and that there is an immediate need to close existing protection gaps, regardless of the question of causal attribution.

Freedom of movement is a human right (United Nations, 1948) and migration can be successful in improving people's standard of living and future prospects. When it comes to climate change impacts, it is even necessary to enable people to move out of harm's way. However, the two case studies show that the socio-economic and cultural consequences of migration for people who are leaving because their livelihoods have been affected by climate change can be very negative. It also arose during the interviews that many generally prefer to stay on their own land as long as they possibly can. This fact should also guide adaptation interventions.

Ideally, there would be unlimited resources to provide the maximum of technological in-situ adaptation solutions, to allow for the choice to stay.

However, it must be taken into consideration that presently even adaptation to normal climate conditions is a financial and technological challenge in many countries. Both technology transfers and financial aid from large emitters to strongly affected low-emitters such as through the Green Climate Fund need to be expanded. Nevertheless, the locked-in future warming of at least 1.5°C makes it unlikely that effective in-situ adaptation will be realized for all. For some severely affected and least developed countries, financial restraints such as low government revenues may prompt decisions in favor of the most cost-effective adaptation options. Managed outmigration may be one of the cost-effective options of adaptation or impact response. Although such measures would perhaps not be the most effective in terms of sustaining peoples' way of life including cultural traditions and conservation of communities, it may be the only feasible option given existing financial restraints. This predicament highlights the challenge for decision makers regarding policy formation on climate migration: They have to both guard cultural and land rights and fulfill the obligation to protect citizens from harm under the precautionary principle.

For some regions, balancing interests in the distribution of government adaptation spending may result in the question which regions to protect as human habitats and which to abandon. While the desertion of possibly culturally significant land for strategic resettlement is a strongly unfavorable option, it is not the worst-case scenario. The current reality in Bangladesh, as documented in the field research data, points to the fact that by and large neither effective in-situ adaptation is realized, nor is a dignified outmigration facilitated. This results in basically two strategies for the affected individuals; to stay and suffer impacts, which can lead to effects ranging from impoverishment to loss of life, or to decide for survival migration, which in many cases does not only carry substantial risks for the migrants, but also puts pressures on already overburdened city administrations. Initiatives that would address climate migration such as decreasing people's vulnerability in rural areas or facilitating the transition of migrants into the urban economy would also carry substantial co-benefits for human development in general. Undoubtedly, many efforts have to conjoin to manage the now unavoidable climate risks. While the challenge is substantial, humanity has the civilizational capacity to confront it. In the face of climate change, the international community now multilaterally has to identify ways to endow people with the positive freedom to stay and the right to go.

11. Epilogue: Tales of Hope

The field research has brought to light the distress inflicted by the effects of climate change on livelihoods. But behind the fact that climate change has already caused great human suffering also lies another narrative. It is that of people's resistance and resilience in the face of adversity. It is the extraordinary lengths that people went to protect their families, the many ways they tried to adapt to unpredictable weather patterns, and lastly, their will to live. The potential of those whose daily concern is survival is lost to humanity. However, the agency that is structurally denied to many affected people is being taken up by others who try to stand in their place at international conferences and intergovernmental negotiations. There are evolving movements in Asia and the Pacific promoting ambitious mitigation. One interview partner in the Marshall Islands told me: "*We go out there and we tell the world that we are not sinking. We are fighting to survive. Yes!*" For their efforts not to be in vain, we have to listen and join their call.

12. "It takes a village to raise a child" (Acknowledgements)

"It takes a village to raise a child" tells a proverb and I think of four villages which have given rise to my thesis. The first is my intellectual village, the heart of which is the Potsdam Institute for Climate Impact Research and my supervisors and mentors Prof. Helga Weisz and Prof. Hans Joachim Schellnhuber. They have not only guided me through challenging academic questions, but also offered their support in difficult personal situations. They encouraged me to go to places that had not been researched yet, uncertain of the outcomes. I am deeply thankful for this unusual support.

At PIK there are several other people for whom I am extremely thankful. First is Dr. Maria Martin, who has seen the ups and downs of this endeavor. Through our discussions my work has become richer. She has not only been a wonderful colleague, but also a true friend. I would also like to thank Dr. Ilona Otto, Dr. Tobias Geiger, Sophia Rottmann, Adrian Heilemann, Martin Wodinski, Lennart Lagmöller and Mechthild Becker of PIK. For in-depth discussions I would like to thank Prof. Rainer Sauerborn of Heidelberg University, Prof. Michael Daxner of Freie Universität Berlin and Prof. Thomas Pogge of Yale University. I am very thankful to the Studienstiftung des deutschen Volkes that funded my PhD research.

My home village, my family, my parents Barbara Lange-Vinke and Hermann Vinke form the solid basis on which this work stands. Thiago Garcia, thank you for your support and unwavering encouragement.

Two important villages lie in Bangladesh and the Marshall Islands, where I conducted my field research. For support in Bangladesh I would like to thank the GIZ Dhaka and particularly Fabian Wolff, as well as Rashed Jalal Himal and Naoshin Jahan.

Dieter Paulmann and the Okeanos Foundation for the Sea took me on an adventure in the Pacific which has sharpened my understanding of the world. For the support of my field research in the Marshall Islands I would like to especially thank Dustin Langidrik and Ann Magdeline Chong Gum. Alex Tohitika Sanchez from Tahiti, Iva Nancy Vunikura from Fiji and the

Marshallese Crew of Okeanos, kommol tata for a home in the ocean. Lastly, I would like to thank Alexander Beetz and Raffael Heldt from GIZ Marshall Islands for their help and for giving me a place to write.

13. Bibliography

ADB: Addressing Climate Change and Migration in Asia and the Pacific, Mandaluyong City, [online] Available from: http://www.adb.org/sites/default/files/publication/29662/addressing-climate-change-migration.pdf (Accessed 9 November 2015), 2012.

ADB and Bangladesh Bureau of Statistics: The Informal Sector and Informal Employment in Bangladesh, Mandaluyong City, [online] Available from: https://www.adb.org/sites/default/files/publication/30084/informal-sector-informal-employment-bangladesh.pdf (Accessed 1 September 2017), 2012.

ADB and ILO: Employment and the Labor Market in Bangladesh: Overview of Trends and Challenges, ADB Briefs No. 62, ADB, Manila, [online] Available from: https://www.adb.org/sites/default/files/publication/190595/employment-labor-market-ban.pdf (Accessed 26 February 2018), 2016.

Ades, A. F. and Glaeser, E. L.: Trade and Circuses: Explaining Urban Giants, Q. J. Econ., 110(1), 195-227, doi:10.2307/2118515, 1995.

Adger, W. N., Arnell, N. W. and Tompkins, E. L.: Successful adaptation to climate change across scales, Glob. Environ. Chang., 15(2), 77-86, doi:10.1016/j.gloenvcha.2004.12.005, 2005.

Adger, W. N. and Barnett, J.: Four Reasons for Concern about Adaptation to Climate Change, Environ. Plan. A, 41(12), 2800-2805, doi:10.1068/a42244, 2009.

Adger, W. N., Pulhin, J. M., Barnett, J., Dabelko, G. D., Hovelsrud, G. K., Levy, M., Spring, Ú. O. and Vogel, C. H.: Human Security, in: Climate Change 2014: Impacts, Adaptation, and Vulnerability, Part A: Global and Sectoral Aspects, Contribution of Working Group II to the Fifth Assessment Report of the Intergovernmental Panel on Climate Change, edited by Field, C. B., Barros, V. R., Dokken, D. J., Mach, K. J., Mastrandrea, M. D., Bilir, T. E., Chatterjee, M., Ebi, K. L., Estrada, Y. O., Genova, R. C., Girma, B., Kissel, E.S., Levy, A.N., MacCracken, S., Mastrandrea, P. R. and White, L. L., Cambridge University Press, Cambridge and New York, 755-791, 2014.

Agrawala, S., Ota, T., Ahmed, U. A., Smith, J. and van Aalst, M.: Development and Climate Change in Bangladesh: Focus on Coastal flooding and the Sundarbans, OECD, Paris, [online] Available from: http://www.oecd.org/env/cc/21055658.pdf (Accessed 27 February 2018), 2003.

Ahlgren, I., Yamada, S. and Wong, A.: Rising Oceans, Climate Change, Food Aid, and Human Rights in the Marshall Islands, Health Hum. Rights, 16(1), 69-80, doi:10.2307/healhumarigh.16.1.69, 2014.

Ahmed S. M., Alam B. B., Anwar I., Begum T., Huque R., Khan J. A. M.: Bangladesh Health System Review, 5(3). Manila. World Health Organization, Regional Office for the Western Pacific, 2015.

Ahsan, R., Karuppannan, S. and Kellett, J.: Climate Migration and Urban Planning System: A Study of Bangladesh, Environ. Justice, 4(3), 163-170, doi:10.1089/env.2011.0005, 2011.

Alam, M. M., Hossain, M. A. and Shafee, S.: Frequency of Bay of Bengal cyclonic storms and depressions crossing different coastal zones, Int. J. Climatol., 23(9), 1119-1125, doi:10.1002/joc.927, 2003.

Albrecht, G., Sartore, G.-M., Connor, L., Higginbotham, N., Freeman, S., Kelly, B., Stain, H., Tonna, A. and Pollard, G.: Solastalgia: The Distress Caused by Environmental Change, Australas. Psychiatry, 15(S1), S95-S98, doi:10.1080/10398560701701288, 2007.

Anderson, C.: New Zealand considers creating climate change refugee visas, Guard., 31 October, [online] Available from: https://www.theguardian.com/world/2017/oct/31/new-zealand-considers-creating-climate-change-refugee-visas (Accessed 24 July 2018), 2017.

Ayeb-Karlsson, S., Smith, C. D. and Kniveton, D.: A discursive review of the textual use of 'trapped' in environmental migration studies: The conceptual birth and troubled teenage years of trapped populations, Ambio, 47(5), 557-573, doi:10.1007/s13280-017-1007-6, 2018.

Balaguru, K., Taraphdar, S., Leung, L. R. and Foltz, G. R.: Increase in the intensity of postmonsoon Bay of Bengal tropical cyclones, Geophys. Res. Lett., 41(10), 3594-3601, doi:10.1002/2014GL060197, 2014.

Bangladesh Bureau of Statistics: Bangladesh Population and Housing Census 2011 – Urban Area Report, Statistics and Informatics Division, Ministry of Planning, Government of Bangladesh, Dhaka, 2014.

Bangladesh Bureau of Statistics: Census of Slum Areas and Floating Population Programe 2014, Statistics and Informatics Division, Ministry of Planning, Government of Bangladesh, Dhaka, 2015a.

Bangladesh Bureau of Statistics: Population Density and Vulnerability: A Challenge for Sustainable Development of Bangladesh, Statistics and Informatics Division, Ministry of Planning, Government of Bangladesh Dhaka, 2015b.

Barnard, P. L., Short, A. D., Harley, M. D., Splinter, K. D., Vitousek, S., Turner, I. L., Allan, J., Banno, M., Bryan, K. R., Doria, A., Hansen, J. E., Kato, S., Kuriyama, Y., Randall-Goodwin, E., Ruggiero, P., Walker, I. J. and Heathfield, D. K.: Coastal vulnerability across the Pacific dominated by El Niño/Southern Oscillation, Nat. Geosci., 8(10), 801-807, doi:10.1038/ngeo2539, 2015.

Barnes, B., Cao, H., Drab, T. and Pearson, J.: Design of Sustainable Relief Housing in Ethiopia: An Implementation of Cradle to Cradle Design in Earthbag Construction, Am. J. Environ. Sci., 5(2), 137-144, doi:10.3844/ajessp.2009.137.144, 2009.

Barnett, J. and Adger, W. N.: Climate Dangers and Atoll Countries, Clim. Change, 61(3), 321-337, doi:10.1023/B:CLIM.0000004559.08755.88, 2003.

Baron, K.: Top threat? Pacific commander clarifies climate change remarks, Foreign Policy, [online] Available from: https://foreignpolicy.com/2013/04/09/top-threat-pacific-commander-clarifies-climate-change-remarks/ (Accessed 2 August 2018), 2013.

Basten, S., Lutz, W. and Scherbov, S.: Very long range global population scenarios to 2300 and the implications of sustained low fertility, Demogr. Res., 28(5) 1145-1166, doi:10.4054/DemRes.2013.28.39, 2013.

Behrman, S., Kent, A. (Eds.): Climate Refugees – Beyond the Legal Impasse, Routledge, New York, 2018.

Beine, M. and Jeusette, L.: A Meta-Analysis of the Literature on Climate Change and Migration, CREA Discussion Paper Series, 18-05, Center for Research in Economic Analysis, University of Luxembourg, Luxembourg, 2018.

Bender, B.: Chief of US Pacific forces calls climate biggest worry, Boston Globe, 9 March [online] Available from: https://www.bostonglobe.com/news/nation/2013/03/09/admiral-samuel-locklear-commander-pacific-forces-warns-that-climate-change-top-threat/BHdPVCLrWEMxRe9IXJZcHL/story.html (Accessed 2 August 2018), 2013.

Berchin, I. I., Valduga, I. B., Garcia, J. and de Andrade Guerra, J. B. S. O.: Climate change and forced migrations: An effort towards recognizing climate refugees, Geoforum, 84, 147-150, doi:10.1016/J.GEOFORUM.2017.06.022, 2017.

Berlin, I.: Freiheit – Vier Versuche, Fischer, Frankfurt am Main, 2006.

Berry, H. L., Butler, J. R. A., Burgess, C. P., King, U. G., Tsey, K., Cadet-James, Y. L., Rigby, C. W. and Raphael, B.: Mind, body, spirit: co-benefits for mental health from climate change adaptation and caring for country in remote Aboriginal Australian communities, N. S. W. Public Health Bull., 21(6), 139-145, doi:10.1071/NB10030, 2010.

Bertaux, D.: Biography and Society: The Life History Approach in the Social Sciences, 29-45, Sage, London, 1981.

Better Shelter: About Better Shelter, [online] Available from: http://www.bettershelter.org/about/ (Accessed 3 August 2018), 2018.

Betts, A.: Survival Migration: Failed Governance and the Crisis of Displacement. Cornell University Press, Ithaca, 2013.

Bhattacharyya, A. and Werz, M.: Climate Change, Migration, and Conflict in South Asia. Rising Tensions and Policy Options across the Subcontintent, [online] Available from: http://citeseerx.ist.psu.edu/viewdoc/summary?, doi=10.1.1.306.3971 (Accessed 2 August 2016), 2012.

Bhugra, D.: Migration, distress and cultural identity, Brit. Med. Bull., 69(1), 129-141, doi:10.1093/bmb/ldh007, 2004a.

Bhugra, D.: Migration and mental health, Acta Psychiatr. Scand., 109(4), 243-258, doi:10.1046?/j.0001-690X.2003.00246.x, 2004b.

Biermann, F. and Boas, I.: Protecting Climate Refugees: The Case for a Global Protocol, Environ. Sci. Policy Sustain. Dev., 50(6), 8-17, 2008.

Black, R.: Environmental refugees: myth or reality?, New Issues in Refugee Research, Working Paper No. 34,UNHCR, 2001.

Black, R., Bennett, S. R. G., Thomas, S. M. and Beddington, J. R.: Migration as adaptation, Nature, 478, 447-449,doi:10.1038/478477a, 2011.

Borroto, R. J.: Global warming, rising sea level, and growing risk of cholera incidence: a review of the literature and evidence, GeoJournal, 44(2), 111-120, doi:10.1023/A:1006821725244, 1998.

Bourque, F. and Cunsolo Willox, A.: Climate change: The next challenge for public mental health?, Int. Rev. Psychiatry, 26(4), 415-422, doi:10.3109/09540261.2014.925851, 2014.

Braun, T.: Stocktake of the gender mainstreaming capacity of Pacific Island governments - Republic of the Marshall Islands - , Noumea, [online] Available from: https://pacificwomen.org/wp-content/uploads/2017/09/rmi-gender-stocktake1.pdf (Accessed 8 March 2018), 2012.

de Brauw, A., Mueller, V. and Lee, H. L.: The Role of Rural–Urban Migration in the Structural Transformation of Sub-Saharan Africa, World Dev., 63, 33-42, doi:10.1016/J.WORLDDEV.2013.10.013, 2014.

Brettell, C. and Hollifield, J. (Eds.): Migration Theory: Talking across Disciplines, 3, Routledge, New York, 2015.

Brooks, N., and Fisher, S.: Tracking adaptation and measuring development, IIED Climate Change Working Paper No. 1, London, [online] Available from: http://pubs.iied.org/pdfs/10031IIED.pdf (Accessed 8 March 2018), 2011.

Brouwer, R., Akter, S., Brander, L. and Haque, E.: Socioeconomic Vulnerability and Adaptation to Environmental Risk: A Case Study of Climate Change and Flooding in Bangladesh, Risk Anal., 27(2), 313-26, doi:10.1111/j.1539-6924.2007.00884.x, 2007.

Brown, O.: Climate change and forced migration: Observations, projections and implications, UNDP Human Development Report Office, Geneva 2007.

Burke, M., González, F., Baylis, P., Heft-Neal, S., Baysan, C., Basu, S. and Hsiang, S.: Higher temperatures increase suicide rates in the United States and Mexico, Nat. Clim. Chang., 8(8), 723-729, doi:10.1038/s41558-018-0222-x, 2018.

Burkett, V. R., Suarez, A. G., Bindi, M., Conde, C., Mukerji, R., Prather, M. J., St Clair, A. L., Yohe, G. W.: Point of departure, in: Climate Change 2014: Impacts, Adaptation, and Vulnerability, Part A: Global and Sectoral Aspects, Contribution of Working Group II to the Fifth Assessment Report of the Intergovernmental Panel on Climate Change, edited by Field, C.B., Barros, V.R., Dokken, D.J., Mach, K.J., Mastrandrea, M.D., Bilir, T.E., Chatterjee, M., Ebi, K.L., Estrada, Y.O., Genova, R.C., Girma, B., Kissel, E.S., Levy, A.N., MacCracken, S., Mastrandrea, P.R. and White, L.L., Cambridge University Press, Cambridge and New York, 169-194, 2014.

Cardona, O.D., van Aalst, M., Birkmann, J., Fordham, M., McGregor, G., Perez, R., Pulwarty, R., Schipper, E.L.F., Sinh, B.T.: Determinants of Risk: Exposure and Vulnerability, in: Managing the Risks of Extreme Events and Disasters to Advance Climate Change Adaptation, A Special Report of Working Groups I and II of the Intergovernmental Panel on Climate Change (IPCC), edited by Field, C.B., Barros,V., Stocker, T.F., Qin, D., Dokken, D.J., Ebi, K.L., Mastrandrea, M.D., Mach, K.J., Plattner, G.K, Allen, S.K., Tignor, M. and Midgley, P.M., Cambridge University Press, Cambridge and New York, 65-108, 2012.

Carvajal, L. and Pereira, I.: Evidence on the Link between Migration, Climate Shocks, and Adaptive Capacity, in: Risk, Shocks, and Human Development, 257-283, Palgrave Macmillan, London, 2010.

Castles, S.: Towards a Sociology of Forced Migration and Social Transformation, Sociology, 37(1), 13-34, doi:10.1177/0038038503037001384, 2003.

Castles, S.: Understanding Global Migration: A Social Transformation Perspective, J. Ethn. Migr. Stud., 36(10), 1565-1586, doi:10.1080/1369183X.2010.489381, 2010.

Castles, S., de Haas, H. and Miller, M. J.: The Age of Migration: International Population Movements in the Modern World, 5, Palgrave Macmillan, New York, 2013.

Chand, S. S., Tory, K. J., Ye, H. and Walsh, K. J. E.: Projected increase in El Niño-driven tropical cyclone frequency in the Pacific, Nat. Clim. Chang., 7(2), 123-127, doi:10.1038/nclimate3181, 2017.

Choi, J. Y.: Seeking health care: Marshallese migrants in Hawai'i, Ethn. Heal., 13(1), 73-92, doi:10.1080/13557850701803171, 2008.

CIA World Factbook: Bangladesh Country Profile, U.S. Central Intelligence Agency, [online] Available from: https://www.cia.gov/library/publications/the-world-factbook/geos/bg.html (Accessed 12 September 2017), 2017a.

CIA World Factbook: Marshall Islands Country Profile, U.S. Central Intelligence Agency, [online] Available from: https://www.cia.gov/library/publications/the-world-factbook/geos/rm.html (Accessed 18 October 2017), 2017b.

Clayton, S., Manning, C., Krygsman, K. and Speiser, M.: Mental Health and Our Changing Climate: Impacts, Implications, and Guidance, American Psychological Association & ecoAmerica, Washington D.C., [online] Available from: http://ecoamerica.org/wp-content/uploads/2017/03/ea_apa_mental_health_report_web.pdf, 2017.

Coker, R. J., Hunter, B. M., Rudge, J. W., Liverani, M. and Hanvoravongchai, P.: Emerging infectious diseases in southeast Asia: regional challenges to control, Lancet, 377(9765), 599-609, doi:10.1016/S0140-6736(10)62004-1, 2011.

Constable, A. L.: Climate change and migration in the Pacific: options for Tuvalu and the Marshall Islands, Reg. Environ. Chang., 17(4), 1029-1038, doi:10.1007/s10113-016-1004-5, 2017.

Corbin, J. and Strauss, A.: Basics of Qualitative Research: Techniques and Procedures for Developing Grounded Theory, 4, Sage, London, 2015.

Coutin, S. B.: Being En Route, Am. Anthropol., 107(2), 195-206, doi:10.1525/aa.2005.107.2.195, 2005.

Cramer, W., Yohe, G. W., Auffhammer, M., Huggel, C., Molau, U., Da Silva Dias, M. A. F., Solow, A., Stone, D. A., Tibig, L., Leemans, R., Seguin, B., Smith, N. and Hansen, G.: Detection and attribution of observed impacts, in: Climate Change 2014: Impacts, Adaptation, and Vulnerability, Part A: Global and Sectoral Aspects, Contribution of Working Group II to the Fifth Assessment Report of the Intergovernmental Panel on Climate Change, edited by Field, C.B., Barros, V.R., Dokken, D.J., Mach, K.J., Mastrandrea, M.D., Bilir, T.E., Chatterjee, M., Ebi, K.L., Estrada, Y.O., Genova, R.C., Girma, B., Kissel, E.S., Levy, A.N., MacCracken, S., Mastrandrea, P.R. and White, L.L., Cambridge University Press, Cambridge and New York, 979-1037, 2014.

Cunsolo, A. and Ellis, N. R.: Ecological grief as a mental health response to climate change-related loss, Nat. Clim. Chang., 8(4), 275-281, doi:10.1038/s41558-018-0092-2, 2018.

Dekker, R. and Engbersen, G.: How social media transform migrant networks and facilitate migration, Glob. Networks, 14(4), 401-418, doi:10.1111/glob.12040, 2014.

Dekker, R., Engbersen, G., Klaver, J. and Vonk, H.: Smart Refugees: How Syrian Asylum Migrants Use Social Media Information in Migration Decision-Making, Soc. Media + Soc., 4(1), doi:10.1177/2056305118764439, 2018.

Doherty, T. J. and Clayton, S.: The psychological impacts of global climate change, Am. Psychol., 66(4), 265-276, doi:10.1037/a0023141, 2011.

Durkin, M. S., Khan, N., Davidson, L. L., Zaman, S. S. and Stein, Z. A.: The effects of a natural disaster on child behavior: evidence for posttraumatic stress, Am. J. Public Health, 83(11), 1549-1553, [online] Available from: http://www.ncbi.nlm.nih.gov/pubmed/8238676 (Accessed 18 July 2017), 1993.

Edenhofer, O., Vinke, K. and Schewe, J.: Why Security Policy is Reliant on Effective Climate Policy, in Germany and the World 2030, edited by Mair, S., Messner,D. and Meyer, L., 138-146, Econ, Berlin., 2018.

Eisenhardt, K. M.: Building Theories from Case Study Research, Acad. Manage. Rev., 14(4), 532-550, 1989.

Ellis, P. and Roberts, M.: Leveraging Urbanization in South Asia – Managing Spatial Transformation for Prosperity and Livability, The World Bank, Washington D.C., [online] Available from: https://openknowledge.worldbank.org/bitstream/handle/10986/22549/9781464806629.pdf?sequence=17&isAllowed=y (Accessed 26 June 2017), 2016.

Embassy of the Republic of the Marshall Islands to the United States of America: Marshall Islands Geography, [online] Available from: http://www.rmiembassyus.org/index.php/about/marshall-islands/geography (Accessed 13 March 2018), 2018.

FAO: Burkina Faso Country Fact Sheet on Food and Agriculture Policy Trends - Socio-economic context and role of agriculture, [online] Available from: http://www.fao.org/docrep/field/009/i3760e/i3760e.pdf, 2014a.

FAO: Fisheries and Aquaculture Country Profiles – The People's Republic of Bangladesh [online] Available from: http://www.fao.org/fishery/facp/BGD/en (Accessed 6 September 2017), 2014b.

FAO: Migration, Agriculture and Rural Development: Addressing the root causes of migration and harnessing its potential for development, Food and Agriculture Organization of the United Nations, Rome, [online] Available from: http://www.fao.org/3/a-i6064e.pdf (Accessed 26 June 2017), 2016.

Farber, D. A.: Basic Compensation for Victims of Climate Change, Univ. PA. Law Rev., 155 (6), 1605-1656, doi:10.2307/40041375, 2007.

Fay, M. and Opal, C.: Urbanization without Growth: A Not-So-Uncommon Phenomenon, The World Bank, Washington D.C., 2000.

Feagin, J. R., Orum, A. M. and Sjoberg, G.: A Case for the Case Study, University of North Carolina Press, Chapel Hill, 1991.

Fellenius, K.: Republic of the Marshall Islands Coral Bleaching Report, Marshall Islands Coastal Management Advisory Council & NOAA Coral Watch, Majuro, 2014.

Felli, R.: Managing Climate Insecurity by Ensuring Continuous Capital Accumulation: 'Climate Refugees' and 'Climate Migrants', New Polit. Econ., 18(3), 337-363, doi:10.1080/13563467.2012.687716, 2013.

Fenton, A., Wright, H., Afionis, S., Paavola, J. and Huq, S.: Debt relief and financing climate change action, Nat. Clim. Chang., 2014 48(4), 2014.

Field, C. B., Barros, V. R., Mach, K. J., Mastrandrea, M. D., van Aalst, M., Adger, W. N., Arent, D. J., Barnett, J., Betts, R., Bilir, T.E., Birkmann, J., Carmin, J., Chadee, D. D. , Challinor, A.J., Chatterjee, M., Cramer, W., Davidson, D.J., Estrada, Y.O., Gattuso, J.-P., Hijioka, Y., Hoegh-Guldberg, O., Huang, H. Q., Insarov, G. E., Jones, R. N., Kovats, R.S. , Romero-Lankao, P., Larsen, J. N., Losada, I.J., Marengo, J.A., McLean, R. F., Mearns, L.O., Mechler, R., Morton, J.F., Niang, I., Oki, T., Olwoch, J. M., Opondo, M., Poloczanska, E. S., Pörtner, H.-O., Redsteer, M. H., Reisinger, A., Revi, A., Schmidt, D. N., Shaw, M. R., Solecki, W., Stone, D. A., Stone, J. M. R., Strzepek, K. M., Suarez, A. G., Tschakert, P., Valentini, R., Vicuña, S., Villamizar, A., Vincent, K.E., Warren, R., White, L.L., Wilbanks, T. J., Wong, P. P. and Yohe, G. W.: Technical summary, in: Climate Change 2014: Impacts, Adaptation, and Vulnerability, Part A: Global and Sectoral Aspects, Contribution of Working Group II to the Fifth Assessment Report of the Intergovernmental Panel on Climate Change, edited by Field, C.B., Barros, V. R., Dokken, D. J., Mach, K. J., Mastrandrea, M. D., Bilir, T. E., Chatterjee, M., Ebi, K. L., Estrada, Y. O., Genova, R. C., Girma, B., Kissel, E. S., Levy, A. N., MacCracken, S., Mastrandrea, P. R. and White, L. L., Cambridge University Press, Cambridge and New York, 35-94, 2014.

Fields, G. S.: Rural-urban migration, urban unemployment and underemployment, and job-search activity in LDCs, J. Dev. Econ., 2(2), 165-187, doi:10.1016/0304-3878(75)90014-0, 1975.

Figueres, C., Schellnhuber, H. J., Whiteman, G., Rockström, J., Hobley, A. and Rahmstorf, S.: Three years to safeguard our climate, Nature, 546(7660), 593–595, doi:10.1038/546593a, 2017.

Findley, S. E.: Does Drought Increase Migration? A Study of Migration from Rural Mali during the 1983-1985 Drought, Int. Migr. Rev., 28(3), 539-553, doi:10.2307/2546820, 1994.

FMO: What is forced migration?, [online] Available from: http://www.forcedmigration.org/about/whatisfm (Accessed 21 February 2016), 2012.

Ford, M.: Shoreline changes interpreted from multi-temporal aerial photographs and high resolution satellite images: Wotje Atoll, Marshall Islands, Remote Sens. Environ., 135, 130-140, doi:10.1016/J.RSE.2013.03.027, 2013.

Ford, M., Merrifield, M. A. and Becker, J. M.: Inundation of a low-lying urban atoll island: Majuro, Marshall Islands, Nat. Hazards, 91(3), 1273-1297, doi:10.1007/s11069-018-3183-5, 2018.

Foresight: Migration and Global Environmental Change – Future Challenges and Opportunities, The Government Office for Science., London, 2011.

Frailing, K., Harper, D. W. and Serpas, R.: Changes and Challenges in Crime and Criminal Justice After Disaster, Am. Behav. Sci., 59(10), 1278-1291, doi:10.1177/0002764215591184, 2015.

Frieler, K., Meinshausen, M., Golly, A., Mengel, M., Lebek, K., Donner, S. D. and Hoegh-Guldberg, O.: Limiting global warming to 2 °C is unlikely to save most coral reefs, Nat. Clim. Chang., 3(2), 165-170, doi:10.1038/nclimate1674, 2013.

Froschauer, U. and Lueger, M.: Das qualitative Interview: Zur Praxis interpretativer Analyse sozialer Systeme, UTB, Wien, 2003.

Gautam, P. K.: Climate Change and Conflict in South Asia, Strateg. Anal., 36(1), 32-40, doi:10.1080/09700161.2012.628482, 2012.

Gemenne, F.: Climate-induced population displacements in a 4°C+ world., Philos. Trans. A. Math. Phys. Eng. Sci., 369 (1934), 182-195, doi:10.1098/rsta.2010.0287, 2011.

Gemenne, F. and Blocher, J.: How can migration serve adaptation to climate change? Challenges to fleshing out a policy ideal, Geogr. J., 183(4), 336-347, doi:10.1111/geoj.12205, 2017.

German, E. and Pyne, S.: Disasters drive mass migration to Dhaka, Global Post, Agence France-Presse, 8 September, [online] Available from: https://www.pri.org/stories/2010-09-08/disasters-drive-mass-migration-dhaka (Accessed 14 August 2017), 2010.

Gifford, E. and Gifford, R.: The largely unacknowledged impact of climate change on mental health, Bull. At. Sci., 72(5), 292-297, doi:10.1080/00963402.2016.1216505, 2016.

Gill, N.: "Environmental refugees": Key Debates and the Contributions of Geographers, Geogr. Compass, 4(7), 861-871, doi:10.1111/j.1749-8198.2010.00336.x, 2010.

Glaser, B. G. and Strauss, A. L.: The discovery of grounded theory, Int. J. Qual. Methods, 5, 1-10, doi:10.2307/588533, 1967.

Graeme, H.: Climate Change-Induced Mobility and the Existing Migration Regime in Asia and the Pacific, in: Climate Change and Displacement: Multidisciplinary Perspectives, edited by McAdam, J., Hart Publishing, Oxford, 9-36, 2010.

Greiner, C., Peth, S. A. and Sakdapolrak, P.: Deciphering migration in the age of climate change. Towards an understanding of translocal relations in social-ecological systems, TransRe Working Paper No. 2, Department of Geography, University of Bonn, Bonn, doi: 10.13140/2.1.4402.976, 2015.

Guiraudon, V.: Before the EU Border: Remote Control of the "Huddled Masses," in Immigration and asylum law and policy in Europe, in: In search of Europe's borders, edited by Groenendijk, C. A., Guild, E. and Minderhoud, P. E., Kluwer Law International, London and The Hague, 2003.

Halaweh, M., Fidler, C. and McRobb, S.: Integrating the Grounded Theory Method and Case Study Research Methodology Within IS Research: A Possible "Road Map", 29th International Conference on Information Systems, [online] Available from: http://aisel.aisnet.org/icis2008 (Accessed 23 January 2016), 2008.

Hansen, G. and Cramer, W.: Global distribution of observed climate change impacts, Nat. Clim. Chang., 5(3), 182-185, doi:10.1038/nclimate2529, 2015.

Hare, W. L., Cramer, W., Schaeffer, M., Battaglini, A. and Jaeger, C. C.: Climate hotspots: key vulnerable regions, climate change and limits to warming, Reg. Environ. Chang., 11(S1), 1-13, doi:10.1007/s10113-010-0195-4, 2011.

Harris, J. R. and Todaro, M. P.: Migration, Unemployment and Development: A Two-Sector Analysis, The Am. Econ. Rev., 60(1), 126-142, 1970.

Hartmann, B.: Rethinking climate refugees and climate conflict: Rhetoric, reality and the politics of policy discourse, J. Int. Dev., 22(2), 233-246, doi:10.1002/jid.1676, 2010.

Herriott, R. E. and Firestone, W. A.: Multisite Qualitative Policy Research: Optimizing Description and Generalizability, Educ. Res., 12(2), 14-19, doi:10.3102/0013189X012002014, 1983.

Hingley, R.: 'Climate Refugees': An Oceanic Perspective, Asia Pacific Policy Stud., 4(1), 158-165, doi:10.1002/app5.163, 2017.

Hirata, A. J.: Postcolonialism and the Marshallese Diaspora: Structural Violence and Health in the Marshallese Community in Springdale, Arkansas, Master's Thesis, The University of San Francisco, San Francisco, 2015.

Hoegh-Guldberg, O.: Coral reefs in the Anthropocene: persistence or the end of the line?, Geol. Soc. London, Spec. Publ., 395(1), 167-183, doi:10.1144/SP395.17, 2014.

Holthus, P., Crawford, M., Makroro, C. and Sullivan, S.: Vulnerability assessment to accelerated sea level rise. Case study: Majuro Atoll, Republic of the Marshall Islands, South Pacific Reg. Environ. Program, 60, Apia, 1992.

Hugo, G.: Circular Migration: Keeping Development Rolling?, Migration Information Source, Migration Policy Institue, [online] Available from:

https://www.migrationpolicy.org/article/circular-migration-keeping-development-rolling (Accessed 12 August 2018), 2003.

ILO: Informal economy, [online] Available from: http://www.ilo.org/employment/units/emp-invest/informal-economy/lang--en/index.htm (Accessed 23 August 2017), 2017.

Imbert, C. and Papp, J.: Short-term Migration, Rural Workfare Programs and Urban Labor Markets: Evidence from India, The Warwick Economics Research Paper Series, 1116, University of Warwick, Coventry, 2016.

Internal Displacement Monitoring Center: Bangladesh Country Information, [online] Available from: http://www.internal-displacement.org/countries/bangladesh/ (Accessed 26 June 2017), 2017.

Internal Displacement Monitoring Center: Global Internal Displacement Database Methodology, [online] Available from: http://www.internal-displacement.org/database/methodology (Accessed 12 August, 2018), 2018.

International Federation of Red Cross and Red Crescent Societies: Final Report – Bangladesh: Cyclone Sidr, [online] Available from: http://www.ifrc.org/docs/appeals/07/mdrbd003fr.pdf (Accessed 20 November 2014), 2010.

International Federation of the Red Cross and Crescent Societies: Operations update – Bangladesh: Cyclone Aila. [online] Available from: http://www.ifrc.org/docs/appeals/09/MDRBD004_OU2.pdf (Accessed 20 November 2014), 2009.

International Monetary Fund: Republic of the Marshall Islands: 2016 Article IV Consultation – Press Release; Staff Report; and Statement by the Executive Director for Republic of the Marshall Islands, IMF Country Report No. 16/260, IMF, Washington D.C., 2016.

International Monetary Fund: Burkina Faso – Economic Development Documents, IMF Country Report No. 18/85, IMF, Washington D.C., 2018.

International Organization for Migration: World Migration Report 2015 – Migrants and Cities: New Partnerships to Manage Mobility, edited by Lee, J. J. H., IOM, Geneva, 2015.

International Organization for Migration: World Migration Report 2018, edited by McAuliffe, M. and Ruhs, M., IOM, Geneva, 2017.

International Organization for Migration: Global Compact for Migration, [online] Available from: https://www.iom.int/global-compact-migration (Accessed 12 April 2018), 2018.

Ionesco, D., Mokhnacheva, D. and Gemenne, F.: Atlas der Umweltmigration, Oekom, München, 2017.

IPCC: Climate Change - The IPCC Scientific Assessment, edited by Houghton, J.T., Jenkins, G.J. and Ephraums, J.J., Cambridge University Press, Cambridge, 1990.

IPCC: Glossary of terms, in: Managing the Risks of Extreme Events and Disasters to Advance Climate Change Adaptation, A Special Report of Working Groups I and II of the Intergovernmental Panel on Climate Change (IPCC), edited by Field, C.B., Barros,V., Stocker, T.F., Qin, D., Dokken, D.J., Ebi, K.L., Mastrandrea, M.D., Mach, K.J., Plattner, G.K, Allen, S.K., Tignor, M. and Midgley, P.M., Cambridge University Press, Cambridge and New York, 555-564, 2012.

IPCC: Global warming of 1.5°C, An IPCC Special Report on the impacts of global warming of 1.5°C above pre-industrial levels and related global greenhouse gas emission pathways, in the context of strengthening the global response to the threat of climate change, sustainable development, and efforts to eradicate poverty, edited by Masson-Delmotte,V., Zhai, P., Pörtner, H.-O., Roberts, D., Skea, J., Shukla P. R., Pirani, A., Moufouma-Okia, W., Péan, C., Pidcock, R., Connors, S., Matthews, J. B. R., Chen, Y., Zhou, X., Gomis, M. I., Lonnoy, E., Maycock, T., Tignor, M. and Waterfield, T., Cambridge University Press, Cambridge and New York, 2018.

Jacobson, C., Crevello, S., Chea, C. and Jarihani, B.: When is migration a maladaptive response to climate change?, Reg. Environ. Chang., doi:10.1007/s10113-018-1387-6, 2018.

Jedwab, R., Christiaensen, L. and Gindelsky, M.: Rural Push, Urban Pull and... Urban Push? New Historical Evidence from Developing Countries, Institute for International Economic Policy, Washington D.C., 2014.

Jetñil-Kijiner: United Nations Climate Summit Opening Ceremony – A Poem to my Daughter, [online] Available from: https://www.kathyjetnilkijiner.com/united-nations-climate-summit-opening-ceremony-my-poem-to-my-daughter/ (Accessed 20 June 2018), 2014.

Jimeno, R. A.: A Profile of the Marshallese Community in Arkansas, 3, Winthrop Rockefeller Foundation and University of Arkansas, Little Rock and Fayetteville, [online] Available from: http://www.wrfoundation.org/media/1355/immigrantstudy_vol3_resources.pdf (Accessed 15 June 2017), 2013.

Jisan, M. A., Bao, S. and Pietrafesa, L. J.: Ensemble projection of the sea level rise impact on storm surge and inundation at the coast of Bangladesh, Nat. Hazards Earth Syst. Sci., 18, 351-364, doi: 10.5194/nhess-18-351-2018, 2018.

Johnson, G.: Pacific's high teen pregnancy rates, Pacific Institute of Public Policy, [online] Available from: http://pacificpolicy.org/2014/04/pacifics-high-teen-pregnancy-rates/ (Accessed 8 March 2018), 2014.

Johnson, G.: Idyllic No More: Pacific Island Climate, Corruption, and Development Dilemmas, Pacific Institute of Public Policy, Majuro, 2015.

Johnson, G.: Philippines Fishing Boat Detained, Prevented From Entering Marshall Islands, Pacific Islands Report, 2 May, [online] Available from: http://www.pireport.org/articles/2017/02/05/philippines-fishing-boat-detained-prevented-entering-marshall-islands (Accessed 5 June 2018), 2017.

Kälin, W.: Natural disasters and IDPs' rights, Forced Migr. Rev., 11-12, 2005.

Kartiki, K.: Climate change and migration: a case study from rural Bangladesh, Gend. Dev., 19(1), 23-38, doi:10.1080/13552074.2011.554017, 2011.

Karyotis, G.: European Migration Policy in the Aftermath of September 11 – The security–migration nexus, Innov. Eur. J. Soc. Sci. Res., 20(1), 1-17, doi:10.1080/13511610701197783, 2007.

Kates, R. W., Travis, W. R. and Wilbanks, T. J.: Transformational adaptation when incremental adaptations to climate change are insufficient, Proc. Natl. Acad. Sci., 109(19), 7156-7161, doi:10.1073/pnas.1115521109, 2012.

Keju-Johnson, D.: "For the Good of Mankind", Seattle J. Soc. Justice, 2(1), 309-314, 2003.

Kelley, C., Mohtadi, S., Cane, M., Seager, R. and Kushnir, Y.: Commentary on the Syria case: Climate as a contributing factor, Polit. Geogr., 60, 245-247, doi:10.1016/j.polgeo.2017.06.013, 2017.

Kelley, C. P., Mohtadi, S., Cane, M. A., Seager, R. and Kushnir, Y.: Climate change in the Fertile Crescent and implications of the recent Syrian drought, P. Natl. Acad. Sci. USA, 112(11), 3241-3246, doi:10.1073/pnas.1421533112, 2015.

Keown, M.: Children of Israel: US Military Imperialism and Marshallese Migration in the Poetry of Kathy Jetnil-Kijiner, Interventions, 19(7), 930-947, doi:10.1080/1369801X.2017.1403944, 2017.

Kessler, R. C., Galea, S., Gruber, M. J., Sampson, N. A., Ursano, R. J. and Wessely, S.: Trends in mental illness and suicidality after Hurricane Katrina, Mol. Psychiatry, 13(4), 374-384, doi:10.1038/sj.mp.4002119, 2008.

Khan, A. E., Ireson, A., Kovats, S., Mojumder, S. K., Khusru, A., Rahman, A. and Vineis, P.: Drinking Water Salinity and Maternal Health in Coastal Bangladesh: Implications of Climate Change, Environ. Health Perspect., 119(9), 1328-1332, 2011a.

Khan, A. E., Xun, W. W., Ahsan, H. and Vineis, P.: Climate Change, Sea-Level Rise, & Health Impacts in Bangladesh, Environ. Sci. Policy Sustain. Dev., 53(5), 18-33, 2011b.

Kili/ Bikini / Ejit Local Government Council: Resolution Number 2015-46 of the Kili/ Bikini / Ejit Local Government Council, [online] Available from: https://www.bikiniatoll.com/KBE%20CLIMATEresolution%202015-46.pdf (Accessed 8 March 2018), 2015.

Kjellstrom, T., Lemke, B. and Otto, M.: Mapping Occupational Heat Exposure and Effects in South-East Asia: Ongoing Time Trends 1980-2011 and Future Estimates to 2050, Ind. Health, 51, 56-67, doi:10.2486/indhealth.2012-0174, 2013.

Kjellstrom, T., Briggs, D., Freyberg, C., Lemke, B., Otto, M. and Hyatt, O.: Heat, Human Performance, and Occupational Health: A Key Issue for the Assessment of Global Climate Change Impacts, Annu. Rev. Public Health, 37, 97-112, doi:10.1146/annurev-publhealth-032315-021740, 2016.

Knutson, T. R., Delworth, T. L., Dixon, K. W., Held, I. M., Lu, J., Ramaswamy, V., Schwarzkopf, M. D., Stenchikov, G., Stouffer, R. J., Knutson, T. R., Delworth, T. L., Dixon, K. W., Held, I. M., Lu, J., Ramaswamy, V., Schwarzkopf, M. D., Stenchikov, G. and Stouffer, R. J.: Assessment of Twentieth-Century Regional Surface Temperature Trends Using the GFDL CM2 Coupled Models, J. Clim., 19(9), 1624-1651, doi:10.1175/JCLI3709.1, 2006.

Krieger, J. and Higgins, D. L.: Housing and health: time again for public health action, Am. J. Public Health, 92(5), 758-768, [online] Available from: http://www.ncbi.nlm.nih.gov/pubmed/11988443 (Accessed 30 January 2018), 2002.

Kumari Rigaud, K., de Sherbinin, A., Jones, B., Bergmann, J., Clement, V., Ober, K., Schewe, J., Adamo, S., McCusker, B., Heuser, S. and Midgley, A.: Groundswell: Preparing for Internal Climate Migration, The World Bank, Washington D.C., [online] Available from: https://openknowledge.worldbank.org/handle/10986/29461 (Accessed 12 April 2018), 2018.

Kunkle, T. and Ristvet, B.: Castle Bravo: Fifty Years of Legend and Lore – A Guide to Off-Site Radiation Exposures, Defense Threat Reduction Agency, Defense Threat Reduction Information Analysis Center, Fort Belvoir, VA, [online] Available from: http://www.dtic.mil/dtic/tr/fulltext/u2/a572278.pdf (Accessed 6 March 2018), 2013.

Laczko, F. and Aghazarm, C., (Eds.): Migration, Environment and Climate Change: Assessing the Evidence, International Organization for Migration, Geneva, 2009.

Lagmay, A. M. F., Agaton, R. P., Bahala, M. A. C., Briones, J. B. L. T., Cabacaba, K. M. C., Caro, C. V. C., Dasallas, L. L., Gonzalo, L. A. L., Ladiero, C. N., Lapidez, J. P., Mungcal, M. T. F., Puno, J. V. R., Ramos, M. M. A. C., Santiago, J., Suarez, J. K. and Tablazon, J. P.: Devastating storm surges of Typhoon Haiyan, Int. J. Disaster Risk Reduct., 11, 1-12, doi:10.1016/j.ijdrr.2014.10.006, 2015.

Lall, S. V., Selod, H., Shalizi, Z.: Rural-urban migration in developing countries: A survey of theoretical predictions and empirical findings, World Bank Policy Research Working Paper 3915, doi: /10.1596/1813-9450-3915, 2006.

Lee, E. S.: A Theory of Migration, Demography, 3(1), 47-57, doi:10.2307/2060063, 1966.

Leenders, N., Holland, P. and Taylor, P.: Republic of the Marshall Islands Post Disaster Needs Assessment of the 2015-2016 Drought, Republic of the Marshall Islands, Majuro, 2017.

Lenton, T. M., Pichler, P.-P. and Weisz, H.: Revolutions in energy input and material cycling in Earth history and human history, Earth Syst. Dynam., 7(2), 353-370, doi:10.5194/esd-7-353-2016, 2016.

Levy, J. S.: Case studies: Types, designs, and logics of inference, Confl. Manag. Peace Sci., 25(1), 1-18, doi:10.1080/07388940701860318, 2008.

Linnerooth-Bayer, J. and Mechler, R.: Insurance for assisting adaptation to climate change in developing countries: A proposed strategy, Clim. Policy, 6(6), 621-636, doi: 10.1080/14693062.2006.9685628, 2006.

Lu, X., Wrathall, D. J., Sundsøy, P. R., Nadiruzzaman, M., Wetter, E., Iqbal, A., Qureshi, T., Tatem, A., Canright, G., Engø-Monsen, K. and Bengtsson, L.: Unveiling hidden migration and mobility patterns in climate stressed regions: A longitudinal study of six million anonymous mobile phone users in Bangladesh, Glob. Environ. Chang., 38, 1-7, doi:10.1016/j.gloenvcha.2016.02.002, 2016.

Malkki, L.: National Geographic: The Rooting of Peoples and the Territorialization of National Identity Among Scholars and Refugees, Cult. Anthropol., 7(1), 24-44, doi:10.1525/can.1992.7.1.02a00030, 1992.

Mallick, B.: Cyclone-Induced Migration in Southwest Coastal Bangladesh, in: Environment Migration and Adaptation – Evidence and Politics of Climate Change in Bangladesh, edited by Mallick, B. and Etzold, B, 119-139, A H Development Publishing House, Dhaka, 2015.

Mallick, B. and Etzold, B. (Eds.): Environment, Migration and Adaptation – Evidence and Politics of Climate Change in Bangladesh, A H Development Publishing House, Dhaka, 2015.

Marshall, R. and Rahman, S.: Internal Migration in Bangladesh: Character, Drivers and Policy Issues, United Nations Development Programme, Bangladesh, Dhaka, 2013.

Martin, S. and Warner, K.: Climate Change, Migration, and Development, in: Global Perspectives on Migration and Development: GFMD Puerto Vallarta and Beyond, edited by Omelaniuk, I., Springer, Dordrecht, 153-172, 2012.

McAdam, J.: Climate Change Displacement and International Law: Complementary Protection Standards, Legal and Protection Policy Research Series No.19, United Nations High Commissioner for Refugees (UNHCR), Geneva, 2011.

McAdam, J. and Saul, B.: Displacement with Dignity: International Law and Policy Responses to Climate Change Migration and Security in Bangladesh, in: German Yearbook of International Law, 53, 233-288, [online] Available from: http://papers.ssrn.com/sol3/papers.cfm?abstract_id=1701486 (Accessed 30 January 2016), 2010.

McIver, L., Kim, R., Woodward, A., Hales, S., Spickett, J., Katscherian, D., Hashizume, M., Honda, Y., Kim, H., Iddings, S., Naicker, J., Bambrick, H., McMichael, A. J. and Ebi, K. L.: Health Impacts of Climate Change in Pacific Island Countries: A Regional Assessment of Vulnerabilities and Adaptation Priorities, Environ. Health Perspect., 124(11), 1707-1714, doi:10.1289/ehp.1509756, 2016.

McKechnie, S., Pilling, G. and Hampton, J.: Stock assessment of bigeye tuna in the western and central Pacific Ocean, Western and Central Pacific Fisheries Commission, Scientific Committee, Rarotonga, [online] Available from: https://www.wcpfc.int/system/files/SC13-SA-WP-05%5Bbet-assessment%5D REV1.pdf (Accessed 15 January 2018), 2017.

McLeman, R. and Smit, B.: Migration as an adaptation to climate change, Clim. Change, 76(1-2), 31-53, doi:10.1007/s10584-005-9000-7, 2006.

McLeman, R. A. and Hunter, L. M.: Migration in the context of vulnerability and adaptation to climate change: insights from analogues, Wiley Interdiscip. Rev. Clim. Chang., 1(3), 450-461, doi:10.1002/wcc.51, 2010.

Melde, S., Laczko, F., & Gemenne, F. (Eds.): Making Mobility Work for Adaptation to Environmental Changes: Results from the MECLEP Global Research, IOM, Geneva, 2017.

Mengel, M., Levermann, A., Frieler, K., Robinson, A., Marzeion, B. and Winkelmann, R.: Future sea level rise constrained by observations and long-term commitment, Proc. Natl. Acad. Sci., 113(10), 2597-2602, doi:10.1073/pnas.1500515113, 2016.

Merlin, M.: Plants and Environments of the Marshall Islands, Center for Pacific Islands Study, University of Hawai`i at Manoa, Honolulu, 2005.

de Mesquita, E. B.: The Quality of Terror, Am. J. Pol. Sci., 49(3), 515-530, 2005.

Michael,K, Deshpande, T., Ziervogel, G.: Examining vulnerability in a dynamic urban setting: the case of Bangalore's interstate migrant waste pickers, Clim. Dev., doi: 10.1080/17565529.2018.1531745, 2018.

Mill, J. S.: A System of Logic: Ratiocinative and Inductive – Being a Connected View of the Principles of Evidence and the Methods of Scientific Investigation, 8, Harper & Brothers, New York, 1882.

Ministry of Environment and Forests Government of the People's Republic of Bangladesh: National Adaptation Programme of Action (NAPA), 2005.

Ministry of Environment and Forests Government of the People's Republic of Bangladesh: Climate Change and Fisheries & Livestock in Bangladesh, [online] Available from: http://cmsdata.iucn.org/downloads/frsheries.pdf (Accessed 6 September 2017), 2010.

Mirza, M. M. Q.: Climate change, flooding in South Asia and implications, Reg. Environ. Chang., 11(S1), S95-S107, doi:10.1007/s10113-010-0184-7, 2010.

Mitchell-Eaton, E.: New Destinations of Empire: Imperial Migration from the Marshall Islands to Northwest Arkansas, Dissertation, Syracuse University, [online] Available from: https://surface.syr.edu/etd/645 (Accessed 5 March 2018), 2016.

Mitlin, D. and Satterthwaite, D.: Reducing Urban Poverty in the Global South, Routledge, New York, 2014.

Mitlin, D., Colenbrander, S. and Satterthwaite, D.: Editorial: Finance for community-led local, city and national development, Environ. Urban., 30(1), 3-14, doi:10.1177/0956247818758251, 2018.

Mohsena, M., Goto, R. and Mascie-Taylor, C.G.N.: Regional variation in maternal and childhood undernutrition in Bangladesh: evidence from demographic and health surveys, WHO South-East Asia J. Public Heal., 4(2), 139-149, [online] Available from: http://www.searo.who.int/publications/journals/seajph/issues/seajphv4n2p139.pdf?ua=1 (Accessed 1 September 2017), 2015.

Mora, C., Dousset, B., Caldwell, I. R., Powell, F. E., Geronimo, R. C., Bielecki, C. R., Counsell, C. W. W., Dietrich, B. S., Johnston, E. T., Louis, L. V., Lucas, M. P., McKenzie, M. M., Shea, A. G., Tseng, H., Giambelluca, T. W., Leon, L. R., Hawkins, E. and Trauernicht, C.: Global risk of deadly heat, Nat. Clim. Chang., 7(7), 501-506, doi:10.1038/nclimate3322, 2017.

Moreno Ródenas, A., Cecinati, F., ten Veldhuis, M.-C., Langeveld, J. and Clemens, F.: Effect of spatiotemporal variation of rainfall on dissolved oxygen depletion in integrated catchment studies, in: Proceedings of the 8th International Conference on Sewer Processes and Networks, Rotterdam, 31 August - 2 September 2016, 1-8, 2016.

Morris, M., Diaz Rios, L. B., Sebastian, A. R., Vega, G. F., Miranda, J. J., Valdes, A., Frewer, F., Escudero, D., Msellati, L., Ahuja, P. S. and Rodriguez, A.: Gaining Momentum in Peruvian Agriculture: Opportunities to Increase Productivity and Enhance Competitiveness, World Bank Group, Washington D.C., 2017.

Muller, P. H.: Republic of the Marshall Islands: Views regarding the Possible Security Implications of Climate Change, Permanent Mission of the Republic of the Marshall Islands to the United Nations, New York, [online] Available from: https://sustainabledevelopment.un.org/content/dsd/resources/res_pdfs/ga-64/cc-inputs/Marshall_Islands_CCIS.pdf (Accessed 23 April 2018), 2009.

Myers, N.: Environmental refugees in a globally warmed world: Estimating the scope of what could well become a prominent international phenomenon, BioScience, 43(11), 752-761, doi:10.2307/1312319, 1993.

Myers, N.: Environmental Refugees: An Emergent Security Issue, 13th Economic Forum, Prague, 23-27 May 2005, EF.NGO/4/05, 2005.

Nature: Climate-Change impacts, Nature, [online] Available from: https://www.nature.com/subjects/climate-change-impacts (Accessed 17 August 2018), 2018.

Nelson, D. R., Adger, W. N. and Brown, K.: Adaptation to Environmental Change: Contributions of a Resilience Framework, Annu. Rev. Environ. Resour., 32(1), 395-419, doi:10.1146/annurev.energy.32.051807.090348, 2007.

Nett, K. and Rüttinger, L.: Insurgency, Terrorism and Organised Crime in a Warming Climate – Analysing the Links Between Climate Change and Non-State Armed Groups, adelphi, Berlin, 2016.

Noble, I. R., Huq, S., Anokhin, Y. A., Carmin, J. A., Goudou, D., Lansigan, F. P., Osman-Elasha, B., Villamizar, A.: Adaptation needs and options, in: Climate Change 2014: Impacts, Adaptation, and Vulnerability, Part A: Global and Sectoral Aspects, Contribution of Working Group II to the Fifth Assessment Report of the Intergovernmental Panel on Climate Change, edited by Field, C.B., Barros, V.R., Dokken, D.J., Mach, K.J., Mastrandrea, M.D., Bilir, T.E., Chatterjee, M., Ebi, K.L., Estrada, Y.O., Genova, R.C., Girma, B., Kissel, E.S., Levy, A.N., MacCracken, S., Mastrandrea, P.R. and White, L.L., Cambridge University Press, Cambridge and New York, 833-868, 2014.

Ober, K.: How the IPCC views migration – An assessment of migration in the IPCC AR5 WGII Report, TransRE Fact Sheet No. 1, Department of Geography, University of Bonn, Bonn, 2014.

OCHA: Guiding Principles on Internal Displacement, United Nations, Geneva, [online] Available from: https://www.unocha.org/sites/dms/Documents/GuidingPrinciplesDispl.pdf (Accessed 17 August 2018), 2004.

Ochoa-Rodriguez, S., Wang, L.-P., Gires, A., Pina, R. D., Reinoso-Rondinel, R., Bruni, G., Ichiba, A., Gaitan, S., Cristiano, E., van Assel, J., Kroll, S., Murlà-Tuyls, D., Tisserand, B., Schertzer, D., Tchiguirinskaia, I., Onof, C., Willems, P. and ten Veldhuis, M.-C.: Impact of spatial and temporal resolution of rainfall inputs on urban hydrodynamic modelling outputs: A multi-catchment investigation, J. Hydrol., 531(part 2), 389-407, doi:10.1016/J.JHYDROL.2015.05.035, 2015.

OECD: Integrating Climate Change Adaptation into Development Co-operation: Policy Guidance, OECD Publishing, Paris, 2009.

Olsson, L., Opondo, M., Tschakert, P., Agrawal, A., Eriksen, S. H., Ma, S., Perch, L. N., Zakieldeen, S. A., Jampel, C., Kissel, E., Mara, V., Marin, A., Satterthwaite, D., Lera St Clair, A., Sumner, A., Cutter, S., Piguet, E., Kaijser, A., Barros, V., Dokken, D., Mach, K., Bilir, T., Chatterjee, M., Ebi, K., Estrada, Y., Genova, R., Girma, B., Kissel, E., Levy, A. and MacCracken, S.: Livelihoods and Poverty, in: Climate Change 2014: Impacts, Adaptation, and Vulnerability, Part A: Global and Sectoral Aspects, Contribution of Working Group II to the Fifth Assessment Report of the Intergovernmental Panel on Climate Change, edited by Field, C. B., Barros, V. R., Dokken, D. J., Mach, K. J., Mastrandrea, M. D., Bilir, T. E., Chatterjee, M., Ebi, K. L., Estrada, Y. O., Genova, R. C., Girma, B., Kissel, E. S., Levy, A. N., MacCracken, S., Mastrandrea, P. R. and White, L. L., Cambridge University Press, Cambridge and New York, 793-832, 2014.

UN Economic and Social Council (ECOSOC): Supplementary Convention on the Abolition of Slavery, the Slave Trade, and Institutions and Practices Similar to Slavery, [online] Available from: http://www.ohchr.org/EN/ProfessionalInterest/Pages/SupplementaryConventionAbolitionOfSlavery.aspx (Accessed 20 November 2014), 1956.

Okeanos Foundation for the Sea: Okeanos Foundation for the Sea - Overview, [online] Available from: http://okeanos-foundation.org/ (Accessed 5 March 2018), 2018.

Opitz Stapleton, S., Nadin, R., Watson, C. and Kellett, J.: Climate change, migration, and displacement: The need for a risk-informed and coherent approach, Overseas Development Institute and United Nations Development Programme, London and New York, 2017.

Oxfam: Extreme Carbon Inequality: Why the Paris climate deal must put the poorest, lowest emitting and most vulnerable people first, [online] Available from https://www.oxfam.org/en/research/extreme-carbon-inequality (Accessed 5 March 2018), 2015.

Pacific Climate Change Science Program: Current and future climate of the Marshall Islands, Marshall Islands National Weather Service Office, Australian Bureau of Meteorology and Commonwealth Scientific and Industrial Research Organisation (CSIRO), Majuro, 2011.

Pacific Sea Level Monitoring Project: Monthly Sea Level and Meteorological Statistics, Australian Government Bureau of Meteorology, [online] Available from: http://www.bom.gov.au/oceanography/projects/spslcmp/data/monthly.shtml (Accessed 18 April 2018), 2018.

Piguet, E.: Climate change and forced migration, Policy Development and Evaluation Service, New Issues in Refugee Research, Research Paper No. 153, United Nations High Commissioner for Refugees, Geneva, [online] Available from: http://www.unhcr.org/47a316182.html (Accessed 4 February 2015), 2008.

Piguet, E.: Linking climate change, environmental degradation, and migration: a methodological overview, Wiley Interdiscip. Rev. Clim. Chang., 1(4), 517-524, doi:10.1002/wcc.54, 2010.

Piguet, E.: From "Primitive Migration" to "Climate Refugees": The Curious Fate of the Natural Environment in: Migration Studies, Ann. Assoc. Am. Geogr., 103(1), 148-162, doi:10.1080/00045608.2012.696233, 2013.

Piguet, E., Kaenzig, R. and Guélat, J.: The uneven geography of research on "environmental migration", Popul. Environ., 39(4), 357-383, doi:10.1007/s11111-018-0296-4, 2018.

Pillinger, J.: Running an Effective Migrant Resource Centre: A Handbook for Practitioners, IOM, Budapest, 2015.

Poelhekke, S.: Urban growth and uninsured rural risk: Booming towns in bust times, J. Dev. Econ., 96(2), 461-475, doi:10.1016/J.JDEVECO.2010.07.007, 2011.

Polk, W. R.: Understanding Syria: From Pre-Civil War to Post-Assad – How drought, foreign meddling, and long-festering religious tensions created the tragically splintered Syria we know today., The Atlantic, 10 December, [online] Available from: https://www.theatlantic.com/international/archive/2013/12/understanding-syria-from-pre-civil-war-to-post-assad/281989/ (Accessed 31 July 2018), 2013.

Pope, C. and Mays, N.: Qualitative Research: Reaching the parts other methods cannot reach: an introduction to qualitative methods in health and health services research, BMJ, 311, 42-45, doi:10.1136/bmj.311.6996.42, 1995.

Price, M. and Benton-Short, L.: Immigrants and world cities: From the hyper-diverse to the bypassed, GeoJournal, 68(2-3), 103-117, doi:10.1007/s10708-007-9076-x, 2007.

Rahman, M. M., Giedraitis, V. R., Lieberman, L. S., Akhtar, T. and Taminskienė, V.: Shrimp Cultivation with Water Salinity in Bangladesh: The Implications of an Ecological Model, Univers. J. Public Heal., 1(3), 131-142, doi:10.13189/ujph.2013.010313, 2013.

Raleigh, C., Jordan, L. and Salehyan, I.: Assessing the Impact of Climate Change on Migration and Conflict, Social Development Department, The World Bank, Washington D.C., [online] Available from: http://siteresources.worldbank.org/EXTSOCIALDEVELOPMENT/Resources/SDCCWorkingPaper_MigrationandConflict.pdf (Accessed 30 June 2017), 2008.

Rao, N. D., Riahi, K. and Grubler, A.: Climate impacts of poverty eradication, Nat. Clim. Chang., 4(9), 749-751, doi:10.1038/nclimate2340, 2014.

Rashid, H., Hunt, L. M. and Haider, W.: Urban Flood Problems in Dhaka, Bangladesh: Slum Residents' Choices for Relocation to Flood-Free Areas, Environ. Manage., 40(1), 95-104, doi:10.1007/s00267-006-0233-7, 2007.

Revi, A., Satterthwaite, D., Aragón-Durand, F., Corfee-Morlot, J., Kiunsi, R., Pelling, M., Roberts, D. and Solecki, W.: Urban areas, in: Climate Change 2014: Impacts, Adaptation, and Vulnerability, Part A: Global and Sectoral Aspects, Contribution of Working Group II to the Fifth Assessment Report of the Intergovernmental Panel on Climate Change, edited by Field, C. B., Barros, V. R., Dokken, D. J., Mach, K. J., Mastrandrea, M. D., Bilir, T. E., Chatterjee, M., Ebi, K. L., Estrada, Y. O., Genova, R. C., Girma, B., Kissel, E. S., Levy, A. N., MacCracken, S., Mastrandrea, P. R. and White, L. L., Cambridge University Press, Cambridge and New York, 535-612, 2014.

Reyer, C. P. O., Adams, S., Albrecht, T., Baarsch, F., Boit, A., Canales Trujillo, N., Cartsburg, M., Coumou, D., Eden, A., Fernandes, E., Langerwisch, F., Marcus, R., Mengel, M., Mira-Salama, D., Perette, M., Pereznieto, P., Rammig, A., Reinhardt, J., Robinson, A., Rocha, M., Sakschewski, B., Schaeffer, M., Schleussner, C.-F., Serdeczny, O. and Thonicke, K.: Climate change impacts in Latin America and the Caribbean and their implications for development, Reg. Environ. Chang., 17(6), 1601-1621, doi:10.1007/s10113-015-0854-6, 2017.

Rockström, J., Gaffney, O., Rogelj, J., Meinshausen, M., Nakicenovic, N. and Schellnhuber, H. J.: A roadmap for rapid decarbonization, Science, 355(6331), 1269-1271, doi: 10.1126/science.aah3443, 2017.

Rooney, P., Schönhofen, C., Wiebusch, M.: Adapting to Climate Change, Reducing Poverty – a German Financial Cooperation project in Khulna, KfW, [online] Available from: http://resilient-cities.iclei.org/fileadmin/sites/resilient-cities/files/Resilient_Cities_2011/Presentations/B/B2_Rooney.pdf (Accessed 20 November 2014), 2011.

Roudier, P., Sultan, B., Quirion, P. and Berg, A.: The impact of future climate change on West African crop yields: What does the recent literature say?, Glob. Environ. Chang., 21(3), 1073-1083, doi:10.1016/j.gloenvcha.2011.04.007, 2011.

Roy, M., Cawood, S., Hordijk, M. and Hulme, D. (Eds.): Urban poverty and climate change: life in the slums of Asia, Africa and Latin America, Routledge, London and New York, [online] Available from: https://www.routledge.com/Urban-Poverty-and-Climate-Change-Life-in-the-slums-of-Asia-Africa-and/Roy-Cawood-Hordijk-Hulme/p/book/9781138860506 (Accessed 30 July 2018), 2016.

Sakdapolrak, P., Naruchaikusol, S., Ober, K., Peth, S., Porst, L., Rockenbauch, T. and Tolo, V.: Migration in a changing climate. Towards a translocal social resilience approach, Erde, 147(2), 81-94, doi:10.12854/erde-147-6, 2016.

Sala, E., Mayorga, J., Costello, C., Kroodsma, D., Palomares, M. L. D., Pauly, D., Sumaila, U. R. and Zeller, D.: The economics of fishing the high seas, Sci. Adv., 4(6), doi:10.1126/sciadv.aat2504, 2018.

Saroar, M. and Routray, J. K.: In situadaptation against sea level rise (SLR) in Bangladesh: does awareness matter?, Int. J. Clim. Chang. Strateg. Manag., 2(3), 321-345, doi:10.1108/17568691011063079, 2010.

Saroar, M. and Routray, J. K.: Impacts of climatic disasters in coastal Bangladesh: why does private adaptive capacity differ?, Reg. Environ. Chang., 12(1), 169-190, doi:10.1007/s10113-011-0247-4, 2012.

Schellnhuber, H. J.: Selbstverbrennung – Die fatale Dreiecksbeziehung zwischen Klima, Mensch und Kohlenstoff, 2, C. Bertelsmann, München, 2015.

Schellnhuber, H. J. and Susantono, B.: Asian Cities' Endless Summer, Proj. Synd., 11 September, [online] Available from: https://www.project-syndicate.org/commentary/asia-climate-risk-coastal-cities-by-hans-joachim--schellnhuber-and-bambang-susantono-2017-09 (Accessed 13 September 2017), 2017.

Schwerdtle, P., Bowen, K. and McMichael, C.: The health impacts of climate-related migration, BMC Med., 16(1), 1, doi:10.1186/s12916-017-0981-7, 2018.

Secretariat of the Pacific Community: Republic of the Marshall Islands 2011 Census report, Economic Policy, Planning and Statistics Office, Republic of the Marshall Islands, and the SPC Statistics for Development Programme, Noumea, 2012.

Seidman, I.: Interviewing as Qualitative Research, 4, Teachers College Press, New York, 2013.

Seto, K. C.: Exploring the dynamics of migration to mega-delta cities in Asia and Africa: Contemporary drivers and future scenarios, Glob. Environ. Chang., 21(S1), S94-S107, doi:10.1016/j.gloenvcha.2011.08.005, 2011.

Sharp, R., Vas Dev, S., Elson, D. and Costa, M.: The Republic of the Marshall Islands – Gender Responsive Budgeting in the Asia Pacific Region, University of South Australia, Adelaide, [online] Available from: https://www.unisa.edu.au/Documents/EASS/HRI/gender-budgets/marshalls.pdf (Accessed 3 April 2018), 2009.

Sheuya, S., Howden-Chapman, P. and Patel, S.: The Design of Housing and Shelter Programs: The Social and Environmental Determinants of Inequalities, J. Urban Heal., 84(S1), S98-S108, doi:10.1007/s11524-007-9177-3, 2007.

Siegele, L.: Loss and damage: the theme of slow onset impact, The Loss and Damage in Vulnerable Countries Initiative, Germanwatch, Berlin, 2012.

Sinha, A.: Bikini Islanders Demand Move to the U.S. Due to Nuclear Testing, Guardian Liberty Voice, 23 March, [online] Available from: http://guardianlv.com/2015/03/bikini-islanders-demand-move-to-the-u-s-due-to-nuclear-testing/, 2015.

Skeldon, R.: Rural-to-urban migration and its implications for poverty alleviation., Asia-Pacific Popul. J., 12(1), 3-16, [online] Available from: https://www.unescap.org/sites/default/files/APPJ-Vol-12-No-1.pdf (Accessed 23 August 2018), 1997.

Spearman, M. and McGray, H.: Making Adaptation Count: Concepts and Options for Monitoring and Evaluation of Climate Change Adaptation, Deutsche Gesellschaft für Internationale Zusammenarbeit (GIZ) GmbH, Eschborn, 2011.

Stark, O. and Bloom, D. E.: The New Economics of Labor Migration, Am. Econ. Rev., 75(2), 173-178, 1985.

Steffen, W., Rockström, J., Richardson, K., Lenton, T. M., Folke, C., Liverman, D., Summerhayes, C. P., Barnosky, A. D., Cornell, S. E., Crucifix, M., Donges, J. F., Fetzer, I., Lade, S. J., Scheffer, M., Winkelmann, R. and Schellnhuber, H. J.: Trajectories of the Earth System in the Anthropocene., Proc. Natl. Acad. Sci., 115(33), 8252–8259, doi:10.1073/pnas.1810141115, 2018.

Stern, N.: The Economics of Climate Change, Government of the United Kingdom, Cambridge University Press, Cambridge, 2007.

Stocker, T. F., Qin, D., Plattner, G.-K., Alexander, L. V., Allen, S. K., Bindoff, N. L., Bréon, F.-M., Church, J. A., Cubasch, U., Emori, S., Forster, P., Friedlingstein, P., Gillett, N., Gregory, J.M., Hartmann, D.L., Jansen, E., Kirtman, B., Knutti, R., Krishna Kumar, K., Lemke, P., Marotzke, J., Masson-Delmotte, V., Meehl, G.A., Mokhov, I. I., Piao, S., Ramaswamy, V., Randall, D., Rhein, M., Rojas, M., Sabine, C., Shindell, D., Talley, L. D., Vaughan D. G. and S.-P. Xie, 2013: Technical Summary, in: Climate Change 2013: The Physical Science Basis. Contribution of Working Group I to the Fifth Assessment Report of the Intergovernmental Panel on Climate Change, edited by Stocker, T. F., Qin, D., Plattner, G.-K., Tignor, M., Allen, S. K., Boschung, J., Nauels, A., Xia, Y., Bex, V. and Midgley, P. M., Cambridge University Press, Cambridge and New York, 2013.

Stokes, C. J.: A Theory of Slums, Land Econ., 38(3), 187-197, doi:10.2307/3144581, 1962.

Storlazzi, C. D., Gingerich, S. B., van Dongeren, A., Cheriton, O. M., Swarzenski, P. W., Quataert, E., Voss, C. I., Field, D. W., Annamalai, H., Piniak, G. A. and McCall, R.: Most atolls will be uninhabitable by the mid-21st century because of sea-level rise exacerbating wave-driven flooding, Sci. Adv., 4(4), 1-9, 2018.

Strübing, J.: Theoretisches Sampling, in: Hauptbegriffe qualitativer Sozialforschung, edited by Bohnsack, R., Marotzki, W. and Meuser, M, Leske + Budrich, Opladen, 2001.

Sussex Centre for Migration Research and Refugee and Migratory Movements Research Unit: Making Migration Decisions amid Climate Change in Bangladesh, Briefing Paper No.1, Sussex Centre for Migration Research and Refugee and Migratory Movements Research, Sussex and Dhaka, 2012.

Sutherland, P.: Report of the Special Representative of the Secretary-General on Migration, UN Doc. A/71/28, 2017.

Swilling, M. and Annecke, E.: Just Transitions – Explorations of sustainability in an unfair world, United Nations University Press, Tokyo, 2012.

Tacoli, C.: Crisis or adaptation? Migration and climate change in a context of high mobility, Environ. Urban., 21(2), 513-525, doi:10.1177/0956247809342182, 2009.

Taylor, J. E. and Martin, P. L.: Human capital: Migration and rural population change, in: Handbook of Agricultural Economics, vol. 1, part A, edited by Gardner, B. L. and Rausser, G. C., 457-511, Elsevier, Amsterdam, 2001.

Taylor, R., Badcock, J., King, H., Pargeter, K., Zimmet, P., Fred, T., Lund, M., Ringrose, H., Bach, F. and Wang, R. L.: Dietary intake, exercise, obesity and noncommunicable disease in rural and urban populations of three Pacific Island countries, J. Am. Coll. Nutr., 11(3), 283-293 doi:10.1080/07315724.1992.10718229, 1992.

Termeer, C. J. A. M., Dewulf, A. and Biesbroek, G. R.: Transformational change: governance interventions for climate change adaptation from a continuous change perspective, J. Environ. Plan. Manag., 60(4), 558-576, doi:10.1080/09640568.2016.1168288, 2017.

The Economist Intelligence Unit: A Summary of the Liveability Ranking and Overview, [online] Available from: http://www.eiu.com/Handlers/WhitepaperHandler.ashx?fi=Liveability+Ranking+Summary+Report+-+August+2016.pdf&mode=wp&campaignid=Liveability2016 (Accessed 26 June 2017), 2017.

The World Bank: Migration and Remittances Factbook 2008, The World Bank,Washington D.C., 2008.

The World Bank: The Cost of Adapting to Extreme Weather Events in a Changing Climate, Bangladesh Development Series No. 28, The World Bank, Dhaka, [online] Available from: http://documents.worldbank.org/curated/en/716231468014361142/pdf/678450NWP0Box3000BDS28ClimateChange.pdf (Accessed 27 February 2018), 2011.

The World Bank: Turn Down The Heat: Why a 4°C Warmer World Must be Avoided, A report for the World Bank by the Potsdam Institute for Climate Impact Research and Climate Analytics, Washington D.C., 2012.

The World Bank: Turn Down the Heat: Climate Extremes, Regional Impacts, and the Case for Resilience, a report for the World Bank by the Potsdam Institute for Climate Impact Research and Climate Analytics, Washington D.C., 2013.

The World Bank: Turn Down the Heat: Confronting the New Climate Normal, a report for the World Bank by the Potsdam Institute for Climate Impact Research and Climate Analytics, Washington D.C., 2014.

The World Bank: Climate Change Poses Urgent Threat to Poor of Coastal Bangladesh, 24 June, [online] Available from: http://www.worldbank.org/en/news/feature/2016/06/24/climate-change-poses-urgent-threat-to-poor-of-coastal-bangladesh (Accessed 26 June 2017), 2016.

The World Bank: DataBank, [online] Available from: http://databank.worldbank.org/data/home.aspx (Accessed 10 December 2017), 2017a.

The World Bank: Worldwide Governance Indicators, [online] Available from: http://info.worldbank.org/governance/wgi/index.aspx#reports (Accessed 16 August 2017), 2017b.

Thiede, B., Gray, C. and Mueller, V.: Climate variability and inter-provincial migration in South America, 1970-2011, Glob. Environ. Chang., 41, 228-240, doi:10.1016/j.gloenvcha.2016.10.005, 2016.

Thomas, G.: A Typology for the Case Study in Social Science Following a Review of Definition, Discourse, and Structure, Qual. Inq., 17(6), 511-521, doi:10.1177/1077800411409884, 2011.

Titus, A. C.: Bombs in the Backyard: Atomic Testing and American Politics, 2, Nevada Studies in History and Political Science No. 25, University of Nevada Press, Reno and Las Vegas, 2001.

Tsamenyi, B. M. and Hanich, Q. A.: Addressing Corruption in Pacific Islands Fisheries, a report prepared for IUCN PROFISH Law Enforcement, Corruption and Fisheries Project, 2008.

TUBS: Bangladesh on the globe, Wikipedia, [online] Available from: https://de.wikipedia.org/wiki/Datei:Bangladesh_on_the_globe_(Asia_centered).svg, 2011a.

TUBS: Location of Marshall Islands, Wikipedia, [online] Available from: https://commons.wikimedia.org/w/index.php?curid=15176198, 2011b.

U.S. Department of State: 2017 Trafficking in Persons Report – Marshall Islands, Office to Monitor and Combat Trafficking in Persons, U.S. Department of State, [online] Available from: https://www.state.gov/j/tip/rls/tiprpt/countries/2017/271239.htm (Accessed 28 May 2018), 2017.

Udomratn, P.: Mental health and the psychosocial consequences of natural disasters in Asia, Int. Rev. Psychiatry, 20(5), 441-444, doi:10.1080/09540260802397487, 2008.

Ullah, A.: Bright City Lights and Slums of Dhaka city: Determinants of rural-urban migration in Bangladesh, Migration Letters, 1(1), 26-41, [online] Available from: https://www.ceeol.com/search/article-detail?id=496475 (Accessed 12 February 2018), 2004.

UN Habitat: Streets as public spaces and drivers of urban prosperity, UN Habitat, Nairobi, 2013.

UN Department of Economic and Social Affairs: World Urbanization Prospects: The 2014 Revision, UN DESA, Population Division, New York, 2014.

UN Department of Economic and Social Affairs: World Population Prospects: The 2017 Revision – Key Findings and Advance Tables, Working Paper No. ESA/P/WP/248, UN DESA, Population Division, New York, 2017.

UN Department of Economic and Social Affairs: World Urbanization Prospects: The 2018 Revision, UN DESA, Population Division, New York, 2018.

UNDP: Human Development Index (HDI), UNDP, [online] Available from: http://hdr.undp.org/en/content/human-development-index-hdi (Accessed 3 April 2018), 2018.

UN General Assembly: International Covenant on Economic, Social and Cultural Rights, 16 December 1966, United Nations, Treaty Series, vol. 993, 3, [online] Available from: https://www.refworld.org/docid/3ae6b36c0.html (Accessed 27 March 2018), 1966.

UNHCR: The Convention and Protocol Relating To the Status of Refugees, UNHCR, Geneva, 2010.

UNHCR: The State of the World's Refugees – In Search of Solidarity, The Office of the United Nations High Commissioner for Refugees, Geneva, 2012.

UNHCR: Planned Relocation, Disasters and Climate Change: Consolidating Good Practices and Preparing for the Future, UNHCR, Division of International Protection, Sanremo, [online] Available from: http://www.unhcr.org/54082cc69.html (Accessed 27 March 2018), 2014.

United Nations: United Nations Framework Convention on Climate Change, UNFCCC, FCCC/INFORMAL/84, 1992.

United Nations Environment Programme and Sabin Center for Climate Change Law: The Status of Climate Change Litigation: A Global Review, United Nations Environment Programme, Law Division, Nairobi, [online] Available from: http://wedocs.unep.org/handle/20.500.11822/20767, 2017.

United Nations ESCAP: Climate Change and Migration Issues in the Pacific, United Nations ESCAP, Suva, 2014.

United Nations: Universal Declaration of Human Rights, UN General Assembly, [online] Available from: http://www.un.org/en/universal-declaration-human-rights/ (Accessed 27 March 2018), 1948.

Vinke, K.: Survival Strategies of Migrants in Southern Bangladesh, unpublished GIZ background paper, 2014.

Vinke, K.: Gradwanderungen, in: Gesucht: Weltumweltpolitik – Herausforderungen im Anthropozän, Jahrbuch Ökologie 2016, edited by Simonis, U.E., Leitschuh, H., Michelsen, G., Sommer, J. and von Weizsäcker, E.U., Hirzel, Stuttgart 45-55, 2015.

Vinke, K., Martin, M. A., Adams, S., Baarsch, F., Bondeau, A., Coumou, D., Donner, R. V, Menon, A., Perrette, M., Rehfeld, K., Robinson, A., Rocha, M., Schaeffer, M., Schwan, S., Serdeczny, O. and Svirejeva-Hopkins, A.: Climatic risks and impacts in South Asia: extremes of water scarcity and excess, Reg. Environ. Chang., 17(6), 1569-1583, doi:10.1007/s10113-015-0924-9, 2016.

Vinke, K., Schellnhuber, H. J., Laplante, B., Coumou, D., Geiger, T., Glanemann, N., Huber, V., Kropp, J., Kriewald, S., Lehmann, J., Levermann, A., Lobanova, A., Lu, X., Knaus, M., Otto, C., Reyer, C., Robinson, A., Rodgers, C., Rybski, D., Schewe, J., Willner, S., Wortmann, M., Zhao, F. and Zhou, B.: A Region At Risk – The Human Dimensions of Climate Change in Asia and the Pacific, Asian Development Bank, Manila, 2017.

Waha, K., Müller, C., Bondeau, A., Dietrich, J. P., Kurukulasuriya, P., Heinke, J. and Lotze-Campen, H.: Adaptation to climate change through the choice of cropping system and sowing date in sub-Saharan Africa, Glob. Environ. Chang., 23(1), 130-143, doi:10.1016/j.gloenvcha.2012.11.001, 2013.

Walling, D. E.: The Impact of Global Change on Erosion and Sediment Transport by Rivers: Current Progress and Future Challenges, Scientific Side Paper Series from WWDR-3, UNESCO, Paris, 2009.

Walsh, I., Holton, J. A, Bailyn, L., Fernandez, W., Levina, N. and Glaser, B.: What Grounded Theory Is . . . A Critically Reflective Conversation Among Scholars, Organ. Res. Methods, 18(4), 581-599, doi:10.1177/1094428114565028, 2015.

Walsham, M.: Assessing the Evidence: Environment, Climate Change and Migration in Bangladesh, IOM, Dhaka, 2010.

Wang, G., Cai, W., Gan, B., Wu, L., Santoso, A., Lin, X., Chen, Z. and McPhaden, M. J.: Continued increase of extreme El Niño frequency long after 1.5 °C warming stabilization, Nat. Clim. Chang., 7(8), 568-572, doi:10.1038/nclimate3351, 2017.

Warner, K.: Climate Change Induced Displacement: Adaptation Policy in the Context of the UNFCCC Climate Negotiations, Legal and Protection Policy Research Series, UNHCR, Divsision of International Protocol, Geneva, 2011.

Warner, K., Afifi, T., Henry, K., Rawe, T., Smith, C. and de Sherbinin, A.: Where the Rain falls: Climate Change, Food and Livelihood Security, and Migration, CARE and UNU-EHS, Bonn, 2012.

Watts, N., Adger, W. N., Agnolucci, P., Blackstock, J., Byass, P., Cai, W., Chaytor, S., Colbourn, T., Collins, M., Cooper, A., Cox, P. M., Depledge, J., Drummond, P., Ekins, P., Galaz, V., Grace, D., Graham, H., Grubb, M., Haines, A., Hamilton, I., Hunter, A., Jiang, X., Li, M., Kelman, I., Liang, L., Lott, M., Lowe, R., Luo, Y., Mace, G., Maslin, M., Nilsson, M., Oreszczyn, T., Pye, S., Quinn, T., Svensdotter, M., Venevsky, S., Warner, K., Xu, B., Yang, J., Yin, Y., Yu, C., Zhang, Q., Gong, P., Montgomery, H. and Costello, A.: Health and climate change: policy responses to protect public health, Lancet, 386(10006), 1861-1914, doi:10.1016/S0140-6736(15)60854-6, 2015.

WBGU: World in Transition: The Research Challenge, German Advisory Council on Global Change, Berlin, 1997.

WBGU: World in Transition: Fighting Poverty through Environmental Policy, German Advisory Council on Global Change, Berlin, 2004.

WBGU: Humanity on the Move: Unlocking the Transformative Power of Cities, German Advisory Council on Global Change, Berlin, 2016.

WBGU: Just & In-Time Climate Policy: Four Initiatives for a Fair Transformation, Policy Paper No. 9, German Advisory Council on Global Change, Berlin, 2018.

Weisz, H., Koch, H., Lasch, P., Walkenhorst, O., Peters, V., Hattermann, F., Huang, S., Eich, V., Büchner, M., Gutsch, M., Pichler, P.-P., Suckow, F. and Vögele, S.: Methode einer integrierten und erweiterten Vulnerabilitätsbewertung: Konzeptionell-methodische Grundlagen und exemplarische Umsetzung für Wasserhaushalt, Stromerzeugung und energetische Nutzung von Holz unter Klimawandel, Umweltbundesamt, Dessau-Roßlau, 2013.

WFP: The Food Security Atlas of Bangladesh: Towards a poverty and hunger free Bangladesh, Bangladesh Planning Commission and United Nations World Food Programme, Dhaka, 2005.

Wheeler, D.: Quantifying Vulnerability to Climate Change: Implications for Adaptation Assistance, Working Paper 240, Center for Global Development,Washington D.C., 2011.

WHO: Internally Displaced Persons, Health and WHO, Humanitarian Affairs Segment of ECOSOC 2000, New York, 19-20 July, [online] Available from: www.who.int/disasters/repo/5666.doc, 2000.

WHO Kobe Centre: A Billion Voices: Listening and Responding to the Health Needs of Slum Dwellers and Informal Settlers in the New Settings, An Analytic and Strategic Review Paper for the Knowledge Network on Urban Settings, WHO Commission on Social Determinants of Health, WHO Kobe Centre, Kobe, [online] Available from: http://www.who.int/entity/social_determinants/resources/urban_settings.pdf, 2005.

WHO: Is violence a problem after disasters?, World Health Organization, Department of Injuries and Violence Prevention, Geneva, [online] Available from: http://www.who.int/violence_injury_prevention/publications/violence/violence_disasters.pdf (Accessed 23 February 2018), 2005.

WHO: Body mass index - BMI, [online] Available from: http://www.euro.who.int/en/health-topics/disease-prevention/nutrition/a-healthy-lifestyle/body-mass-index-bmi (Accessed 2 August 2018), 2018.

Woodward, A., Hales, S. and Weinstein, P.: Climate change and human health in the Asia Pacific region: who will be most vulnerable ?, Clim. Res., 11(31-38), 1998.

Yamada, S., Burkett, M. and Maskarinec, G. G.: Sea-Level Rise and the Marshallese Diaspora, Environ. Justice, 10(4), 93-97, doi:10.1089/env.2016.0038, 2017.

Yin, R. K.: Case Study Research: Design and Methods, 3, Applied Social Research Method Series, Vol. 5, Sage Publications, Thousand Oaks, London and New Delhi, 2003.

Yohe, G. and Tol, R. S. J.: Indicators for social and economic coping capacity—moving toward a working definition of adaptive capacity, Glob. Environ. Chang., 12(1), 25-40, doi:10.1016/S0959-3780(01)00026-7, 2002.

Yonetani, M.: Global Estimates 2014: People Displaced by Disasters, Norwegian Refugee Council Internal Displacement Monitoring Centre, Geneva, 2014.

Yu, W. H., Alam, M., Hassan, A., Khan, A. S., Ruane, A. C., Rosenzweig, C., Major, D. C. and Thurlow, J.: Climate Change Risks and Food Security in Bangladesh, Earthscan, Washington D.C., 2010.

Yuki, K.: Urbanization, informal sector, and development, J. Dev. Econ., 84(1), 76-103, doi:10.1016/J.JDEVECO.2006.09.004, 2007.

Zander, K. K., Botzen, W. J. W., Oppermann, E., Kjellstrom, T. and Garnett, S. T.: Heat stress causes substantial labour productivity loss in Australia, Nat. Clim. Chang., 5(7), 647-651, doi:10.1038/nclimate2623, 2015.

Zetter, R.: Protecting People Displaced by Climate Change: Some Conceptual Challenges, in: Climate Change and Displacement: Multidisciplinary Perspectives, edited by McAdam, J., 131-151, Hart Publishing, Oxford, 2012.

14. Annex

14.1. Summary / Zusammenfassung

English

The nexus between climate change and migration is complex and its investigation leads to crucial implications for mitigation, adaptation and development policies. In developing countries the general trend of rural-urban migration may be amplified by the negative effects of climate change on agricultural production as sources of livelihoods in the countryside, and on human health and safety. In Asia and the Pacific many people are highly vulnerable to climate change. Deltaic regions such as the Bay of Bengal and island nations like the Marshall Islands are at the forefront of expected climate impacts. Already, in many cities informal and poor settlements are growing, leaving little capacity to absorb migrants with no skills for the urban labor market. This leads to the question of this dissertation: **Is migration an effective adaptation to the impacts of climate change?**

Following a Grounded Theory approach, a theory building multilevel qualitative systems analysis, which takes into account empirical data from two case studies, is carried out. As different actors employ different criteria for effectiveness, three levels of analysis are included: the individual migrant, the sending community and the receiving community. Methods include semi-structured qualitative interviews with migrants, sending communities and relevant experts, focus group discussions, participatory observation, a literature review and a critical discussion of the existing scientific debate. Hypotheses are generated on the specific circumstances under which migration can be considered an effective adaptation strategy. A key insight of this study is that individual agency in migration decision-making and in shaping migration outcomes is strongly limited by the vulnerabilities of the social group to which the individual belongs. Therefore, migration effectiveness is determined by wider structural inequalities.

The study also arrives at the conclusion that migration should only be categorized as adaptation if it is of a preventative nature. If it is a reaction to the already occurred effects of climate change, it should be seen as an impact response. These two categories of migration serve different purposes. Migration as adaptation aims to maintain or improve the standard of living which the household had prior to the climate impact, whereas migration as an impact response has the objective of exploiting beneficial opportunities in face of a hazard, or just to ensure survival. This study ultimately intends to inform policies of climate mitigation, adaptation and migration management.

German
Die Untersuchung der komplexen Zusammenhänge zwischen Klimawandel und Migration führt zu wichtigen Implikationen für Entwicklungs- und Anpassungspolitik sowie für die Minderung globaler Treibhausgasemissionen. Durch voranschreitende Klimafolgen verstärkt sich insbesondere in Entwicklungsländern der Migrationstrend von ländlichen Gebieten in die Städte. Die Auswirkungen des Klimawandels auf die Landwirtschaft können die Existenzgrundlagen von Kleinbauern zerstören und schwerwiegende Konsequenzen für die Gesundheit und Sicherheit der Menschen zur Folge haben.

Im asiatisch-pazifischem Raum sind bereits viele vulnerable Gruppen vom Klimawandel unmittelbar betroffen. Flussdeltas wie die Bay of Bengal und Kleininselstaaten wie die Marshallinseln stehen an der vordersten Front klimawandelgetriebener Umweltveränderungen. Gleichzeitig verzeichnen viele Städte, die Zielorte für Migranten aus dem ländlichen Raum sind, schon jetzt ein rapides Anwachsen informeller Armutssiedlungen. In einem Großteil dieser Städte bieten sich für Migranten, die keine Qualifikationen für den urbanen Arbeitsmarkt aufweisen können, nur wenige Möglichkeiten der ökonomischen Integration. Dieser Punkt führt zur Forschungsfrage dieser Dissertation**: Ist Migration eine effektive Form der Anpassung an den Klimawandel?** Einem Grounded Theory Ansatz folgend, steht im Mittelpunkt dieser Arbeit eine theoriebildende, qualitative Mehrebenen-Systemanalyse, die sich auf empirische Daten zweier Fallstudien stützt.

Da verschiedene Akteure unterschiedliche Kriterien für Effektivität anwenden, wird eine dreistufige Analyse vorgenommen: und zwar auf der Ebene des einzelnen Migranten, ferner der Entsendegemeinschaft und schließlich am Aufnahmeort. Die Methoden umfassen semi-strukturierte qualitative Interviews mit Migranten, den Entsendegemeinschaften sowie Experten. Ferner sind Fokusgruppendiskussionen, partizipatorische Beobachtung und eine kritische Auseinandersetzung mit der bestehenden wissenschaftlichen Literatur Bestandteil der Arbeit. Auf dieser Basis werden Hypothesen zu den spezifischen Bedingungen, unter denen Migration als effektive Anpassungsstrategie betrachtet werden kann, generiert. Eine wesentliche Erkenntnis dabei ist, dass die individuelle Kapazität zum Handeln stark abhängt von der Vulnerabilität der sozialen Gruppe, der der Migrant bzw. der Haushalt angehört. Diese äußeren Bedingungen begrenzen sowohl die Entscheidungsfreiheit zur Migration bzw. zum Verbleib wie auch die Fähigkeit des Einzelnen, sein Leben nach der Migration und damit auch den Erfolg der Migrationsentscheidung selbst zu gestalten. Daher wird die Effektivität von Migration durch strukturelle Ungleichheiten bestimmt.

Die Studie kommt auch zu dem Schluss, dass Migration nur als eine Form der Anpassung kategorisiert werden kann, wenn sie präventiver Natur ist. Wenn sie eine Reaktion auf bereits eingetretene Effekte des Klimawandels darstellt, handelt es sich um eine Entgegnung auf eine durch den Klimawandel verursachte Gefahrensituation. Den beiden Kategorien liegen unterschiedliche Ziele zugrunde. Bei einer Anpassung an den Klimawandel wird versucht, den Lebensstandard, den die Person oder der Haushalt vor Eintritt der Klimafolge hatte, zu halten oder noch zu verbessern. Bei einer Entgegnung auf eine Klimafolge geht es oft nur darum, verbleibende Möglichkeiten während einer Gefährdungslage zu nutzen oder schlicht das eigene Überleben zu sichern. Die Ergebnisse der Studie sollen helfen, die Informationsbasis für zukünftige Anpassungsstrategien zu erweitern und somit auch eine menschenwürdige Migration zu ermöglichen. Ebenso verdeutlicht die Arbeit die Notwendigkeit einer raschen und weitreichenden Klimaschutzpolitik.

14.2. Interview Guide

- Introduction of interviewers and project, state name, affiliation and position.
- Explanation of project scope: To capture the experience of rural migrants who had migrated because of environmental changes to urban settlements.
- Goals of the interview: Learning about interviewee's migration history and experiences, getting to know whether or not the migration has helped them to make up for losses of income caused by meteorological stress. Analyzing under which circumstances migration is effective or ineffective in terms of acquiring access to additional income as well as keeping or improving ones living standard on the whole, including aspects of wellbeing, education, health, etc.
- Technical Aspects: Interviews will be audiotaped and later on transcribed.
- Informed Consent: Interviewers are required to read the informed consent form out loud in the language of the interviewee. They ask whether everything was understood by the potential respondent and whether they wish to participate in the study. If yes, the respondent is asked to sign the form and answer the questions regarding audiotaping, use of transcriptions and anonymity. If no, the interviewers say that this is fine and thank the respondent for their time.
- Questions should be asked in sequence, however, if some questions are already answered as part of a reply to a previous question, the questions are not repeated. Probing and additional questions for understanding and elaboration of new insights are possible.
- At the end of each interview the interviewer thanks the respondents for their time and participation.

14.3. Annex Bangladesh

Overview Bangladesh Migrant Interview Partners[8]

ID Number	Place	Urban Livelihoods	None Rural Livelihoods	Gender
1	Dhaka	Housemaid	None/Subsistence Agriculture	F
2	Dhaka	Housewife / Husband Rickshaw	Housewife/Van Puller	F
3	Khulna	Housemaid	None	F
4	Khulna	Van Puller	Fishermen	M
5	Khulna	Rickshaw Puller	Forester	M
6	Khulna	None/Husband Rice Mill Laborer	Small Business/Subsistence Agriculture	F
7	Khulna	Husband Tea Stall Worker	Tea Stall Owner	F
8	Khulna	Housemaid/ Husband Vendor	Rickshaw Puller	F
9	Khulna	Student	Student	F
10	Khulna	Son is Vendor	Subsistence Agriculture	F
11	Khulna	Rickshaw Puller	Agricultural Day Labor	M
12	Khulna	Husband Auto Rickshaw Driver	Agricultural Day Labor	F
13	Khulna	Husband Rickshaw Puller	Shrimp Cultivator	F

[8] In cases in which women were interviewed who were not the primary breadwinner of the household, the husband's or children's occupation is listed.

14	Khulna Focus Group	Housewives / Husbands Day Laborers	Honey Collector / Subsistence Agriculture	F
16	Satkhira	Rice Mill Worker	Rickshaw Puller	M
17	Satkhira	Associate Mason	Soil Digger	M
18	Satkhira	Day Laborer / Rickshaw Puller	Rice Mill Mason	M
19	Satkhira	Rice Mill Worker	Subsistence Agriculture / Fisheries / Soil	M
20	Satkhira	Rice Mill Worker	Fishery	M
25	Satkhira	Rice Mill Worker	Housewife	F
26	Barisal	None/Son works in Iron Factory	Subsistence Agriculture	M
27	Barisal	Housewife / Husband Rickshaw and Small Business	Subsistence Agriculture	F
28	Barisal	Husband Rickshaw Puller	Subsistence Agriculture	F
29	Barisal	Beggar	Day Laborer	F
31	Barisal	Daughters Housemaids	Subsistence Agriculture	F
32	Barisal	Brick Field Worker	Brick Field Worker	F
33	Barisal	Beggar	No Response	F
34	Barguna	Husband Carpenter	Carpenter	F
35	Barguna	Husband Fish Dealer	Rickshaw Puller	F

Overview Bangladesh Sending Communities Interview Partners

ID Number	Place	Urban Livelihoods	Rural Livelihoods	Gender
21	Satkhira	-	Fishery	M
22	Satkhira	-	Fishery	M
23	Satkhira	-	Fishery / Embankment Building	F
24	Satkhira	-	Agricultural Day Labor	M
30	Barisal	-	Subsistence Agriculture / Construction	M
36	Barguna	In Dhaka: Construction / Rickshaw (returned to village)	Fishery	M
37	Barguna	-	Fish Vendor	M

Bangladesh Coding Sheet

Sex
- Female
- Male

Rural Livelihood
- Housewife
- Rickshaw / Van Puller
- Nothing
- Fishing
- Forester
- Subsistence Farming
- Small Business
- Daily Labour Agriculture
- Mill

Urban Livelihood
- Rice / Jute Mill
- Rickshaw
- Brick Field
- Maid
- Tea Stall / Shop/ Small Business
- Day Laborer

Reason for Migration
- River Erosion
- Cyclone Aila
- Cyclone Sidr
- Work
- Flooding

Impact Natural Disaster on Village
- Food Security
- Income
- Property Damage

Return Migration
- After Storm

Perceived Reason for Climate Change
- Deforestation
- Don't know
- Global Warming
- Infrastructure
- No response
- Religious

Return to Village Circumstance
- Financial Aid
- Land / Shelter
- Work Opportunity
- Environmental Improvement
- Debt cancellation
- There is no possibility

Problems in the City
- Debt
- Environment
- Health
- Lack of Income
- Shelter
- Costs
- Crowded / Chaos

Land rights
- No (rented but fear of eviction)
- Yes (rented)
- Yes (house owner)

Remittances
- Rural remittance to Urban
- Urban remittance to rural
- No remittance

Primary School Access
- Yes - NGO
- Yes - government
- Yes (paid school)
- Madrasa
- No (too expensive)

Access to Basic Medical Care
- Yes (paid)
- Yes (hospital)

Access to Water
- Fetch from well (far)
- Collective tube well
- Supply at home

Access to Toilets
- Unimproved
- improved
- Open Defecation

Self-Determination
- Trapped in urban slum

Perceived governmental support
- Bad
- Others receiving support

Stated Preference
- Urban (because of lack of land)
- Rural (under prior circumstance)
- Urban (because of income)
- Urban (unspecified)
- Urban (because of environmental risks)
- Rural (unspecified)

Informed Consent English

Informed Consent Form

Resilient and Inclusive Urban Development Study

DESCRIPTION: You are invited to participate in a research study on Resilient and Inclusive Urban Development. The study aims at identifying typical livelihood patterns, social situations and motivations for migration from rural to urban areas in order to provide sufficient background for the formulation of adequate support measures to migrants. You will be asked to answer a questionnaire and you will be audiotaped. The tapes will be used for written analysis and will be kept by the interviewer. Transcripts will also be kept by GIZ. If you wish to stay anonymous, your name will not be mentioned in the analysis or transcriptions.

TIME INVOLVEMENT: Your participation will take approximately 30 minutes.

RISKS AND BENEFITS: There are no foreseeable risks associated with this study. There are no direct benefits of the study outcome to the participants.

PARTICIPANT'S RIGHTS: If you have read this form and have decided to participate in this project, please understand your participation is voluntary and you have the right to withdraw your consent or discontinue participation at any time without penalty or loss of benefits to which you are otherwise entitled. The alternative is not to participate. You have the right to refuse to answer particular questions. The results of this research study may be presented at scientific or professional meetings or published in scientific journals. With your permission, your identity will be made known in written materials resulting from the study.

CONTACT INFORMATION:

Questions: If you have any questions, concerns or complaints about this research and its procedures you can ask the interviewer at any point during the interview or afterwards.

Independent Contact: If you are not satisfied with how this study is being conducted, or if you have any concerns, complaints, or general questions about the research or your rights as a participant, please contact the GIZ Office Bangladesh.

Indicate ***Yes*** or ***No***:
I give consent to be audiotaped during this study.

___Yes ___No

I give consent for tapes resulting from this study to be used for transcription and evaluation of the study.

___Yes ___No

I give consent for my identity to be revealed in written materials resulting from this study.

___Yes ___No

The extra copy of this signed and dated consent form is for you to keep.

SIGNATURE ______________________________ **DATE** ____________

Informed Consent Bangla

সম্মতিপত্র

Resilient and Inclusive Urban Development Study

বর্ননা: Resilient and Inclusive Urban Development Study তে অংশগ্রহণের জন্য আপনাকে আমন্ত্রণ। অভিবাসীদের পর্যাপ্ত সহায়তা প্রদান কার্যক্রম প্রণয়নের জন্য যথেষ্ট পটভূমি প্রদান করার লক্ষ্যে তাদের জীবিকা, সামাজিক অবস্থা এবং গ্রাম থেকে শহরে আসার কারণ সমূহ চিহ্নিত করাই হচ্ছে এই গবেষনার উদ্দেশ্য। আমরা আপনার কাছে কিছু প্রশ্নের উত্তর জানতে চাইব এবং এই কথোপকথনটি রেকর্ড করা হবে। এই টেপটি লিখিত বিশ্লেষণের জন্য ব্যবহৃত হবে এবং সাক্ষাৎকার গ্রহণকারীর কাছে এটা সংরক্ষিত থাকবে। অনুলিপিটি GIZ সংরক্ষণ করবে। আপনি যদি বেনামী থাকতে চান, তাহলে আপনার নাম বিশ্লেষণ বা অনুলিপিতে উল্লেখ করা হবে না।

প্রয়োজনীয় সময়: আপনার অংশগ্রহণে আনুমানিক ৩০ মিনিট লাগবে।

ঝুঁকি ও সুবিধা সমূহ: এই গবেষণার ক্ষেত্রে তেমন কোন ঝুঁকির সম্ভাবনা নেই । এই গবেষণার ফলাফল থেকে অংশগ্রহণকারীদের জন্য সরাসরি কোন সুবিধা নেই।

অংশগ্রহনকারীর অধিকার: আপনি যদি এই সম্মতিপত্রটি পড়ে এই প্রকল্পে অংশগ্রহণ করার সিদ্ধান্ত নিয়ে থাকেন তাহলে অনুগ্রহপূর্বক আপনার এই অংশগ্রহণকে স্বেচ্ছাশ্রম হিসাবে বিবেচনা করবেন এবং আপনি যে কোন মুহূর্তে, কোন জরিমানা বা আপনার অধিকারভুক্ত কোন সুবিধার উপর প্রভাব ছাড়াই, সম্মতি প্রত্যাহার বা অংশগ্রহণ থেকে বিরত থাকতে পারবেন। এর বিকল্প হচ্ছে অংশগ্রহণ না করা। প্রতিটি প্রশ্নের উত্তর প্রদানে আপনি বাধ্য নন। এই গবেষনার ফলাফল বৈজ্ঞানিক বা পেশাদারি অধিবেশনে উপস্থাপিত হতে পারে বা বৈজ্ঞানিক জার্নালে প্রকাশিত হতে পারে। আপনার অনুমতি সাপেক্ষে, এই গবেষণার ফলাফলে আপনার পরিচয় তুলে ধরা হবে।

যোগাযোগের তথ্য:

প্রশ্ন: এই গবেষণা ও তার পদ্ধতি সম্পর্কে আপনার যদি কোন প্রশ্ন, মতামত অথবা অভিযোগ থাকে, তাহলে আপনি যে কোন মুহূর্তে, সাক্ষাৎকারের সময় বা তার পরে, সাক্ষাৎকার গ্রহণকারীর কাছে জানতে চাইতে পারবেন।

স্বতন্ত্র যোগাযোগ: যদি আপনি এই গবেষণার পদ্ধতিতে সন্তুষ্ট না হন অথবা এই গবেষণা বা একজন অংশগ্রহণকারী হিসেবে আপনার অধিকার সম্পর্কে আপনার যদি কোনও ধরণের মতামত, অভিযোগ বা সাধারণ প্রশ্ন থাকে তাহলে দয়া করে আপনি GIZ বাংলাদেশ অফিসে যোগাযোগ করুন।

হ্যাঁ অথবা না নির্ধারণ করুন:

আমি এই সাক্ষাতকারটি রেকর্ড করার জন্য আমার সম্মতি জ্ঞাপন করছি।

___হ্যাঁ / ___না

আমি এই গবেষণা থেকে তৈরি টেপটি প্রতিলিপিকরণ ও মূল্যায়নের জন্য সম্মতি জ্ঞাপন করছি।

___হ্যাঁ / ___না

আমি এই গবেষণা থেকে তৈরি লিখিত নথিতে আমার পরিচয় প্রদানে সম্মতি জ্ঞাপন করছি।

___হ্যাঁ / ___না

স্বাক্ষর ও তারিখ সম্বলিত অতিরিক্ত সম্মতিপত্রটি আপনার জন্য।

স্বাক্ষর ______________________________ **তারিখ** ____________

Set of Questions: English

Place and date of interview	
Name of Interviewee	
Age of Participant	
Male / Female	
Number of people in the household Number of children if any	
Where did you migrate from?	
Did you come directly here or did you stay somewhere else in between?	
When did you move here?	
Why did you migrate?	
Are environmental factors in your home community a problem? (Please identify)	
If so, have they increased / intensified over the past decade(s)? Why have they increased / Why do they occur?	
Did you know someone here before deciding to come?	
What is your current occupation?	
Is it different from the work you did beforehand?	

Do you live or are in touch with people here who are from your home community?	
For how long are you planning to stay here? If you are leaving, where are you planning to go?	
Under what conditions would you go back to your place of origin?	
Are you in contact with family members from your place of origin?	
If yes, do you support them monetarily?	
Are there people from your place of origin who are planning to migrate as well?	
Do you go back home during the year? (seasonal work, for example)	
How is your living situation? Are there problems with living in the city?	
How could these problems be solved?	
What facilities are lacking?	
Do you have (Yes / No): Shelter Tap (running) water Access to electricity Access to toilets Access to primary education for children	

Land rights to the place in which you live Access to basic medical care	
What did you need most when you first came here?	
Are environmental factors such as rainfall, mud slides etc. affecting your life in the city?	

Observation Points of Living Conditions (by interviewer)

Set of Questions Bangla

সাক্ষাৎকারের স্থান ও তারিখ	
সাক্ষাৎকার প্রদানকারীর নাম (পরে anonymized করা হবে)	
অংশগ্রহণকারীর বয়স	
নারী / পুরূষ	
পরিবারে সদস্য সংখ্যা শিশুদের সংখ্যা (যদি থাকে)	
আপনি কোন অঞ্চল থেকে স্থানান্তরিত হয়েছেন?	
আপনি কি সরাসরি এখানে এসেছেন নাকি এখানে আসার আগে অন্য কোথাও থেকেছিলেন?	
আপনি কখন এখানে এসেছেন?	
আপনি কেন স্থানান্তর করেছেন?	
পরিবেশ গত বিষয়গুলো কি আপনার নিজ সম্প্রদায়ে কোন সমস্যা তৈরী করছে? (নির্দিষ্ট করে বলুন)	
যদি তাই হয় ,সেগুলো কি বিগত দশকে বৃদ্ধি পেয়েছে বা তীব্রতর হয়েছে? কেন বৃদ্ধি পেয়েছে বা কেন এগুলো হচ্ছে বলে আপনার মনে হয়?	
আপনি এখানে আসার সিদ্ধান্ত নেয়ার আগে এখানকার কাউকে কি চিনতেন?	
আপনার বর্তমান পেশা কি?	

এটা কি আপনার পূর্বের পেশা থেকে ভিন্ন?	
আপনি কি এখানে আপনার নিজ সম্প্রদায়ের সাথে বসবাস করছেন বা তাদের সাথে আপনার যোগাযোগ আছে?	
আপনি এখানে কতদিন যাবত থাকার পরিকল্পনা করছেন? যদি আপনি এখান থেকে যেতে চান ,তবে কোথায় যাওয়ার পরিকল্পনা করেছেন?	
কোন পরিস্থিতিতে আপনি আপনার আদি আবাসস্থলে ফিরে যেতে পারতেন?	
আপনার সাথে কি নিজ আবাসস্থলের পরিজনদের সাথে যোগাযোগ আছে?	
যদি থাকে, আপনি কি তাদের আর্থিক ভাবে কোন ধরনের সহায়তা প্রদান করেন?	
আপনার নিজ আবাসস্থলের কেউ কি একই ভাবে স্থানান্তর হতে চায়?	
আপনি কি এ বছর বাড়ি গিয়েছেন? (উদাহরণসরূপ, মৌসুমী কোন কাজে?)	
আপনার বাসস্থানের বর্তমান পরিস্তিতি কি? শহরে বসবাস করতে কি কোন সমস্যা হয়?	
কি ভাবে এ সমস্যাগুলির সমাধান হতে পারে?	
এখানে কি ধরনের সুযোগ/সুবিধার ঘাটতি রয়েছে?	

আপনি কি নিম্নলিখিত সুবিধাগুলি পানঃ আশ্রয়স্থল (হ্যাঁ / না) পানির ট্যাপ (সচল অবস্থায়) (হ্যাঁ / না) বিদ্যুৎ সুবিধা (হ্যাঁ / না) টয়লেট সুবিধা (হ্যাঁ / না) শিশুদের জন্য প্রাথমিক শিক্ষা সুবিধা (হ্যাঁ / না) বসবাসরত ভূমির উপর অধিকার (হ্যাঁ / না) মৌলিক চিকিৎসা সুবিধা (হ্যাঁ / না)	
যখন আপনি প্রথম এখানে এসেছেন আপনার সবচেয়ে প্রয়োজনীয় চাহিদা কি ছিল?	
পরিবেশগত বিষয় যেমন বৃষ্টিপাত, ভূমি ধ্বস, ইত্যাদি আপনার শহর জীবন যাত্রার ক্ষেত্রে কি কোন প্রভাব ফেলছে?	

জীবন যাত্রার মান / পরিস্থিতি (সাক্ষাৎকার গ্রহণকারীর অনুধাবন)

14.4. Annex Marshall Islands

Overview Marshall Islands Migrant Interview Partners

ID	Urban Occupation	Previous Occupation	Gender	Island of Origin
Migrant Interview 1	Cleaner	Copra Production	M	Utirik
Migrant Interview 2	Misc. / Carpenter / Unemployed	Copra Production & Fisheries	M	Wotje
Migrant Interview 3	Security Guard	n/a (School)	M	Wotje
Migrant Interview 4	Cashier	n/a (School)	F	Arno
Migrant Interview 5	Cleaner	Copra Production	M	Ailinglaplap
Migrant Interview 6	Misc. / Warehouse Worker	Copra Production	M	Arno
Migrant Interview 7	Packaging	Copra Production	M	Ailuk
Migrant Interview 8	Construction	Copra Production	M	Namu

Overview Marshall Islands Sending Communities Interview Partners

ID	Position / Occupation	Group	Gender
Ailuk Interview 1	Traditional Leader	Leader	M
Ailuk Interview 2	Handicraft Maker	Handicrafts	F
Ailuk Interview 3	Handicraft Maker	Handicrafts	F
Ailuk Interview 4	Handicraft Maker	Handicrafts	F

Ailuk Interview 5	Handicraft & Copra Maker	Handicrafts & Agriculture	F
Ailuk Interview 6	Teacher Elementary School Ailuk	Educator	M
Ailuk Interview 7	Copra Maker	Agriculture	F
Ailuk Interview 8	Copra Maker & Carpenter	Agriculture & Construction	M
Ailuk Interview 9	Copra Maker	Agriculture	M
Ailuk Interview 10	Religious Leader	Leader	M
Ailuk Interview 11	Classroom Teacher	Educator	M
Ailuk Interview 12	Councilman Ailuk	Councilmen	M
Ailuk Interview 13	Councilman Ailuk and Shop Owner	Councilmen and Small Business	M
Ailuk Interview 14	Health Assistant	Health Worker	M
Ailuk Interview 15	Retired / Copra	Elderly (Agriculture)	M
Ailuk Interview 16	Traditional Leader	Leader	M
Ailuk Interview 17	Copra Producer	Agriculture	M
Ailuk Interview 18	Copra Producer	Agriculture	M
Ailuk Interview 18a	Handicraft Maker	Handicrafts	F
Ailuk Interview 19	Handicraft Maker	Handicrafts	F
Maloelap Interview 1	Shop and Ship Owner Maloelap	Local Business / Transport	M

Maloelap Interview 2	Political Leader	Outer Island Administration	M
Maloelap Interview 3	Copra Maker	Agriculture	F
Maloelap Interview 4	Councilman / Previous Political Leader	Councilmen	M
Maloelap Focus Group Discussant 1	Copra Maker	Agriculture	M
Maloelap Focus Group Discussant 2	Copra Maker	Agriculture	M
Maloelap Focus Group Discussant 3	Copra Maker & Pastor	Agriculture & Religious Leader	M
Maloelap Focus Group Discussant 4	Copra Maker & Church Worker	Agriculture & Religious Leader	M
Maloelap Focus Group Discussant 5	Copra Maker & Church Worker	Agriculture & Religious Leader	M
Maloelap Focus Group Discussant 6	Copra Maker & Policeman	Agriculture & Police	M
Maloelap Focus Group Discussant 7	Copra Maker & Teacher	Agriculture & Educator	M
Maloelap Focus Group Discussant 8	Copra Maker & Teacher	Agriculture & Educator	M

Marshall Islands Coding Sheet Migrants

- **Typical Urban Livelihoods**
  - Tuna Industry
  - Cleaning
  - Temporary Jobs
  - Construction
- **Reason for Migration**
  - Visit then stayed
  - Drought induced harvest loss
  - Education
  - Healthcare
- **Effectiveness**
  - Economic
  - Working Conditions
  - Loss of Culture
  - Better Access to Education
  - Better Access to Healthcare
  - Identity
  - Living Situation
- **Problems on the Outer Islands**
  - Drought
  - King Tides
  - None
  - Adaptation Options
- **Problems in the City**
  - Health
  - No Problems
- **Perceived Reason for Climate Change**
  - Don't know
  - No response
- **Prefer to Stay or Return**
  - Return
  - Stay
- **Remittances**
  - Yes, used for food
  - No
  - Yes, regularly
- **Environmental Problems on Intensified**
  - Yes
- **Previous Job**
  - Copra Production

Marshall Islands Coding Sheet Sending Communities

Environmental Problems Outer Islands
- Extreme Heat
- Soil degradation
- Decrease in Food Production / Hunger
- Effects on Livestock
- Effects on Plant Growth
- Coastal Erosion
- Increase of Severity / Frequency
- Effects on Livelihoods
- High Tides / Inundation / Sea Water Intrusion
- Freshwater Scarcity
- Sea Level Rise
- Health
- Drought
- Changing Winds
- Change in Seasons
- Coral Bleaching / Fisheries
- Salinization
- No problems

Effects of Migration
- Lack of Workforce
- More Challenges
- Positive for the Migrants because of Work Opportunities
- Reduction of Pressure on Land
- Foreign Influence on Sending Community
- Negative Effects on the Community

Other problems on the Outer Islands
- Effects of Nuclear Testing
- People would prefer to stay
- Lack of Inter Atoll Sea Transport
- Lack of Medical Supplies
- Lack of Food Supplies
- Dependency on Outside Supplies
- Low Copra Price

Knowledge about Climate Change
- Knowledge about the Term Climate Change
- No Knowledge
- Some Knowledge
- No response

Remittances
- Yes

Reason for Migration
- Climate Change / Environmental Degradation
- Work Opportunities
- To be with Family
- Education
- Resource Depletion
- Better Life

Destination of Migration of Family Members
- US
- Majuro

Situation of Migrants Abroad
- Coping Challenges
- No good Jobs

Future on the Outer Islands
- It will be the same
- Adaptation Options
- Further Outmigration
- Solutions have to come from Outside
- Complete Outmigration
- Situation will improve
- Don't Know / No Answer
- Challenges due to intensified Climate Change
- Situation will get worse

Marhall Islands Coding Sheet Experts

- **Climate Impacts**
  - Drought
  - Coping Mechanisms
  - King Tides
  - Salinization
  - Health
  - Agriculture
  - Handicraft Production
  - Fisheries
  - Violence
  - Urban
  - Storms
  - Short Recovery between Impacts
  - Increase of Severity / Frequency
- **Problems Outer Islands**
  - Freshwater
  - Lack of Research
  - Lack of CC Knowledge
  - Lack of Agency on CC
  - Dependency
  - Overfishing
- **Reasons for Migration**
  - Complexity
  - Trafficking
  - Climate Change
  - Compact of Free Association
  - Employment
  - Evolving Patterns
  - Resource Limitations
  - Cultural Change / Outside Influence
- **Adaptation Options**
  - Tourism
  - Infrastructural
  - Finance
  - Choosing to Stay
  - Community and Livelihoods Projects
  - Improved Education
  - Responsibility of other Nations to help
  - Impoved Awareness of Local Assets
  - Improved Transport
- **Migration Problems & Opportunities**
  - Knowledge about Destination
  - Connection to the Land
  - Lack of Job Opportunities / Low Wages
  - Lack of Meaning
  - Losing Culture
  - Trapped at Destination
  - Losing Identity
  - Comparison Nuclear Legacy
- **Effectiveness for Migrants**
  - Typical Livelihoods at Destination
- **Effectiveness for Sending Communities**
  - Knowledge Transfer
  - Future of the Community
  - Changing Social Order
- **Receiving Communities**
  - Remittances
  - Provision of Services
  - Additional Purchasing Power
  - Lack of Work Permits
  - Family Networks
  - Land Scarcity

Informed Consent English

Informed Consent Form

Climate Change Impacts on Livelihoods and Human Mobility

DESCRIPTION: You are invited to participate in a research study on Climate Change Impacts on Livelihoods and Human Mobility. The study aims at identifying typical livelihood patterns, social situations and motivations for migration from outer-islands to Majuro or overseas. You will be asked to answer a questionnaire and you will be audiotaped. The tapes will be used for written analysis and will be kept by the interviewer. If you wish to stay anonymous, your name will not be mentioned in the analysis or transcriptions.

TIME INVOLVEMENT: Your participation will take approximately 30 minutes.

RISKS AND BENEFITS: There are no foreseeable risks associated with this study. There are no direct benefits of the study outcome to the participants.

PARTICIPANT'S RIGHTS: If you have read this form and have decided to participate in this project, please understand your participation is voluntary and you have the right to withdraw your consent or discontinue participation at any time. The alternative is not to participate. You have the right to refuse to answer particular questions. The results of this research study may be presented at scientific or professional meetings or published in scientific journals. With your permission, your identity will be made known in written materials resulting from the study.

CONTACT INFORMATION:

Questions: If you have any questions, concerns or complaints about this research and its procedures you can ask the interviewer at any point during the interview or afterwards.

Independent Contact: If you are not satisfied with how this study is being conducted, or if you have any concerns, complaints, or general questions about the research or your rights as a participant, please contact the Okeanos Foundation for the Sea Marshall Islands or the University of the South Pacific Sustainable Sea Transport Department.

Indicate ***Yes*** or ***No***:
I give consent to be audiotaped during this study.

___Yes ___No

I give consent for tapes resulting from this study to be used for transcription and evaluation of the study.

___Yes ___No

I give consent for my identity to be revealed in written materials resulting from this study.

___Yes ___No

The extra copy of this signed and dated consent form is for you to keep.

SIGNATURE ______________________________ **DATE** ____________

Informed Consent Marshallese

FORM IN MALIM

MEN KO REJELET MOUR IM MAKITKIT IN ARMEJ ITOK JEN UKOKTAK IN MEJATOTO

KOMLELE: Kwoj ruwainnene in bok konaam ilo ekkatak in ikijeen Men Ko Rejelet Mour im Makitkit in Armej Itok Jen Ukoktak in Mejatoto. Kottopar eo an ekkatak in ej nan kalikar wawein mour, ta ko rejelet kej, im un ko me rekomman menin ad emmakit jen aelon kein nan ko jet enwot Majuro ako likin. Jenaaj kajitok waj jet kajitok me jej aikuj rekooti. Melele kein naaj kojerbali nan jeik juon ekkatak im naaj ped ilo kejparok eo an rikkatok eo. Ne koknaan, Jenaaj kejparok eok im etam bwe enjab walok ilo ekkatak in.

IEN EO AM: Ien in am enaaj bolen bok 30 minit.

JORRAAN AK TOPRAK KO KEMLETI ILO AM BOK KONAAM: Ilo katak in eban lon jorraan enaaj walok nan kwe, im eban lon menoknok in jeraman naaj lewaj jen ekkatak in.

JIMWE IM MARON AN RO REJ BOK KONAER: Ne emoj am reati im melele kon ekkatak in im erra in bok konaam, kwoj melelel im jela ke am make eddo kalet in am im komaron kabojrak ijo am bok konaam jabdewot ien. Komaron bar kalikar ne kwojjab maron bok konaam. Komaron jab uwaak jet kajitok ko kojjab konaan uwaki. Toprak in ekkatak in naaj lelok nan jikin ekkatk ko rellap nan kwelok koi m jerbal in ekkatak ko jet. Ne kokemalimi, jenaaj kojerbal bwinnum ilo katako naaj jeiki im toprak ko jen ekkantak in.

KILEN TOPAR RIKKATOK RO: KAJTIOK: Ne elon am kajitok im abnono ikijeen ekkatak in, komaron kajiotk ippen eo ej kommane ekkatak in jabdewot ien ilo ien bwebwenato in ako alikin bwebwenato in.

KILEN TOPAR RIKKATOK EO: Ne ejjab bun burwom ikijeen ad kar kommane ekkatak in, ak ne elon am abonono ako inepata, im ne ebar lon kajitok ko jet, jouj im leloki nan Okeanos Marshall Islands im GIZ – USP Low Carbon Sea Transport.

Kalikar Aet ak Jaab:

Naij kemalimi rekoote ekkatak in.

____AET _____JAAB

Naij komalim kojerbal melele kein jen ekkatak in nan kameeji ilo jeje im nan ekkatok ko jet kaki.

____AET _____ JAAB

Naij komalim bwe bwinnu en alikar ilo jeje ko remeej im walok jen ekkatak in

____AET _____ JAAB

PEPA EO JUON JEN IN EM EWALOK IEN EO KWAR LIKIT ELTAN PEIM IN KEMALIM EJ AM.

SIGNATURE___________________________

DATE_____________________________________

Set of Questions English – Migrants

Place and date of interview	
Name of Interviewee	
Age of Participant	
Male / Female	
Number of people in the household Number of children if any	
Where did you migrate from?	
Did you come directly here or did you stay somewhere else in between?	
When did you move here?	
Why did you migrate?	
Are environmental factors in your home community a problem? (Please identify)	
If so, have they increased / intensified over the past decade(s)? Why have they increased / Why do they occur?	
Did you know someone here before deciding to come?	
What is your current occupation?	
Is it different from the work you did beforehand?	

Do you live or are in touch with people here who are from your home community?	
For how long are you planning to stay here? If you are leaving, where are you planning to go?	
Under what conditions would you go back to your place of origin?	
Are you in contact with family members from your place of origin?	
If yes, do you support them monetarily?	
Are there people from your place of origin who are planning to migrate as well?	
Do you go back home during the year? (seasonal work, for example)	
How is your living situation? Are there problems with living in the city?	
How could these problems be solved?	
What facilities are lacking?	
Do you have (Yes / No): Shelter Tap (running) water Access to electricity Access to toilets Access to primary education for children	

Land rights to the place in which you live Access to basic medical care	
What did you need most when you first came here?	
Are environmental factors such as rainfall, mud slides etc. affecting your life in the city?	

Set of Questions English – Home Communities Outer Islands

Place and date of interview	
Name of Interviewee	
Age of Participant	
Male / Female	
Number of people in the household Number of children, if any	
Are environmental factors in your home community a problem? (Please identify) (Flooding, extreme rain, sea water intrusion, Storms)	
If so, have they increased / intensified over the past decade(s)?	
Why have they increased?	
What is your current occupation?	
Have changes in the environment affected your livelihood or income?	
Did someone of your family migrate?	
If yes, where did they go? (Majuro, abroad etc.)	
Why did they leave this island?	
How are they doing now? What work do they do?	
Do they support you by sending money or products?	

Do they visit, if yes, how often do they visit?	
Are there other people from this island who are planning to migrate as well?	
If yes, why are they leaving?	
If yes, what do you think about this that people are leaving? (Is it good or bad?)	
How is your living situation?	
Do you have (Yes / No):	
Shelter (What type)	
Tap (running) Water	
Access to electricity	
Access to toilets (how many people per toilet)	
Access to primary education for children	
Access to secondary education (high school)	
Land rights to the place in which you live (Secure lease)	
Access to medical care	
Are there any problems you are facing here?	
How could these problems be solved?	

Do you want to stay here?	
How do you see the future for this community in the next ten or twenty years in terms of livelihoods? Do you see any challenges?	

Set of Questions English – Experts & Community Leaders (Chiefs)

Place and date of interview	
Name of Expert	
Profession / Institution	
Male / Female	
Are environmental factors in the Marshall Islands /this community a problem? (Please identify) (Flooding, extreme rain, sea water intrusion, Storms)	
If so, have they increased / intensified over the past decade(s)?	
Why have they increased?	
How are the people here dealing with these changes?	
Is it affecting their livelihoods?	
Are they migrating because of these changes?	
If yes, where do they go? (Majuro, abroad etc.)	
How are they doing after the migration? What work do they do?	
How is their living situation?	
Are they able to support their families back home (by sending money etc)?	

How is this migration affecting the home communities?	
How is this migration affecting the places where they go to? (Majuro)	
Do you see any problems with this migration?	
What do you think is the future of the outer islands where people come from? Will there be more people migrating?	
What could be done to help people stay?	
How do you see the future for this community in the next ten or twenty years in terms of livelihoods? Do you see any challenges?	

Set of Questions Marshallese Outer Islands

Jikin/Aelon/Bukwon	
Etan Armej eo	
Drettan	
Emmaan/Kora	
Jonan Armej ro rej jokwe ilo mweo/Jete ajiri	
Elon ke jorraan ewalok nan jukjuk in ped eo am jen (Iuwe in den jen wot, Lojet ako lan ko jet?)	
Ne Aet, ilo iio ko jonoun remootlok rej ke ikkutlok?	
Rejaam ikkutlok?	
Jerbal rot eo am ilo tore in?	
Oktak kein ilo Jukjuk in ped eo am rejelet ke mour eo am kab am komman jaan?	
Elon ke ilo baamle eo am emoj aer emmakit jen aniin?	
Ne aet, rekar etal nan ia? (Majuro, likin, etc)	
Rejaam kar emmakit jen aelon in?	
Ejet aer ped kio? Jerbal rot ko aer likin?	

Rej ke jipan tok kwe ak rimwiin jilkin tok jaan ak jeraman ko jet jet likin?	
Renanin ke bar rooltok? Ewi ikkut in aer kijon lotok kom ak aelon in?	
Elon ke armej ilo aelon kojela rej lomnak in emmakit jen aelon in?	
Ne aet, kojela ke rejaam emmakit?	
Ne aet, Kolak lale emman ke enana menin ilo a er emmakit ?	
Komaron ke kwalok ewi wot jokkin mour eo am im family eo am kio?	
Elon ke men kein (AET/Jaab)	
Jikin Kepped	
Den/Nien den	
Jarom	
Mon bwidej	
Jikin jikuul nan ajiri ro	
Elon ke am maron ilo bwidej ion aelon in?	
Jikin ajmour/takto	
Elon ke apan ko rejelet kwe kio?	
Ta mejlan aban kein ak elmen bwe ren jako?	

Ilo jenoul ak ronoul iio jen kio, ewi wawein mour nej ilo jukjuk in ped in? Kwoj ke ello aban ko?	

Wolfgang Gieler; Hakan Cetinyilmaz
Die Klimapolitik der Türkei zwischen Anspruch und Wirklichkeit
Dieser Band untersucht die türkische Klimapolitik und ihre wichtigsten Einflussfaktoren. In welchem Politikbereich sind die Prioritäten der Türkei zwischen Umwelt-, Klima-, und Wachstumspolitik zu verorten? Welches sind die prägenden Faktoren türkischer Klimapolitik? Welche Antriebsmomente? In türkischen wie auch internationalen politikwissenschaftlichen Analysen ist das Thema bisher nur in Ansätzen behandelt worden, so dass der Band als grundlegende Einführung in die türkische Klimapolitik verstanden werden kann.
Bd. 16, 2015, 186 S., 39,90 €, br., ISBN 978-3-643-12780-8

Lutz Wicke; Hans Joachim Schellnhuber; Daniel Klingenfeld
Die 2° max.-Klimastrategie – Ein Memorandum
Dieses Jahrzehnt entscheidet über Erfolg oder Misserfolg der globalen Klimapolitik: Wollen Deutschland und die Europäische Union das Zwei-Grad-Klimaziel nicht verloren geben, dann muss jetzt eine wirksamere und gerechtere Klimaschutzstrategie entwickelt und umgesetzt werden. In diesem Buch legen die Autoren ein Gesamtkonzept vor, das Wege aufzeigt, gravierende Konstruktionsfehler im bestehenden internationalen Klimaregime zu überwinden und die globale Emissionstrendwende im Jahr 2015 herbeizuführen.
Bd. 13, 2010, 64 S., 19,90 €, gb., ISBN 978-3-643-10817-3

LIT Verlag Berlin – Münster – Wien – Zürich – London
Auslieferung Deutschland / Österreich / Schweiz: siehe Impressumsseite